ISBN 978-1-332-57794-1
PIBN 10182358

JOURNALS

OF

MAJOR ROBERT ROGERS:

CONTAINING

N ACCOUNT OF THE SEVERAL EXCURSIONS HE MADE
UNDER THE GENERALS WHO COMMANDED UPON
THE CONTINENT OF *NORTH AMERICA*,
DURING THE LATE WAR;

FROM WHICH MAY BE COLLECTED

HE MOST MATERIAL CIRCUMSTANCES OF EVERY CAMPAIGN UPON THAT
CONTINENT, FROM THE COMMENCEMENT TO THE CONCLUSION OF THE WAR.

WITH AN INTRODUCTION AND NOTES,

AND AN APPENDIX CONTAINING NUMEROUS DOCUMENTS AND PAPERS
RELATING TO THE DOINGS OF MAJOR ROGERS WHILE COM-
MANDING AT MICHILIMACKINACK, IN 1767; AND HIS
CONDUCT IN THE EARLY PART OF THE
REVOLUTIONARY WAR.

By FRANKLIN B. HOUGH.

ALBANY:

INTRODUCTION.

The Journals of Major Robert Rogers, giving the details of his services as a partizan officer in the French and Indian war of 1755-60, have been very generally regarded as forming a work of unquestionable historical value. The volume does not ·profess to be in any sense, a general history of the events of that war, nor a connected account of the military operations of a particular frontier; but simply a narrative of what he himself saw and did, with here and there a brief allusion to the doings of others, where they seemed in some way to have had relation to his own. Being evidently written with a view of promoting his own military reputation, as he may have doubtless felt that he deserved, it would be surprising if he had been uniformly as fair in his account of others as of himself, or if his narratives were in all respects such as another, as well acquainted with every fact and circumstance, and without personal motives, would have written. An author in describing his own acts, does not naturally seek to expose his own errors, nor always to conceal those of others; nor can we expect, in scenes and circumstances like those which our author describes, that no jealousies, or rivalries, or disappointments were encountered, that might sometimes influence his conduct, and show themselves in his writings. Such, upon several occasions, will be noticed by the careful reader of his Journals nor should they be regarded as exceptional, in publications of this class, where the exploits of the written form the principal theme.

The general tenor of the narrative, and details in abundance, are however well verified by independent authorities, and justify the belief that the accounts of services here given, are in the main reliable, and that the work fairly presents the condition of affairs, as they existed, and the events, as they occurred, in the time and manner described.

In annotating this work for a new edition, no

attempt has been made to supply the links in the chain of events which the author omitted; but simply to illustrate by citation and reference, such passages and allusions as appeared to admit of annotation or enlargement, from such sources of information as came within our reach.

The incidents in the early life of this partizan soldier, are for the most part lost; but from his own statement, the rude and rugged hardships of a frontier settlement, were of such a character that he could hardly avoid gaining a thorough practical knowledge of the manners, customs and language of the Indians near whom he was reared, and a general acquaintance with the wild and hardy forest life of the pioneers. He mentions the twelve years that immediately preceded the war in which he served, as full of hardships, and particularly well calculated to qualify him for the arduous duties of the service in which he engaged.

Of the ancestry of this celebrated Ranger we have few details. He was the son of James Rogers[1]

---

[1] Major Roger's father perished in a very singular manner. Mr. Rogers was going to a hunter's camp, in order to invite some gentle-

originally from Ireland, or of Irish descent, and one
of the first settlers of Dunbarton, now in Merrimack
county, New Hampshire, first known as " Starks-
Town." The settlement of this town began some
years before 1746, but at what time cannot now
be ascertained. Robert Rogers was born in Lon-
donderry, N. H., (or Methuen Mass.), in 1727, and
was probably fourteen or fifteen years of age, when
his father began a settlement in the wilderness.
From his youth, he was inured to the hardships of
the frontier, acquiring that character of decision,
self-reliance and boldness, which distinguished him

---

men who were making surveys to dine with him. The hunter,
[Ebenezer Ayer of Haverhill, Mass.] saw him approaching through
the bushes at a distance, and not expecting a visit from others than
wild animals, fired upon him, mistaking him for a bear, and killed
him on the spot. It is reported of Major Rogers, that while in London after the French war, and in company with several other persons,
it was agreed that the one who should tell the most improbable story
or the greatest lie, should be exempt from paying his fare. When his
turn came, he related, that his father was shot in the woods of America by a person who supposed him to be a bear; and that his mother
was followed several miles through the forest by hunters, who mistook
her track for that of some animal. It was acknowledged by all, that he
was entitled to the prize, although he had told nothing but the truth.
Farmer and Moore's Hist. Coll., i, 240, In the memoir of Gen. John
Stark by Caleb Stark, (1860) the details of this singular accident are
related. *Memoir and Correspondence of Gen. Stark, p.* 386.

in after life. He was six feet in statute, well pro-
portioned, and one of the most athletic men of his
time, well known in all the trials of strength and
activity among the young men of his vicinity, and
for several miles around.[1]

Of his entrance into the military service, at the
age of twenty-eight years, and his perilous adventures
until the final surrender of the French posts in the
West, ample details are given, mostly from his own
pen, in the following pages. His name and fame
appear to have become familiar throughout the
country, and in both armies ; and in a military point
of view, his services must be regarded as of the first
importance to the British cause. The brutal warfare
of his day, resulting from a century of murderous
invasion and vindictive reprisal, had grafted upon
the system every custom that was horrid and barbar-

---

[1] *Potter's Hist. of Manchester*, p. 488. *Caleb Stark's Memoir of Gen.
John Stark*, p. 387.

An engraved full length portrait of Major Rogers, was published in
London, in 1776. He is represented as a tall, strong man, dressed in the
costume of a Ranger, with a powder horn slung at his side, a gun resting
in the hollow of his hand arm, and a countenance by no means pre-
possessing. Behind him at a little distance, stand his Indian followers,
Parkman's Pontiac, i, 164.

ous. Each of the nationalities then contending for the mastery of the Continent, had brought to its aid the cunning and cruel Savage ; had taught him the use of arms more destructive than his native weapons, and had stimulated his passions by every art and motive, until humanity to the wounded, or mercy to the captive were unknown; and if the prisoner escaped the scalping knife and the stake, he was led off into a captivity often worse than death.

Through scenes of peril and danger which threatened every step, our partizan soldier passed without serious harm ; but we can scarcely believe that the attractions of home, or the ease of private life, had many charms for him, when the war was over, and not an enemy could be found throughout the length and breadth of the Continent, which the winning Government found it necessary to repress.

Nor is there room for doubt, but that amidst the scenes of bloodshed of which he witnessed so much, and took so active a part, the finer sensibilities of humanity were lost in moments when expediency or policy dictated to the contrary ; for in the reports made immediately upon his return from a scout, we find it mentioned, that he had scalped the dead within sight of a French garrison, and murdered a prisoner when too badly wounded to march.[1]

Major Rogers married, but at what period is unknown, a Miss Elizabeth Browne, or as some accounts give it, Elizabeth Furness, of Portsmouth. She obtained a divorce, and afterwards married Capt. John Roche, or Roach of Concord.[2]

In the troubled times which preceded and attended the seige of Detroit, by Pontiac, in 1763, Major Rogers was sent with a body of troops to the relief of that garrison, and he assisted in the sortie upon the occasion that Captain Dalyel was killed.[3]

After the surrender of the western posts, Rogers engaged in an expedition against the Cherokees in

---

[1] These statements were omitted in the volume published by Major Rogers, but appear over his own signature, in the Journals printed in the fourth volume of Documentary History which we have introduced as notes — the originals being found among Johnson Manuscripts in the New York State Library.

[2] Mrs. Rogers appears to have been living with her husband, when commandant at Michilimackinac, in 1767. Roach died May 11, 1811.—*Bouton's Hist of Concord*, p. 351.—*Stark's Memoirs*, p. 389.

[3] *Seige of Detroit*, edited by F. B. Hough (Munsell's Historical Series, No. IV), p.

the south under the orders of General Grant, but no details of this enterprise, have come to our notice: and on leaving the service he was retired upon half pay. His accounts appear to have been embarrassed from want of vouchers, so that it was not until 1763, that he secured a settlement with the Provincial Government of New Hampshire, for services rendered eight years before.[1] The trouble that he encountered in adjusting these claims, appears to have arisen from a negligent habit in the keeping of accounts, and probably in some degree from the death of persons whose living testimony would have sustained his claims.

Not long after this, Rogers went to England, to present his claims for accounts, and while there, published the work which we now reproduce. The title-page of the original edition shows that it was printed for the author, probably on subscription,[2] and in the

---

[1] See appendix, B.

[2] Sold by J. Millan, Bookseller, Whitehall, 1765. 8vo, pp. 237.
In 1769, this was republished in Dublin by R. Acheson, together with the account of Col. Henry Bouquet's Expedition against the Ohio Indians, in 1764, including his Negociations with the Indians relative to the delivery of Prisoners, and the Preliminaries of Peace, and an In-

same year another work,— with still the promise of a continuation, which, so far as we can ascertain, never appeared.

The other work published by Major Rogers in London in 1765, have the following title:

" A Concise Account of North America ; containing a Description of the several British Colonies on that Continent, including the Island of Newfoundland, Cape Breton, &c., as to their Situation, Extent, Climate, Soil, Produce, Rise, Government, Religion, present Boundaries, and the number of Inhabitants supposed to be in each. Also of the Interior, or westerly Parts of the Country, upon the Rivers St.

---

troductory Account of the preceding Campaign and the Battle of Bushy Run. Pages x and 218.

A condensed anonymous edition of Rogers's Journals, was published by Luther Roby, at Concord, N. H., in 1831. (12mo, pp. 276), of which the editor is known to have been Caleb Srark, Jr. The title of this work is as follows :

" Reminiscences of the French War ; containing Rogers's Expeditions with the New England Rangers under his Command, as published in London in 1765 ; with Notes and Illustrations. To which is added an Account of the Life and Military Services of Maj. Gen. John Stark ; with Notices and Anecdotes of Officers distinguished in the French and Revolutionary Wars." Of this volume, the abstract of Rogers's Journals fills 132 pages — and an Appendix 36 more,— the remainder being devoted to the Memoirs of Gᵉⁿ ·ᵃˡ John Stark.

Lawrence, the Mississippi, Christino, and the Great Lakes. To which is subjoined, an Account of the several Nations and Tribes of Indians residing in those Parts, as to their Customs, Manners, Government, numbers, etc. Containing many useful and entertaining Facts, never before treated of. By Major Robert Rogers, London: Printed for the Author, and sold by J. Millan, Bookseller, near Whitehall. MDCCCLXV, 8vo, pp. 264."

In the first of these publications, the author announced his intentions of publishing an account of his travels into the Cherokee country and the Southern Indians; of his second tour into the interior country, upon the Great Lakes; and of the Indian wars in America since the year 1760; together with correct plans of all the British posts upon the continent. In the second, of the above noticed publications, he proposed to issue a volume containing maps of the several colonies, and of the interior country of North America, " more correct, and easier to be understood than any yet published." The price of each, was to be an English guinea, but so far as we are informed, nothing further of this nature appeared under his name, relating to American affairs.[1]

Major Rogers, in 1766, was appointed Commandant at Michilimackinac, which after the conquest of Canada had become the most important military and trading post in the interior.[2]

From its fine location, it naturally intercepted the trade of all the country beyond it to the west and northwest, and as there was no Commissary in special charge of the trade, at the time he received his appointment, the office of Commandant was one of great responsibility, as one also of rare opportunity, which he lost no time in turning to his own advantage. In short, we find him incurring expenses without authority, drawing orders upon the Government which went to protest for non-payment, and falling under charges of a design to plunder the Fort he commanded, and then desert to the French in New Orleans.[3]

---

[1] The fragment of a Journal of the Siege of Detroit, first published in Munsell's Historical Series, No. IV, in 1860, they have been intended to form a part or the proposed work. His Journal covers the period from May 6 to July 4, 1763.

[2] Letters from Gen. Thomas Gage to Sir Wiliiam Johnson, dated January 25, 1767.— *Doc. Hist. of N. Y.*, iv., 837.

[3] See Appendix C.

He was arrested, and brought a prisoner to Montreal, but managed to acquit himself of these charges, and in 1769 again went to England, where he was presented to the King.[1]

Major Rogers remained abroad on this second occasion until the summer of 1775, and from one of his letters, we learn that he was for a time in the Algerine service. He appears to have become attached to the soldier's profession, in which he had had so long an experience, and for which, on outpost duty and occasions requiring prompt decision, courage and endurance, he had shown himself eminently well fitted.

He was now approaching the age of fifty years — a period of life at which the judgment matured by

---

[1] While in England at this time, the following anecdote is related of him :

A mail coach, in which he was a passenger, was stopped by a highwayman on Hunslow Heath. The robber, thrusting a pistol through the coach window, demanded the purses and watches of the occupants. While others were taking out their valuables, the bold American stranger suddenly seized the man by the collar by main strength, drew him through the window, and ordered the coachman to drive on. The captive was an old offender, for whose apprehension a reward of £50 Sterling has been offered by the Government.— *Stark's Memoir*, p. 385 *Potter's Manchester*, p. 489.

experience operates with clearness, and the physical powers are with many still capable of great achievement. During his six year's absence, his native country had been steadily preparing for the crisis of the Revolution ; and although absent, we may well believe, he could not have been indifferent, as to the tendencies of the times, and the probabilities of a conflict, in which military experience would be sought and valued, and ample opportunities afforded for promotion and reward.

As to his preferences at this time, we have no indication. His long associction with military men and affairs, might have naturally predisposed him to regard the Royal cause as the one of right, as well as the one of power, and his long separation from family and friends of early life, may have failed to inspire him with the patriotic impulses then filling the country with enthusiasm, and hastening it to organized rebellion.

Under all the circumstances of his case, the fact that he was a retired half pay officer of the British army, that he had for many years taken no interest in American civil affairs, and perhaps, the knowledge of his transactions at Michilimackinac, appear to have led his countrymen to distrust him, before he had declared his preference, and possibly before he had formed his own opinions.[1]

Under these suspicions, some regarded him as an enemy in disguise, and even serving as a spy, while others looked upon him as a mercenary soldier, ready to accept the highest bid from either party,.and with no principles that would deter him from selling out his opportunities, if it could be done with probable success.

At any event, his conduct was not such as to invite confidence, from the time of his first arrival in the country, until his preferences were publicly declared. We find him wandering about the country, without visible employment, or plausable pretext,—associating with suspected persons, and visiting places of doubtful reputation,— arrested time and again on suspicion, and

---

[1] Mr. Stark, who afterwards became so efficient in the American service, and who had shared the hardships and dangers of the partizan service with Major Rogers in the war of. 1755–60, visited him when at Medford, Mass , in December, 1775, endeavoring to gain an interview with Washington, and expressed the belief, that if Major Rogers had not been charged with disloyal sentiments before he had expressed them by word or deed, he might have been won to the support of the Continental cause.

giving his parol under oath, to which he paid no regard,—and finally when confined, escaping to the
British lines, and openly accepting a commission as a
partizan officer in the Royal cause. It is now known,
that long before this decision was openly avowed, he
had tendered his servicee to both parties ; and that before he in writing to General Washington said, " I
love North America ; it is my native country, and
that of my family, and I intend to spend the evening
of my days in it," he had pledged the wealth of hi
talent for inroad and destruction, to the commander-
in-chief of thc British army, and had been promised
His Majesty's future favor.[1]

His services as a loyalist, were short and inglorious.
He was commissioned with the rank of Lieutenant
Colonel Commandant, to raise a partizan corps to be-
known as the *Queen's Rangers ;* but on the 21st of
October, 1776, his party was surprised at Mamoranec,
near Long Island Sound, a part were captured, and
Rogers himeelf barely escaped, in the confusion of
the encounter.[2] Not long after this, he returned to

---

[1] See Appendix D.

[2] See Appendix E. The *Queens Rangers,* were afterwards commanded
by Lieut. Colonel Simcoe, subsequently Governor of Upper Canada.

England, where he died about the year 1800. He is said to have lived a wild, improvident and extravagant life, and to have been the victim of bad habits.

Major Rogers was banished from the State by an Act of the New Hampshire Legislature, in November, 1778, but his estate was not confiscated, as was the case of many others.

His son Arthur Rogers, lived with his mother many years upon the family farm near Concord, and died in Portsmouth, N. H., in 1841, leaving three children of respectable standing, in San Domingo.

Long after the death of Major Rogers, some correspondence passed among those who were seeking to learn, and who were willing to inform, concerning his standing and character in the community where he had lived. We cheerfully present this tribute of friendship, from one whose good opinion might well be prized, as tending to show that the wild and rugged traits in the character of this partizan soldier, were relieved by traces of softer tone; and that among those who had no words of approval for the final course of his military career, his memory still retained the sympathies of a friend.

CONCORD, *July* 16, 1842.

DEAR SIR: I have made some inquiry respecting Major R. Rogers, and among our oldest inhabitants I find but *one opinion*, respecting his character, and that is fully expressed in the note enclosed to me and transmitted herewith to you from Govenor Hill.

Mr. Hill has perhaps a better knowledge of Major Roger's character, as an officer, than any other person here; he has been prompted by reasons which could not have operated on others.

Respectfully, your Obedient Servant,

ROBERT A. DAVIS.

Mr. Charles Coffin, N. Y. City.

"GEN. ROBERT DAVIS.

My Dear Sir: I have this moment read Mr. Coffin's letter addressed to you, requesting information in relation to the character of the late Maj. Robert Rogers. Having recently had occasion to make inquiries relative to his early history, I find nothing in the region of his birth, that goes at all to discredit him. One of the last of his blood relations in this vicinity who personally remembered him, a lady, died about a year ago. From her mouth, through Mark Burnham, Esq., a native of the same town with Rogers, I derived the information that all the family were proud of his name, and were reluctant to associate it with a reputation that was not entirely unsullied. Maj. Rogers never resided in this State permanently after the commencement of the Revolutionary war. He was in the British service in Canada, after the close of the old French war, partly in a military and partly in a civil capacity. The only child bearing his name was several years under my care as a guardian. This circumstance, among others, has led me more particularly to mark the character of the celebrated warrior. I consider him to have been one of the most talented men of the country — perhaps the best partizan officer this country ever produced. .I believe him to have been the author of thatiperfect mode of attack and defence which enabled a hundred of the Rangers to do more service than thousands of the British regulars, especially in the winter service of the old war of 1756,

Such safety to troops on fatigue, amid the severest seasons of a sever climate, was never before secured.

such certainty in the results, either on the advance¯ or retreat, perhaps has never realised by any other

force than the Rangers, under the perfect arrangement
and discipline invented by Rogers, I consider him to
have been as great a man in his pecular sphere, as
Napoleon Bonaparte, and for decision and firmness
equal to Andrew Jackson.

Yours truly
ISAAC HILL."

The Author's Introduction.

It would be offering an affront to the public, should I pretend to have no private views in publishing the following journals; but they will excuse me if I leave them to conjecture what my particular views are, and claim the merit of impartially relating matters of fact, without disguise or equivcoation. Most of those which relate to myself can at present be attested by living witnesses.

And should the troubles in America be renewed, and the savages repeat those scenes of barbarity they so often have acted on the British subjects, which there is great reason to believe will happen, I flatter myself, that such as are immediately concerned may reap some advantage from these pages.

Should any one take offence at what they may here meet with, before they venture upon exhibiting a charge, they are desired, in favor to themselves, to consider, that I am in a situation where they cannot attack me to their own advantage; that it is the soldier, not the scholar, that writes; and that many things here were wrote, not with silence and leisure, but in deserts, on rocks and mountains, amidst the hurries, disorders, and noise of war, and under that depression of spirits, which is the natural consequence of exhausting fatigue. This was my situation when the following journals or accounts were transmitted to the generals and commanders I acted under, which I am not now at liberty to correct, except in some very gross and palpable errors.

It would perhaps gratify the curious to have a particular account of my life, preceding the war; but tho' I could easily indulge them herein, without any dishonor to myslelf, yet I beg they will be content with my relating only such circumstances and occurrences as led me to a knowledge of many parts of the country, and tended in some measure to qualify me for the service I have since been employed in. Such, in particular, was the situation of the place in which I received my early education, a frontier town in the province of New Hampshire,[1] where I could hardly avoid obtaining some knowledge of the manners, customs, and language of the Indians, as many of them resided in the neighborhood, and daily conversed and dealt with the English.

Between the years 1743 and 1755 my manner of life was such as led me to a general acquaintance both with the British and French settlements in North America, and especially with the uncultivated desert, the mountains, valleys, rivers, lakes, and several passes that lay between and contiguous to the said settlements. Nor did I content myself with the accounts I received from Indians, or the information of hunters, but travelled over large tracts of the country myself, which tended not more to gratify my curiosity, than to inure me to hardships, and, without vanity I may say, to qualify me for the very service I have since been employed in.

---

[1] Dunbarton, originalley called "Stsrkstown," was granted in 1751, by the Masonian proprietors to Archibald Stark, Caleb Page, and others. Settlement was begun some years before 1746, by Joseph and William Putney, James Rogers and Obadiah Porter. It is included in County Merrimack, New Hampshire, and the country adjacent beonges to tne Abenaque tribe.

About this time the proceedings of the French in America were such as excited the jealousy of the English, especially in New York and New England ; and as Crown Point was the place from which, for many years, the Indians in the French interest had been fitted out against our settlements on the frontiers, a design was formed in the beginning of 1755 to dispossess them of that post ; pursuant to which troops were levied in the several provinces of New England, New York, and New Jersey. The general rendezvous was appointed at Albany in the proinvce of New York, and the troops put under the command of Major General (since Sir William) Johnson.[1] I had the honor of commanding a company in the troops furnished by the province of New Hampshire, with which I made several excursions, pursuant to special orders from the governor of that province, on the northern and western frontiers, with a view to deter the French and their Indians from making inroads upon us that way. In this manner I was employed till the month of July, when I received orders to repair to Albany, at which place I tarried till August

---

[1] See Appendix (A).

26th, and was then ordered with 100 men to escort tha provision waggons from thence to the Carrying-Place, then so called, since Fort Edward. Here I waited upon the General, to whom I was recommended as a person well acquainted with the haunts and passes of the enemy, and the Indian method of fighting, and was by him dispatched with small parties on several tours towards the French posts, and was on one of these up Hudson's River on the 8th of September, when Baron Dieskau was made prisoner, and the French and Indians under his command defeated, at the south-end of Lake George.

The 24th of September I received orderes from the General to proceed with four men to Crown Point, and, if practicable, to bring a prisoner from thence ; and with an account of the manner in which I executed these orders I shall begin my Journals.

A

JOURNAL, &c.

September 24, 1755.

Pursuant to orders of this date from Major General Johnson, Commander in Chief of the Provincial Forces, raised for the reduction of Crown Point,* I embarked with four men·upon Lake George,† to

---

*According to Wm. Brassier's map of Lake Champlain, published in 1762, Crown Point, or Fort St. Frederick was called by the Indians, Tek-ya-dough-nigarigee, which signifies "Two points opposite to each other." The opposite point, on this map, is called the "Dutch Crown Point." The name, "St. Frederick," is said by Kalm, to have been given in honor of Frederick Maurepas, French Secretary of State, in whose hands the direction and management of the Court of Admiralty was, at the time of its erection.

† Lake George is a little over 33 miles long and nearly 4 miles wide at the broadest place; it is 321 feet above tide water and 225 feet above Lake Champlain; the whole of the lake, and all of its islands south of the line of Essex county, lie in Warren county, the east bounds of which, are by statute located along the easterly shore of the lake.

The Iroquois name of the lake was Andia-ti-roc-te. "Where the lake shuts itself." The French called it "St. Sacrament," which was given it by Father Jogue, the Catholic Missionary, in 1646, from the fact that he first came there on the festival of Corpus Christi.

The English name of Lake George, was applied for the first time. by Sir William Johnson, who in a letter to General Shirley under date of Sept. 1, 1755, says,— " I have given the name of LAKE GEORGE, not only in honor of this Majesty, but to assert his undoubted dominion here."—*Johnson* MSS. ii, 199

reconnoitre the strength of the enemy, and proceeding down the lake twenty-five miles. I landed on the
west side, leaving two men in charge of the boat,
while I marched with the other two till the 29th,
when I had a fair view of the fort at Crown Point,
and discovered a large body of Indians round the
fort, and, from their repeated irregular firing, supposed
they were shooting at marks (a diversion much in
use among the savages). At night I crept through
the enemy's guards into a small village lying south
of the fort, and passed their centries to an eminence
south-west of it, from whence I discovered they were
building a battery, and had already thrown up an entrenchment on that side of the fort. The next day,
from an eminence at a small distance from the former,
I discovered an encampment, which extended from
the fort south-east to a wind-mill, at about thirty
yards distance; as near as I could judge, their number amounted to about 500 men ; but finding no opportunity to procure a captive. and that our small party
was discovered, I judged it proper to begin a retreat
homeward the 1st of October. I took my route
within two miles of Ticonderoga, from whence I observed a large smoke to arise, and heard the explosion
of a number of small arms ; but our provisions being
expended, we could not tarry to ascertain the number
of the enemy there. On the 2d we arrived at the
place where we left our boat in the charge of two
men, but to our great mortification found they were
gone, and no provisions left. This circumstance
hastened us to the encampment with all possible
speed, where we arrived the 4th, not a little fatigued
and distressed with hunger and cold.*

---

*The " Journals of Sir William Johnson's Scouts," printed in the
fourth volume of the Documentary History of New York, give a
notice of several of the expeditions described in the text, somewhat

October 7, 1755. I received orders of this date from General Johnson, to embark with five men

---

different in some cases, and more fully in others; for which reasons we insert the more important of those by Capt. Rogers, as notes. In doing this we have not attempted to follow the illiterate orthography which appears in some cases, and have adopted a punctuation and division into sentences that appeared to give most fully the meaning of the writers.

It will be noticed that the dates are usually some ten days behind those given in the text,— evidently from the fact that the Old Style calendar then lately adopted in England and English colonies, had not as yet, come entirely into use.

According to this authority, the party here noticed in the text, set out on the 14th of September,— landed about daylight, left two men of Connecticut in charge of boats and provisions, and in the morning, saw sundry Indian canoes passing in the lower part of the lake. The Journal then adds :

"The 17th day, at evening, discovered the wheat fields, and four. houses, about two miles southerly from Crown Point fort. In the night went to the intrenchment, made from the fort, encompasing a little hill, the trenches not finished, but reached about thirty rods from the fort; which intrenchment begins at the South-west corner of the fort, and trends south-westerly, about two rods wide at the fort, and widens to about fifteen at the other end. Went into the trench, and spent the night, for discovery in and about there till morning, and then retired to a Mountain about a mile west from the fort, where there was a clear view of all the fort and appurtenances — and saw an addition to the fort, from the North-west corner, about twenty-five rods which reached to the water side, inclosing some buildings — many tents were set up in it.

A wind mill about sixty rods south of the fort, in which space many tents were up had clear discovery of the fort and appurtenances; the soldiers were mustered and exercised. The whole of French and Indians we judged were near upon five or six hundred.

Their people, some few were at work at the intrenchments, seemed unconcerned — hunting pidgeons, etc., all around in the wood. Some of which came within about fifteen rods of the scout. We came off the hill at night.

19th. Set homeward, travelled to the lake, about six miles from Tionduroque.

20th. Set up the lake, to where we left the Battoe, found that, and the two men (we left) were gone, and we set homeward. The 23d late at night, arrived at the great camp.

The land is rough and mountainous from the lower end of the lake

under my command to reconnoitre the French troops at Ticonderoga.*   Accordingly I proceeded at night to a point of land on the west side of the lake, where we landed, hid our canoe, and left two men in charge of it.   The next day, with the other three, I marched to the point at Ticonderoga. where we ·arrived about noon.   I here observed a body of men, which I judged to be about 2000 in number, who had thrown up an entrenchment, and prepared large quantities of hewn timber in the adjacent woods.   We remained here the second night, and next morning saw them lay the foundation of a fort, on the point which commands the pass from Lake George to Lake Champlain, and the entrance of South Bay, or Wood Creek. Having made what discoveries we could, we began our return, in which we found that the enemy had a

---

to Crown Point.   The distance about 20 miles, and we apprehend impracticable to get a feasible road there, — which is the general account of the discovery we have made."

The report is signed by Robert Rogers, dated Sept. 24, and transmitted to Gen. Johnson by Joseph Blanchard of the New Hampshire Regiment.—*Doc. Hist.* N. Y., iv, 259.

[In citing from this work, in this volume, the *octavo* edition is referred to, and not the *quarto*.] — *Ed.*

* The orders issued on this occasion were as follows :

CAMP AT LAKE GEORGE,
7 Oct'r, 1755.

You are to embark with the party under your command, and land with them on one of the nearest and most convenient islands in the lake toward the carrying place and Ticonderoga and then send out three or four proper persons to reconnoitre the enemy thereabouts and make what discoverys they can : you are then to send out the Birch Canoe ` as a bait for the enemy, and to remain with the rest of the party, in order to succor and assist them if pursued, or to circumvent the enemy, for which purpose you are to be in constant readiness with your Men and Battoes, and keep a good lookout.

By the General's Command,

PETER WRAXALL,
A.D. Camp.

large advanced guard at the north end of Lake George, where the river issues out of it into Lake Champlain. While we were viewing these, I observed a bark canoe, with nine Indians and a Frenchman in it, going up the lake. We kept sight of them till they passed the point of land, where our canoe and men were left, where, when we arrived, we had information from our people that the above Indians and Frenchman had landed on an island six miles to the south of us, near the middle of the lake. In a short time after, we saw them put off from the island; and steer directly towards us; upon which we put ourselves in readiness to receive them in the best manner we could, and gave them a salute at about 100 yards distance, which reduced their number to four. We then took boat and pursued them down the lake, till they were relieved by two canoes, which obliged us to retreat towards our encampment at Lake George, where we arrived the 10th of October.

October 15, 1755. Agreeable to orders of this date from General Johnson, I embarked with forty men in five boats. Our design was to discover the strength of the enemy's advanced guard, and, if possible, to decoy the whole, or part of them, into an ambush; but tho' we were indefatigable in our endeavours for several days, yet all our attempts of this kind proved abortive; and, as an account of our several movements during this scout would little gratify the reader, I shall omit giving a particular detail of them. We returned safe to our encampment at Lake George on the 19th.*

---

* The report of this tour made to Gen. Johnson, contains many details omitted in the text:

"October 7th, 1755. In the evening embarked by order from the camp at Lake George, with a party of about 50 men to make discovery of the French at Atianderogoe, and we went by three or four

October 21, 1755. I had orders from General
Johnson on this date, to embark for Crown Point,

---

fires, and in sixteen miles sailing, I missed one batoe — it being dark
could not find it. Went on with the rest of the command, and about
brake [of] day landed our battoes on ye east side of ye Lake George,
within twelve miles of the Carrying Place, at Atenderrogo. Lay there
that day; made no discovery. The eighth day at evening, landed our
batoes and bore towards Tianderroge, and discovered a fire on an island. Put to land, and sent off a birch canoe to see what was there.
They, that were on the island discovered ye canoe, and put out their
fires, and, as we supposed, went off in their canoe. Then went
down with ye party within about seven miles of the Carrying Place,
and landed on a point on ye west side of Lake George, and drew up
ye batoes and secured them."

"On the 9th at morning, sent off Capt. Putnam, with one man and
Capt. Hunt with three men more, in order to go to the Carrying
Place and Tiandeeroge and make discoueries there and return to the
party. At evening, Capt. Hunt came back with two men. At night,
sent off Ens'n. Putnam with three men, and ordered them to make
what discovery they could with the birch canoe, and go to the Carrying
Place, tarry there all night, and in ye morning as soon as it was light
come back to their command. This night discouered several fires on
ye shore of ye lake."

"10th day, Sun half an hour high. In ye morning our birch canoe
came in. Kept out small scouts by land, and good guards, for fear of
the enemy coming on our backs. At sun about two hours high there
came up three birch canoes. They came by ye east shore and within
seventy rods of ye point where we were well ambushed for them.
They lay on their oars for the best part of an hour — twenty-three in
number. Then sent out our birch canoe to decoy them up by the
point. Our canoe went; parleyed with them within thirty rods —
then turned and paddled back up by y point — but they did not follow them, but turned down ye lake half a mile and bore over to the
west shore, and there landed their canoes. Our sentry and small
scouts came in, and said that they discovered Indians and heard them
talk. Capt. Putnam instantly came back with ye account [that]
ye Indians were on our backs. We found their party was too strong ,
for us to encounter. Launched our boats and got homewards fifteen
miles and lodged on an island."

"On the 11th we arrived at Lake George encampment, where we
took our departure from."—*Doc. Hist. N. Y.*, iv, 262.

The reports to Capt. Rogers, made by Capt. Israel Putnam, Capt.
Samuel Hunt and Ensign Timothy Putnam, are given in *Doc. Hist.
N. Y.*, iv, 264—266. They are found in *Johnson MSS.* iii, 57, 58, 59.

with a party of four men, in quest of a prisoner.* At
night we landed on the west side of Lake George,
twenty-five miles from the English camp. The remainder of the way we marched by land, and the
26th came in sight of the fort. In the evening we
approached nearer, and the next morning found ourselves within about 300 yards of it. My men lay
concealed in a thicket of willows, while I crept
something nearer, to a large pine log, where I concealed myself by holding bushes in my hand. Soon
after sun-rise the soldiers issued out in such numbers,
that my men and I could not possibly join each other
without a discovery. About 10 o'clock a single man
marched out directly towards our ambush. When I
perceived him within ten yards of me, I sprung over
the log, and met him, and offered him quarters,
which he refused, and made a pass at me with a dirk,
which I avoided, and presented my fusee to his
breast ; but notwithstanding, he still pushed on with
resolution, and obliged me to dispatch him. This
gave an alarm to the enemy, and made it necessary

---

* To CAPTAIN ROGERS :

You are to embark in the boats with the party under your command, and make the best of your way down the lake to within six
miles of the advanced guard of the enemy, and make the best disposition which circumstances will permit, to intercept any scouting parties
of the enemy who may be sent out on the lake for discovery, and
take as many prisoners as you possibly can.

Camp at Lake George, 29th Oct. 1755.

The accounts brought by Capt. Rogers concerning the enemy at
Ticonderoga, differing somewhat from that obtained through other
sources, led Sir William Johnson in writing to Sir Charles Hardy, Oct.
13, 1775, to explain the situation, and in referring to Rogers' account,
speak of him as one whose bravery and sagacity stand very clear in
my opinion, and of all who knew him. Tho' his regiment is gone, he
remains here a volunteer, and is the most active man in our army.

To-morrow he proposes to set off with two or three picked men,
take a review, if he can, of Ticonderoga, and proceed to Crown Point
for a prisoner.—*Johnson MSS.* iii, 83.

for us to hasten to the mountain. I arrived safe at our camp the 30th, with all my party.*

November 4, 1755. Agreeable to orders from General Johnson this day, I embarked for the enemy's advanced guard before mentioned, with a party of thirty men, in four battoes, mounted with two wall-pieces each. The next morning, a little before day-light, we arrived within half a mile of them, where we landed, and concealed our boats; I

---

* A report by "Capt. Rogers and Co." (signed by Robert Rogers, Jonathan Butterfield and Israel Putnam), was addressed to Gen. Johnson, under date of Oct. 22, [O. S.] as follows:

"On the 14th day of October, 1755, I embarked in a birch canoe at the camps on the south end of Lake George, with four men beside myself, and sailed twenty-five miles, and landed on the west side of the lake. Then traveled by land, and on the 18th day I arrived on the mountains on the west side of Crown Point, where I lay that night and all the next day, and observed the enemy's motions there, and about Crown Point. Observed Ambussers built upon the mount, about thirty rods to the south-west of Crown Point post. In the evening went down to the houses that were built upon the lake, to the south of Crown Point, and went into a barn that was well filled with wheat. Left three men and proceeded with one man to make further discoveries at the fort. Found a good place to ambush within sixty rods of the fort, and immediately went back and took our partners and ambushed, at the proper place we had found, and there we lay till about ten o'clock. Observed several canoes passing up and down the lake, and sundry men that went out to work about their secular affairs, and judged the whole that was in the fort to be about five hundred. At length, a Frenchman came out of the fort towards us, with his gun, and came within fifteen rods of where we lay. Then I with another man ran up to him, in order to capture him — but he refused to take quarters — so we killed him, and took his scalp, in plain sight of the fort — then ran, and in plain view, about twenty rods, and made our escape. The same night we came right west of Tianarago, about three miles, and upon a mountain in plain sight of their fort, and saw a large encampments around it, and heard a vast number of small arms fired. Judged there to be two thousand men at Tianarago.

"On the 21st day, got to our canoes about eight o'clock in the morning, and found all safe. About nine o'clock in the evening, arrived all well at our encampments, from whence we had set out."
—*Johnson MSS.* iii, 122 —*Doc. Hist. N. Y.,* iv, 269.

then sent out four men as spies, who returned the next evening, and informed me, that the enemy had no works around them, but lay entirely open to an assault ; which advice I dispatched immediately to the General, desiring a sufficient force to attack them, which, notwithstanding the General's earnestness and activity in the affair, did not arrive until we were obliged to retreat. On our return, however, we were met by a reinforcement, sent by the General, whereupon I returned again towards the enemy,*

---

* The party sent to reinforce Capt. Rogers, was under Capt. Roger Billings, who made a brief report, found in *Doc. Hist.* iv, 274. The original is in *Johnson MSS.* iii, 166.

Billings was the bearer of the following letter to Capt. Rogers :

"Agreeable to your message and desire, I send you a reinforcement of men under the command of Capt. Billings, who with the men, are to put themselves under your command. I would recommend you to act with silent caution, and so to post your men as to cut off their retreat to Ticonderoga. It appears to me most desirable to begin the attack from the water, securing their canoes, and that at break of day. You will consult with the officers upon your proceedings, but the stroke must be struck without delay. If there are any works and time will permit, destroy them. Do your business as soon as possible, and don't delay one moment. When you have done the best you can, suffer no men to delay time by looking after plunder, for if you are dilatory, the enemy from Ticonderoga may come upon you, and be too powerful for you to make a safe retreat."

Camp at Lake George, 2d Nov. 1755.

The instructions to Colonel Billings were as follows :

"You are to embark with the party under your command, in order to join Capt. Rogers. You are to keep the men orderly and silent, upon the pain of death, and not scatter the battoes out of sight of each other. Yourself, and the next officer in command to be in the last battoe, in order to bring up the rear regularly. On your joining Capt. Rogers, you are to be under his command, and deliver him my letter herewith. I have directed him to consult with the officers when occasion requires. Your success depends upon secrecy and silence. Let that be your principal care and attention. Take Connor in the battoe with you as a pilot, and let the officer who brings up the rear have the Indian who came from Capt. Rogers in his battoe.'—*Johnson MSS.* iii, 168.

and the next evening sent two men to see if the enemy's centries were alert, who approached so near as to be discovered and fired at by them, and were so closely pursued in their retreat, that unhappily our whole party was discovered. The first notice I had of this being the case, was from two canoes with thirty men in them, which I concluded came out with another party by land, in order to force us between two fires: to prevent, which I, with Lieutenant McCurdy, * and fourteen men, embarked in two boats, leaving the remainder of the party on shore, under the command of Captain Putnam.† In order to decoy the enemy within the reach of our wall-pieces, we steered as if we intended to pass by them, which luckily answered our expectations ; for they boldly headed us till within about an hundred yards, when we discharged the before mentioned pieces, which killed several of them, and put the rest to flight, in which we drove them so near where our land-party lay, that they were again galled by them ; several of the enemy were tumbled into the water, and their canoes rendered very leaky. At this time I discovered their party by land, and gave our people

---

* John McCurdy, Second Lieutenant of Capt. Rogers' company.

† This was Israel Putnam, afterwards Major-General in the Revolutionary war. He was then in command of a company of Connecticut levies, in Lyman's regiment. Putnam shared with Rogers the hardships and perils of many scouts during this campaign, but he seldom mentions his name, and on one occassion, as "One Captain Putnam, of Connecticut."

Is it not probable that jealousies may have been excited between them, that prevented amicable relations, and generous mention in the work written after the war was over? There are many anecdotes of Putnam, of this, and later periods, related by Mr. David Humphrey's, his biographer, but we consider the statements of this writer so little reliable, as not to be worth quoting.

notice of it, who thereupon embarked likewise, without receiving any, considerable injury from the enemy's fire, notwithstanding it was for some time very brisk upon them. We warmly pursued the enemy, and again got an opportunity to discharge our wall-pieces upon them, which confused them much, and obliged them to disperse. We pursued them down the lake to their landing, where they were received and covered by 100 men, upon whom we again discharged our wall-pieces, and obliged them to retire; but finding their number vastly superior to our's, we judged it most prudent to return to our encampment at Lake George, where we safely arrived on the 8th of November. *

---

* A report signed by Robert Rogers, Israel Putnam and Noah Grant, was addressed to Gen. Johnson, giving the following account of this expedition :

"Pursuant to your orders of ye 29th of October last, I set off with ye party to me ordered, and went down ye lake, and on ye 31st made a discovery of a number of fires, by night, situated on a point of land on ye west side of ye lake, (a) upon which we landed, and secured our battoes, upon ye same side of ye lake, about a mile and a half distance from their encampment. Next morning sent out spies for further discovery. In the evening Captain Fletcher, one of ye spies returned, leaving two of ye spies there, and made a report that there were four tents, and sundry small fires on ye point, and upon that, after consultation, it was concluded advisable to acquaint your Honor of our discovery, and reinforce us if you think it advisable, in order to proceed fu·thei, and make a push upon our enemy. Accordingly Capt. Fletcher was dispatched to you with six men in ye battoe,, and six being returned as invalids — leaving me with nineteen men only:— but being uneasy with the report, I took a battoe with five men, and went down within twenty-five rods of their fires. Discovered a small fort, with several small log camps within ye fort, which I judged to contain about a quarter of an acre — said fort being open towards ye water, the rest picketed. Made no further discovery there, and returned to my party. Found all well except Capt. Putnam and

---

(a)Conjectured by B. C. Butler, in his "*Lake George and Lake Champlain.*" (p 132), to have been at what is now known as "Friends Point," in the town of Hague, Warren Co.

Nov. 10, 1755. Pursuant to orders received this day from Gen. Johnson, in order to discover the enemy's strength and situation àt Ticonderoga, I proceeded on the scout with a party of ten men, on the 12th instant, and on the 14th arrived w:thin view of the fort at that place, and found they had

---

lay upon our oars, and inquired after the circumstances of yᵉ party yᵉ spies with him, who was not returned. The next morning, about 10 o'clock, Capt. Putnam returned, and yᵉ spies with him, who gave much the same account as above given — that yᵉ enemy's sentries were set twenty rods from the fires, and [that] for a more critical examination of yᵉ enemy's proceedings, he went forward till he came so nigh that he was fired upon by one of y sentries within a rod of him. But unfortunately, upon preparing to fire upon him, fell into a clay pit and wet his gun. Then made yᵉ best retreat he was able, having yᵉ enemy close on their heels. They made a tack, and luckily escaped safe to our party. Soon after, there was a discovery made of two Frenchmen upon a hill, a small distance, who called to us. Said hill overlooked our ambush. In a few moments they retreated, and two canoes appeared and went by us, and lay in yᵉ middle of yᵉ lake, about forty rods distance from each other. Judging by their behavior that there was a party coming by land, and that we must inevitably be between two fires."

"Upon which I ordered two battoes into yᵉ water. Lieut. Grant with six men, and I with six more, and put on board of each a wallpiece, and went out towards yᵉ canoes, who seemed to lie by their paddles, as though they had a design to decoy us into some mischief by their party, and that it was designed to surround our people on shore, and then attack us by keeping us between them and their party. Finding their design [we] attacked them first, put them to route and surprised [them] so that they made to yᵉ shore, where Capt. Putnam with yᵉ rest of our party lay. But unhappily for them, he was prepared for them, and shot and killed their cockswain ; and by our wallpieces, etc., killed divers of them. But upon his firing upon their canoe, immediately y enemy that was upon his back, fired and [he] had but just time to shove his battoe out into yᵉ water, and get into it, before yᵉ enemy appeared upon yᵉ water's edge, and made a brisk, fire upon him. [He was] shot through his blanket in divers places, and through yᵉ battoe, and he then made to our battoes for refuge. Upon his escape, we pursued yᵉ canoes with a constant fire upon them till we came within eighty rods of their fires. Discovered a number of men upon each side of yᵉ shore, within about forty rods of us, and gave each a broad side which put them to yᵉ bush, and gave us a clear passsage homewards. After we got fairly into yᵉ lake, [we]

erected three new barracks and four store-houses in the fort, between which and the water they had eighty battoes hauled upon the beach, and about fifty tents near the fort ; they appeared to be very busy at work. Having by these discoveries answered the design of our march, we returned, and arrived at our encampment on the 19th of November.

December 19, 1755. Having had a month's repose, I proceeded, agreeable to orders from General Johnson, with two men, once more to reconnoitre

---

Found none killed, but one wounded, which gave joy to all of us, after so long an engagement, which I judge, was near two hours.

"And then we made ye best of our way to our headquarters. About half way, we met with ye reinforcements — but upon consultation, thought best to report what had happened, without further proceeding, and accordingly arrived here, to ye encampment, ye 3^d instant."—*Johnson MSS.* iii, 172.—*Doc. Hist. N. Y.*, iv, 272.

The correspondence presented in the Johnson MSS., show that there was much diversity of opinion in the enemy's camp, at this period — from the conflicting reports of scouts, spies, and deserters — concerning the strength of the enemy at Ticonderoga and Crown Point.

Sir William Johnson in writing to General Shirley, Nov. 18. 1755, says :

"When Capt. Rogers had his skirmish with the enemy's advance party, he told me he heard the alarm cannon fired at Ticonderoga. I find upon looking over his written report, [that] he has omitted this circumstance. He persists that he was not mistaken, but very plainly, heard the cannon. Now I apprehend, that upon this alarm, the enemy assembled at Crown Point, and from all parts of the country that way, marched to Ticonderoga, imagining our army was coming forwards — posted themselves in some advantageous pass to oppose us, and that this was the army the Indian saw, for I cannot bring myself to think they were mistaken. The oldest of them is to this moment as positive as ever, with regard to the greatness of their fires, and that he clearly saw a vast number of tents. Whether that army remains, if broke up, upon further discovery that their alarm was groundless, or are taking measures to attack us — which of these is the case, I will not pretend to determine. Perhaps before the close of this day, some of our scouts may help us to form some more certain judgment."

Johnson MSS. iii, 215.

Letter to Col. Gradley. *Id.* iii, 204.

the French at Ticonderoga. In our way we discovered a fire upon an island adjacent to the route
we took, which, as we supposed, had been kindled
by some of the enemy who were there. This
obliged us to lie by and act like fishermen, the better
to deceive them, till night came on, when we proceeded and retired to the west side of the lake, fifteen miles north of our fort. Here concealing our
boat, the 20th we pursued our march by land, and
on the 21st, at noon, were in sight of the French
fort, where we found their people still deeply engaged at work, and discovered four pieces of cannon
mounted on the south-east bastion, two at the north-
west towards the woods, and two on the south. By
what I judged, the number of their troops were about
500.* I made several attempts to take a prisoner by
waylaying their paths; but they always passed in
numbers vastly superior to mine, and thereby disappointed me. We approached very near their fort by
night, and were driven by the cold (which now was
very severe) to take shelter in one of their evacuated
huts; before day, there was a fall of snow, which
obliged us with all possible speed to march homeward, lest the enemy should perceive our tracks and
pursue us.

We found our boat in safety, and had the good

---

* A deserter from the French, who was examined at Fort Edward, on
the 27th of December, 1755, reported the number of regulars at Ticonderoga, as 200, and of Canadians, 300 — with 20 Algonquin and
20 Iroquois savages. The latter were employed as scouts, and were
paid 1000 livres for each prisoner they should take. The Commandant of the fort was Mons Le Corn.

At Crown Point, he reported 50 regulars and 50 Canadians. The
French army of 3,000 had recently returned to Canada. The deserter
assigned scarcity of provisions as his reason for quitting the camps, and
reported that this scarcity prevailed throughout Canada.

fortune (after being almost exhausted with hunger, cold, and fatgue) to kill two deer, with which being refreshed, on the 24th we returned to Fort William Henry (a fortress erected in this year's campaign) at the south-end of Lake George. About this time General Johnson retired to Albany, to which place Commissioners were sent from the several governments whose troops had been under his command (New Hampshire only excepted).* These Commissioners were empowered by their respective constituents, with the assent of a council of war, to garrison Fort William Henry and Fort Edward, for that winter, with part of the troops that had served the preceeding year. Accordingly a regiment was formed, to which Boston government furnished a Colonel — Connecticut a Lieutenant-Colonel— and New York a Major: after which it was adjudged, both by Gen. Johnson and these Commissioners, that it would be of great use to leave one company of woodsmen or rangers under my command, to make excursions towards the enemy's forts during the winter; I accordingly remained, and did duty the whole winter, untill called upon by General Shirley.†

January 14, 1756. I this day marched with a party of seventeen men, to reconnoitre the French

---

* The Council assembled at Albany by General Shirley, consisted of Sir Charley Hardy, Mr. Fitch of Connecticut, Mr. Sharp of Maryland, Mr. Morris of Pennsylvania; Col. Peter Schuyler, Col. Dunham Major Craven, Major Rutherford and Sir John St.Clair.

Sir Wiliam Johnson in writing to Gov. Wentworth, Oct. 6, 1755, mentions that Col. Syms and Capt. Rogers, with a few of their men had agreed to stay at Lake George through the winter. He thought they would be of much service in the scouting way, and hoped his Excellency would approve of the arrangement.— *Johnson MSS.*, iii, 44.

† William Shirley, was Commissioned as a Colonel August 31, 1745, and Major General in the British army, Febuary 26, 1755.

forts ; we proceeded down the lake on the ice, upon skates, and halted for refreshment near the fall out of Lake George into Lake Champlain. At night we renewed our march, and, by day-break on the 16th formed an ambush on a point of land on the east shore of Lake Champlain, within gunshot of the path in which the enemy passed from one fort to the other. About sun-rise, two sledges laden with fresh beef were presented to our view, we intercepted the drivers, destroyed their loading, and afterwards returned to Fort William Henry, where I arrived with my prisoners and party in good health the 17th.

January 26, 1756. Pursuant to orders of this date, from Colonel Glasier,* I marched from Lake

---

* The following is doubtless the order here referred to, although of different date :

FORT WILLIAM HENRY, 29th Jany. 1756.
"SIR,

You are hereby ordered to march the party under your command the nighest and best way you can to Crown Point. Then take a view of that fortress and outworks, and make minutes of the same. If you meet Indians, or any enemies on your way, you are to take them prisoners, or kill them, or distress them any other way or means your prudence shall direct. You are to take good care of your men, and not expose them too much. You are to use all imaginable protection not to loose a man. If it should snow, you are to return immediately to this fort. If you discover any large bodies of the enemy, you are to send one of the most active of your men with intelligence to me. As soon as you can perform this service, you are to return to this fort with your party. I heartily wish you success."

—*Johnson* MSS. iv, 26. I am Sir, Your Humble Servant,
B. GLASIER.

To CAPT. ROBT. ROGERS :

The report of Capt. Rogers made upon his return to Fort William Henry, is more minute than as given in the text.

"Set out with a party of fifty men with orders to look into Crown Point and the advanced battery that is built around it. The first day we marched down the Lake George about eighteen miles and camped. So we proceeded by the westward of the great mountains and continued our march until the 2d of February ; then climbed up a great mountain, to the west of Crown Point, about one mile, and gave it the name of Ogden's Mount. There we took a particular view of the

George with a party of fifty men, with a design to discover the strength and works of the enemy at Crown Point.

On the 2d of February, we arrived within a mile of that fortress, where we climbed a very steep mountain, from which we had a clear and full prospect of the fort, and an opportunity of taking a plan of the enemy's works there. In the evening we retired to a small village, half a mile from the fort, and formed an ambuscade on each side of the road leading from the fort to the village. Next morning a Frenchman fell into our hands; soon after we discovered two more, but they unluckily got sight of us

---

fort and the ridouts that is built around it, and a plan of the same. We laid there until the evening, then went down the mountain, marched through a small village about half a mile from the fort to the southward. There we laid in ambush upon each side of the road that leads from the fort through s^d village. There we laid until about nine of the clock in morning, and there came along one Frenchman which we took prisoner, and two more were a coming toward us but discovered our ambush and made a speedy escape to the fort and some of my men pursued them within gunshot of the fort but could not overtake them. So we being discovered thought it needless to wait any longer for prisoners, but immediately set fire to the barns and house, where was abundence of wheat and other grain and we killed their cattle, horses and hogs in number about fifty. Left none living in s^d village to our knowledge.

"About 11 o'clock we marched homeward, leaving the village on fire. The 5th inst., in the morning, one of our men was taken sick, so I stopped with seven men and sent the rest home with Capt. Cushing and Lieut. Ogden. They arrived at our fort about 6 in the evening and I got home the next day about 4 o'clock in ye afternoon with the remainder of my party."

A true account by your humble servant,

Witness,
Seth Cushing.

Doc. Hist. N. Y., iv, 283-284.—*Johnson* MSS. v, 27.

before they were in our power, and hastily retired to the fort. Finding ourselves discovered by the enemy by this accident, we employed ourselves while we dare stay in setting fire to the houses and barns in the village, with which were consumed large quantities of wheat, and other grain; we also killed about fifty cattle, and then retired, leaving the whole village in flames* and arrived safe at our fort, with our prisoner, the 6th of February.

February 29, 1756. Agreeable to orders from Colonel Glasier, I this day marched with a party of fifty-six men down the west side of Lake George. We continued our route northward till the 5th of March, and then steered east to Lake Champlain, about six miles north of Crown Point, where by the intelligence we had from the Indians, we expected to find some inhabited villages. We then attempted to cross the lake, but found the ice too weak. The 17th we returned and marched round by the bay to the west of Crown Point, and at night got into the cleared land among their houses and barns; here we formed an ambush, expecting their labourers out to tend their cattle, and clean their grain of which there were several barns full; we continued there that night, and next day till dark; when discovering none of the enemy, we set fire to the houses and barns,

---

*The remains of a village with its streets, and the cellars of houses is still visible near the ruins of the fortress of Crown Point. The Swedish traveler Kalm, mentions a thriving settlement at this place: Mr. Winslow C. Watson in his history of Essex County, (p. 117), mentions the trace of a French settlement near Crown Point, and from allusions in ancient manuscripts and traditions draws the conclusion that this must have been the seat of an important traffic between the French and Indians, with a resident population estimated in its best days, at from 1,500 to 3,000 inhabitants; and that even before French military occupation, it might have been an important mart of Indian trade.

and marched off. In our return I took a fresh view of Ticonderoga, and reconnoitered the ground between that fort and the advanced guard on Lake George, approaching so near as to see their centries on the ramparts, and obtained all the knowledge of their works, strength and situation, that I desired.

The 14th of March, we returned safe to Fort William Henry.

(The next day, after my return from this scout, I received a letter, dated February 24, 1756, from Mr. William Alexander * of New York, who was secretary to Mr. Shirley, Commander in chief of the troops at Oswego the preceding year, and who now upon the decease of General Braddock,† succeeded to the chief command of all his Majesty's forces in North America, and was now at Boston, preparing for the ensuing campaign, being previously recommended to this gentleman by General Johnson. I was desired by the above mentioned letter to wait on him at Boston ; of which I informed the commanding officer at the fort, and, with his approbation, I set out on the 17th of March, leaving the command of my company to Mr. Noah Johnson,‡ my Ensign ; my brother Richard Rogers, who was my Lieutenant,

---

* Mr. Alexander served on Gen. Shirley's staff as aid-de-camp and private secretary, and after the war accompanied him to England to assist in the settlement of his accounts. He is known in history as Lord Stirling, a Major General of the American Revolution.

† Major General Edward Braddock was killed July 13, 1755, in a battle on the Monongahela near Pittsburgh.

‡ Johnson belonged in Dunstable, and had been in Lovewell's fight, in 1725. At the age of eighty, he went up to Freyburg, to show to the settlers the scene of this engagement.— *Stark's Reminiscences of the French War*, p. 18.

being sent to Boston by the commanding officer, on some dispatches previous to this.[*]

On the 23d, I waited on the General, and met with a very friendly reception; he soon intimated his design of giving me the command of an independent company of Rangers, and the very next morning I received the commission, with a set of instructions.

According to the General's orders, my company was to consist of sixty privates, at 3s. New York currency *per* day, three serjeants at 4s. an Ensign at 5s. a Lieutenant at 7s. and my own pay was fixed at 10s. *per* day. Ten Spanish dollars were allowed to each man towards providing cloaths, arms, and blankets. My orders were, to raise this company as quick as possible, to inlist none but such as were used to travelling and hunting, and in whose courage and fidelity I could confide; they were, moreover, to be subject to military discipline, and the articles of war.

Our rendezvous was appointed at Albany, from thence to proceed in four whale-boats to Lake George, and, "from time to time, to use my best "endeavors to distress the French and alliés, by "sacking, burning, and destroying their houses, "barns, barracks, canoes, battoes, &c., and by killing "their cattle of every kind; and at all times to en- "deavour to way-lay, attack, and destroy their "convoys of provisions by land and water, in any "part of the country, where I could find them."

---

[*] It is stated in Potter's History of Manchester, N. H. (p. 489), that Rogers while engaged in enlisting soldiers in Massachusetts, had become implicated with some others in counterfeiting the paper money of the colony, and was arrested and put under bonds for his appearance at court. The government was in want of troops, and an arrangement was soon made, that the proceedings should be stayed against him and his companions provided they enlisted for the war. Rogers was commissioned as a Captain and in a very short time, had his complement of men and was on his way to Albany.

With these instructions, I received letters to the commanding officers, at Fort William Henry and Fort Edward, directing them to forward the service, with which I was now particularly charged.*

When my company was completed, a part marched under the command of Lieutenant Rogers to Albany; with the remainder, I was ordered to march through the woods to Number Four then a frontier town greatly exposed to the enemy; where,†

April 28, 1756. I received orders to march from thence to Crown Point, in pursuance of which we travelled through deserts and mountains. The second day of our march, my Second Lieutenant, Mr. John Stark, was taken sick, and obliged to return, with whom I sent six men to guard him to Fort Edward.

We continued our march till the 5th of May, when I arrived with nine men at Lake Champlain, four miles south of Crown Point. Here we concealed our packs and marched up to a village on the

---

* The officers of this company were :
ROBERT ROGERS, *Captain.*
RICHARD ROGERS *First Lieutenant.*
JOHN STARK, *Second Lieutenant.*
NOAH JOHNSON. *Ensign.*
The company consisted of sixty privates, and was the nucleus of the famous " Roger's Rangers." — *Report of Adjutant General of N. H.,* 1866, ii, 158.

† " Number Four," now Charlestown, Sullivan Co. N. H., was granted by Massachusetts, and settled about 1736. A fort was built here at an early period, to check the enemy from Canada, in their inroads upon the English settlements. In the spring of 1747, the post was attacked by a large party of French and Indians under Monsieur Debeline, but gallantly and successfully defended by Capt. Phineas Stevens, who with thirty men, sustained a seige of three days, with but small loss. Sir Charles Knowles, who was then at Boston, sent an elegant sword to Captain Stevens, and when the place was incorporated as a town in 1753, it was named Charlestown in compliment to the commodore. The post was subsequently attacked several times by the enemy, and in March 1748, Captain Stevens was killed.

east side, about two miles distant from Crown Point, but found no inhabitants there. We lay in wait the whole day following, opposite to Crown Point, expecting some party to cross the lake; but nothing appeared except about four or five hundred men in canoes and battoes, coming up the lake from St. John's to Crown Point. We kept our station till next day, ten o'clock A M. to observe the motions of the enemy, but finding no opportunity to trapan any of them, we killed twenty-three head of cattle, the tongues of which was a very great refreshment to us on our journey. We at this time discovered eleven canoes manned with a considerable number of French and Indians crossing the lake directly towards us, upon which we retired; and the better to escape our pursuers we dispersed, each man taking a different route. We afterwards assembled at the place where we concealed our packs, and on a raft crossed over to the west side of the lake. In our way we had a view of the French and Indians, encamped at the old Indian carrying place, near Ticonderoga, and the 11th of May arrived safe at Fort William Henry. Mr. Stark, with his party, arrived at Fort Edward three days before. In their way they discovered a scouting party of three or four hundred Indians. Lieutenant Rogers with his party had arrived some days before this, and was at this time out upon a scout.

May 20, 1756. Agreeable to orders from the General, I set out with a party of eleven men to reconnoitre the French advanced guards. The next day, from the top of a mountain, we had a view of them, and judged their number to be about 300; they were busy in fortifying themselves with palisadoes. From the other side of the mountain we had a prospect of Ticonderoga fort, and, from the ground their encampment took up, I judged it to consist of about 1000 men. This night we lodged on the mountain, and next morning marched to the Indian carrying-path, that leads from Lake George to Lake Champlain, and formed an ambuscade between the French guards and Ticonderoga fort. About six o'clock 118 Frenchmen passed by without discovering us; in a few minutes after, twenty-two more came the same road, upon whom we fired, killed six, and took one a prisoner; but the large party returning, obliged us to retire in haste, and we arrived safe, with our prisoner, at Fort William Henry the 23d.

The prisoner we had taken reported, "that a party of 220 French and Indians were preparing to invest the out-parties at Fort Edward," which occasioned my marching the next morning with a party of 78 men to join a detachment of Col. Bayley's* regiment, to scour the woods as far as South Bay, if possible to intercept the enemy; but we could not discover them.

June 13, 1756. Agreeable to orders this evening, I embarked with a party of 26 men in battoes upon Lake George, to revisit the French advanced guard; excessive thunder and lightening obliged us to land at about ten miles distance from our fort, where we spent the night. The next morning, about sun-rise, we heard the explosion of upwards of twenty small arms, on the opposite side of the lake. which we supposed to be a party of French and Indians, cleaning

---

* Col. Jacob Bayley, was a native of Hampstead, to which father had moved from Newbury, Mass. After the close of the " Seven Year's War " he removed to Newbury, Vt., having obtained a grant of that town for himself and associates from Governor Wentworth. He was very influential in the Coös Country in the Revolution and held various important Civil Offices. He died March, 1815, aged 89 years.— *Report of Adjutant General of New Hampshire*, 1866, ii, 182.

their guns after the rain. In the evening we embarked again, and early in the morning of the 16th drew up our battoes about four miles distant from the advanced guard, and afterwards lay in ambush by a path leading from thence to a mountain, in order to surprise the enemy, who went there daily in parties, to take a view of the lake ; but finding they were not at that place, we marched to the spot where the enemy had posted their advanced guard, but they had retired and demolished all their works there ; we then continued our march toward Ticonderoga, near which place we ascended an eminence, and had a clear view of their works. I judged that their garrison and encampment consisted of about 3000 men : We then set out on our return, and arrived at Fort William Henry the 18th instant, except one man, who strayed from us, and who did not get in till the 23d, then almost famished for want of sustenance.*

---

* The report of this expedition made to General Johnson, was as follows :

"Journal of a Scout from Fort William Henry down into Lake Champlain, pursuant to an order from his Excellency, Major General Shirley to Captain Robert Rogers — as followeth, viz.

June ye 20th, 1756, set out with a party of fifty men in five Whale Boats, and proceeded at about twenty miles in Lake George, where we encamped. The next day went five miles further down y Lake and there landed, hauled our boats ashore, and carried them over a mountain about six miles to South Bay, where we arrived on ye 3d July, in the afternoon, and ye same evening went down ye Lake [to] about six miles distance from ye Forts.

July ye 4th towards morning we hauled up ye Boats on the east side of the lake and concealed them, and laid by until evening. Then set out again, and passed by Tiantiroga and found we were not discovered by being so near ye enemy as to hear ye sentry's watch word, we judged from the number of their fires [that] they had a body of about two thousand men, and that ye Lake in this place is about seventy rods [wide]. Continued on till day-light; about five miles from ye Fort; then hauled up ye Boats and concealed all day, on ye same shore, and discovered sundry Battoes, loaded and unloaded,

About this time the General augmented my company to seventy men, and sent me six light whaleboats from Albany, with orders to proceed immediately to Lake Champlain, to cut off, if possible, the provisions and flying parties of the enemy. Accordingly, June 28, 1756, I embarked with fifty men in five whale-boats, and proceeded to an island in Lake

which were coming and going upon yᵉ lake. [In a marginal note is here added — Thirty going loaded from Crown Point to Ticonderoga; two bark canoes, with about twenty Indians; nine empty, returning from Ticonderoga.]

In yᵉ evening of yᵉ fifth day, put off again, and attempted to pass by Crown Point; but thought it imprudent to pursue this intention by reason of the clearness and light of the night — so [we] hauled up boats again, and lay concealed all day, being of 6th current. This day near one hundred boats passed us, seven of which came very near us, and asked to land at the point where we lay, but their officers went further on, and landed about twenty-five rods from us, where they dined in our view; but [we] did not think it advisable to attack them in the situation we were in. [Added in a marginal note.— Thirty of the sailing boats, empty, and going north ward, and three loaded, going to Ticonderoga.] About 9 in yᵉ evening, set out again Passed yᵉ Fort at Crown Point and went ten miles from it down yᵉ Lake and hauled up yᵉ Boats about the break of day.

July 7th about ten in yᵉ morn, thirty boats passed towards Canada, [Supposed in part to be those seen the day before]; also a light schooner of about 35 or 40 tons. Set out again in yᵉ evening, and went fifteen miles further down, and went ashore about 1 o'clock A. M., upon a point on yᵉ east side of — and immediately sent a party further down the Lake for discovery. They saw a schooner at anchor some distance from yᵉ shore, about a mile from us, and, upon this intelligence, lighted our boats and intended to board them, but were prevented. About three o'clock saw two lighters coming up the Lake, who, we found, intended to land in yᵉ place where we were. These vessels we fired upon immediately, and afterwards hailed them, and offered them quarters if they would come ashore — which they said they would comply with — but instead thereof, put off in their boats to yᵉ opposite shore. But we foilowing them in our boats and intercepted them, and after taking them, found twelve men, three of whom were killed and two wounded. One of the wounded could not march therefore [we] put an end to him to preuent discovery. As soon as the prisoners were secure, we employed ourselves in destroying and sinking vessels and cargoes, which were chiefly Wheat, Flour, Rice,

George. The next day, at about five miles distance
from this island, we landed our boats, and carried
them about six miles over a mountain, to South Bay,
where we arrived the 3d of July. The following
evening we embarked again, and went down the bay
to within six miles of the French fort, where we
concealed our boats till the evening. We then embarked again, and passed by Ticonderoga undiscovered, tho' we were so near the enemy as to hear
their centry's watch-word. We judged from the
number of their fires, that they had a body of about
2,000 men, and the lake in this place to be near 400
yards wide. About five miles further down, we
again concealed our boats, and lay by all day. We
saw several battoes going and coming upon the lake.
At night we put off again, with a design to pass by
Crown Point, but afterwards judged it imprudent by
reason of the clearness of the night, so lay concealed

Wine and Brandy — except some few casks of brandy and wine, which
we hid in some very secure places, with our whale boats, at some distance on ye opposite shore. The prisoners informed us, that about
five hundred men, of which they were foremost, were on their passage at about two leagues distance, which occasioned us to get forward
on our return, on ye morning of the 8th inst and pursued our march
till ye 12th, when we arrived on the west side of Lake George, about
twenty-five miles from Fort William Henry. Sent Lieut. Rogers to
said fort for the battoes and provisions to carry us by water. On the
14th, in ye evening. ye Lieut. returned to us with thirty men and
ten battoes, and on the 15th at two o'clock, we arrived safe with all
my party and prisoners at Fort William-Henry."

In a letter from Gen. Winslow to Gov. Wentworh, dated June
27, 1776, the following account is given of this expedition:

"Capt. Rogers has lately returned from reconnoitering the fortress
of Ticonderoga, and informs us that the enemy are retired and under
their Fortress, and that he judges them to be three thousand strong at
that fort, and that they have been out and intirely destroyed their Advance Guard, about six miles on this side. Hope things will succeed
according to the desire of my Constituents, and my Country saved by
this expedition, which I am sensible is not only costly, but hazardous."

—*New Hampshire, Provincial Papers*— vi, 529.

again the next day, when near a hundred boats passed
by us, seven of which came very near the point
where we were, and would have landed there ; but
the officer insisted, in our hearing, upon going about
150 yards further, where they landed, and dined in
our view. About nine o'clock at night we re-im-
barked, and passed the fort at Crown Point, and
again concealed our boats at about 10 miles distance
from it. This day, being July 7th, 30 boats and a
schooner of about 30 or 40 tons, passed by us
towards Canada. We set out again in the evening,
and landed about fifteen miles further down, from
which place I sent a party for further discovery, who
brought intelligence of a schooner at anchor, about a
mile from us ; we immediately lightened our boats,
and prepared to board her ; but were prevented by
two lighters coming up the lake, who, we found, intended to land where we were posted ; these we
fired upon, then hailed them, and offered them quarters, if they would come ashore ; but they hastily
pushed towards the opposite shore, where we pursued and intercepted them ; we found their number
to be twelve, three of which were killed by our fire,
and two wounded, one of them in such a manner
that he soon died. We sunk and destroyed their
vessels and cargoes, which consisted chiefly of wheat
and flour, wine and brandy ; some few casks of the
latter we carefully concealed. The prisoners informed us, that they were a part of 500 men, the
remainder of which were not far behind on their
passage, which induced us to hasten our return to
our garrison, where, with our prisoners we safely
arrived the 15th of July. These prisoners, upon
examination, reported: "That a great number of
regular troops and militia were assembling at Cham-

blee, and destined for Carillon, or Ticonderoga;*
that great quantities of provisions were transporting
there, and a new General† with two regiments lately
arrived from France ; that there was no talk of any
design upon our forts on this side ; but that a party
of 300 French and 20 Indians, had already set out
to intercept our convoys of provisions between Albany and Lake George ; that 60 livres was the reward for an English scalp, and. that the prisoners
were sold in Canada for 50 crowns each; that their
prospect of an harvest was very encouraging, but
that the small-pox make great havoc amongst the
inhabitants." About the time of my setting out
upon this scout, Major-General Shirley was superseded in his command by Major-General Abercrombie,‡
who arrived at the head-quarters in Albany on the
25 of June, and brought with him two regiments of
regular troops from England. I therefore, upon my

----

*The former is the French, the latter the Indian name, signifying
the meeting or confluence of three waters.

Carillon, is a French word, signifying a chime of bells, and doubtless owes it application at Ticonderoga, to the music of the cascade in
the outlet of Lake George, above the modern village of Ticonderoga.
The principal fall is about 100 feet in hight — not in one sheet, but in
a steep descent over rugged rocks that break the stream into a mass of
foam. The outlet is about three miles and a half long, and is naviga-
ble up to the lower falls. The entire fall between the two lakes is 225
feet, the most of which is within a distance of a mile and a half.

The native name "Onderoga," or "Ticonderoga," is said to have
allusion to the music of these falling waters.

Brassiere's Map of Lake Champlain, (1762,) names this place
"Chonderoga" or Three Rivers."

†The Marquis de Montcalm, who commanded in the reduction of
Oswego this year, and of Fort William Henry the year following.
Note by the Author.

‡ James Abercrombie, became a Colonel April 16, 1746 and a Major-General in the British Army February 1, 1756.

return, wrote to his Excellency, desiring leave to lay before him the minutes of my last scout, and to recommend to his consideration an augmentation of the rangers. The General permitted me, with my brother Richard Rogers, to wait upon him at Albany. In this interview we discoursed on the subject of my letter, in consequence of which he immediately ordered a new company of rangers to be raised, and gave the command of it to my brother,* appointed Noah Johnson, my former Ensign, his First Lieutenant, Nathaniel Abbot† his Second Lieutenant,

---

* He completed his company in 28 days, and, by the General's orders, went up Mohawke river, to serve as a scouting party for the troops that way.

Note by the Author.

This second company of Rangers was officered as follows:
Richard Rogers, Captain.
Noah Johnson, First Lieutenant.
Nathaniel Abbott, Second Lieutenant.
Caleb Page, Ensign.
These, as well as the first company, were all of New Hampshire, and the men were mainly of this Province.
Rogers' original company of Rangers was then officered as follows:
Robert Rogers, Captain.
John Stark, First Lieutenant.
John McCurdy, Second Lieutenant.
Jonathan Burbank, Ensign.
    —*Report of Adjutant General of N. H.*, 1866, ii, 158.
About the first of December, 1756, the Corps of Rangers augmented by two companies, was officered in part as follows:
    ———*Hobbs*, Captain.
    ———*Bulkley*, Lieutenant.
    ———*Spikeman*, Captain.
    ———*Kennedy*, Lieutenant.
    ———*Brewer*, Ensign.
In the Spring of 1759, a new company of Rangers was formed, of troops from New Jersey, under the command of Capt. Burgin.

† Nathaniel Abbot, was born in Andover, Mass., in 1709, and when about thirty years old, settled in Penacook, N. H., of which he was an enterprising and useful citizen. He died in 1770.
    —*Bouton's Hist. of Concord* — p. 132.

and Caleb Page his Ensign.* John Stark, formerly my Second Lieutenant, was appointed my First, John McCurdy succeeded to his place, and Jonathan Burbank was appointed my Ensign.

August 2, 1756. Agreeable to orders received of General Abercrombie at Albany, the 23d of July, I embarked this day at Fort William Henry, on board one of the lighters built there this summer, with twenty one of my company, in order to reconnoitre the enemy at Ticonderoga and Crown Point, and sixty men under Capt. Larnard of the provincials, who had General Winslow's† orders to proceed with his men to the French advanced guard; but he not being acquainted with the way thither, put himself under my command. We landed this morning about fifteen miles down Lake George, and proceeded with the party till the 4th in the evening, and encamped about a mile from the advanced guard. The 5th in the morning mustered the whole party and got to the summit of a hill, west of the advanced guard where we discovered two advanced posts which I then imagined was the whole of the guard, one of them on the west side, half a mile southward of Lake Champlain, the other on the east side of the Lake opposite the former, at the old Indian carrying-place. We judged there were about 400 men on the east, and 200 on the west. After 'de-

---

* Caleb Page, Jr., son of a prominent citizen of the same name, was from Dunbarton, N. H., the home of Major Rogers. He was killed in the battle fought Jan'y., 22d, 1757.

He is said to have been the handsomest man of the Page family.

Stark's Hist. of Dunbarton, N. H., 189.

† General Winslow commanded the provincial troops this year, by virtue of a commission from the several provinces, who were concerned in 1755, in the same expedition, and was now with the greatest part of the provincial troops at Lake George.—*Note by the Author*

liberating with Capt. Larnard upon the strength, and disposition of the enemy, and the report of our advanced party, we concluded it unadvisable to continue there any longer. He returned towards Fort William Henry, and I went on with my own party till we came within view of Ticonderoga Fort, where from an eminence, I discovered the situation, but could not ascertain the strength of it to my satisfaction.

August 6, I went down towards Crown Point, by the west side of Lake Champlain, and discovered several battoes passing from that place to Ticonderoga with troops on board. We then proceeded to the place, where we burned the village, as mentioned before, and there encamped, and perceived a party sallying out, driving a number of horses to feed.

The 7th we lay in ambush by the road, with a design to intercept such as might come out to drive in the cattle ; but no one appearing for that purpose, we approached nearer, to within half a mile of the fort, where we were discovered by two Frenchmen, before they were in our power. This accident obliged us to make a retreat, in which we killed upwards of forty cattle. We arrived at Fort William Henry, August 10.

A company of Stockbridge Indians was this year employed in his Majesty's service, commanded by Indian officers, properly commissioned by General Shirley, before he was superseded in his command. General Abercombie was somewhat at a loss how to dispose of this company, and applied to Sir William Johnson, who advised, that a part,* viz.: thirty privates

---

* The remainder of this Indian company with their Captain, were sent to Saratoga, to be under the direction of Colonel Burton.
Note by the Author.

and a Lieutenant, should scout and scour the woods under my direction, which party had arrived while I was out upon my last scout, and Lieutenant Stark had strengthened their party with some of our people, and sent them out with particular directions what route to take, the day before I arrived.

About this time his Excellency, the Earl of Loudoun, arrived in Albany, and had taken upon him the command of the army, to whom I applied as I had done before, to Gen. Abercrombie, transmitting to him an account of the Indian scout above mentioned (who returned the 13th with two French scalps, agreeable to their barbarous custom) and desiring that with them I might attempt to penetrate into Canada and distress the inhabitants, by burning their harvest (now nearly ripe) and destroying their cattle.

Accordingly, August 16, we embarked in whaleboats in two departments, the one commanded by Lieutenant Stark, the other by myself. The next morning we joined each other, at which time also fell in with us a party of eight Mohocks, who had marched out from Fort William Henry the day before. We then marched directly to the place where we left our whale-boats the 7th of July, proceeding about twenty-five miles northward of Crown Point fort, on the west side of Lake Champlain, where we all (excepting one man who strayed from us and returned) arrived safe the 24th. We embarked again in our boats, and steered down the lake towards St. John's. The 25th we proceeded twenty miles further, and about midnight discovered a schooner standing up the lake with a fair wind towards Crown Point; they passed us so swiftly that we could not possibly board her, as we intended.

The 26th we landed, and the Mohocks left us to join another party of theirs, then out on a scout.

The 27th we got on a point, with a design to intercept the enemy's battoes that might pass up and
down the lake; but not discovering any, and our
provisions growing short, we returned up the lake,
and landed eight miles north of the fort at Crown
Point, on the east side of the lake.

The 29th in the morning we marched to a village
lying east of the fort, and in our way took prisoners,
a man, his wife and daughter, (a girl about fourteen
years of age) ; with these prisoners we returned, and
arrived safe at Fort William Henry, Sept. 22, 1756.

The man-prisoner, above mentioned, upon examination, reported : "That he was born at Vaisac, in
"the Province of Guienne, in France; that he had
"been in Canada about fifteen years, and in the colo-
"nies service about six, 'and two years at Crown
"Point; that there were only 300 men at Crown
"Point, and those chiefly inhabitants of the adjacent
"villages ; that there were 4000 men at Ticonderoga
"or Carillon, 1500 of which were regular troops,
"who had a sufficiency of all kinds of provisions ;
"that he never was at Ticonderoga or at the advance
"guard, but heard there were only fifteen men at the
"latter; that the French had 600 Indians at Ticon-
"deroga, and expected 600 more ; that 1200 were
"arrived at Quebec for Carillon, which last 1800
"were under the command of Mons. Scipio de la
"Masure ; that they had a great quantity of cannon,
"mortars, shells, &c., at Ticonderoga, but he did not
"know the number or quantity ; that they expected
" the above reinforcement in two or three days at
" Ticonderoga, having sent boats to Montreal to fetch
" them : that they understood by a letter that Oswego
" had fallen into their hands, but the news was not
" confirmed : that they had heard we intended to in-
" vest Carillon, but did not know what movements

" were intended on their side should we neglect it :
" that they had 150 battoes on Lake Champlain,
" which were kept at Carillon, thirty-five of which
" constantly plied between Montreal and that fortress :
" that Mons. Moncalm commanded at Frontiniac
" with 5,000 men, but did not know whether these
" troops were regulars or provincials : that a great
" number of vessels had arrived at Canada with pro-
" visions and military stores : that they heard we had
" several ships in the river Lawrence : that Mons.
" de Conte de Levi commanded at Carillon, and came
" last May from France ; and that, since the two last
" shallops or lighters (before mentioned) were taken,
" they had augmented the number of men on board the
" large schooner in Lake Champlain from twelve
" to thirty."

Upon my return to the fort, I received orders from
my Lord Loudon to wait upon Col. Burton, of the
48th regiment, for instructions, he being then posted
at Saratoga.   By him I was ordered to return to my
company at Fort William Henry, and march them to
the South Bay, thence east to the Wood Creek, then
to cross it southerly, opposite to Saratoga, and return
and make my report to him.

In this tour we apprehended four deserters from
Otway's regiment, who were going to the enemy,
and whom I sent back to Fort Edward, with a part
of my detachment, under the command of Lieutenant
Stark, and proceeded with the remainder to complete
my orders, after which I returned to Saratoga to make
my report.

There I met my brother Capt. Richard Rogers
with his company, he being ordered back from Mohock river, to join me with the remainder of the
Stockbridge Indians ; and I marched both companies
to Fort Edward, where I was ordered to form an en-

campment. A part of the Indian company were sent out on the east side of Lake Champlain to alarm the enemy at Ticonderoga, whilst I, with a detachment of my own, and Capt. Richard Rogers's company, was ordered on another party down Lake George, in whale-boats, and the remainder of the companies were employed in reconnoitering round the encampment, and also served as flankers to the parties that guarded provisions to Lake George. Capt. Jacob, who commanded the Indian party before mentioned, returned two days before me with four French scalps, which they took opposite to Ticonderoga on the east side.

Sept. 7, 1756. Agreeable to orders, I this day embarked on Lake George, with a party of fourteen men in a whale-boat, which we landed and concealed the evening following, on the east shore, about four miles south of the French advance guard. Here I divided my party, taking seven men with me, leaving the remainder in charge of Mr. Chalmer (a volunteer sent me by Sir John Sinclair) with orders, upon his discovering the enemy's boats going up the lake, &c., to make the best of his way with the intelligence to Fort William Henry.

I was the 9th current within half a mile of Ticonderoga fort, where I endeavored to reconnoitre the enemy's works and strength. They were engaged in raising the walls of the fort, and had erected a large block-house near the south-east corner of the fort, with ports in it for cannon. East from the block-house was a battery, which I imagined commanded the lake. I discovered five houses south of the fort close to the water-side, and 160 tents south-west of the fort, and twenty-seven battoes hauled upon the beach.

Next morning with one private, I went to view the falls betwixt Lake Champlain and Lake George (where I had heard the explosion of several guns the evening before, and had at that time sent Sergeant Henry to discover the reason of it) leaving the remainder of my party in charge of Mr. Gibbs, another volunteer, to wait our return. Sergeant Henry followed soon after me, and reported, " that the French were " building a small fort at the head of the falls on the " east-side of the lake; that he also discovered their " guard to the westward, and imagined both con- " sisted of 500 men." I returned, after finding the French were engaged in building a saw-mill at the lower end of the falls, and found my boats, with provisions left, as I suppose, by Mr. Chalmer and his party, whom I waited for till seven o'clock next day; but he not returning, and I judging from their tracks that they were returned to Fort William Henry, we likewise began our return, and arrived safe the 11th of September, where I found Mr. Chalmer and the party left with him, he having punctually obeyed the orders given him above. Upon my return, I communicated my observations upon the Lakes George and Champlain to my Lord Loudoun, giving him as just a description as I could of their situation.

September 24, General Abercrombie issued out orders, that three commissioned officers of the Rangers, with 20 privates each, should reconnoitre the Wood Creek, South Bay, and Ticonderoga ; and these were alternately sent out, so that a continual scout was kept up for a considerable time.

October 22, 1756. The greatest part of the army was now at Fort Edward, under the command of General Abercrombie, and Lord Loudoun arriving about this time with the remainder, it was generally expected that the army would cross the lake, and endeavour to reduce the French forts, notwithstanding the season was so far advanced ; but his Lordship taking into consideration the probability that those lakes would freeze (which they generally do in the month of December) in which case no supplies could be had from, nor any communication kept up with Fort William Henry ; he deteimined to desist from this design and contented himself with keeping the field till Mons. Montcalm retired to winter-quarters, and accordingly sought all opportunities to learn his situation and movements.

Agreeable to orders from his Lordship, I this day embarked in two whale-boats, with a party of twenty men, upon Lake George, with an intent to bring a prisoner from Ticonderoga. We passed the Narrows twenty miles from our embarkation, when Capt. Shephard (who was made a captive in August last, and carried to Canada) hailed our boat ; I knew his voice, and took him on board with three other men, one of whom was taken with him. He reported, that he left Canada fifteen days before. I went on my course till the 27th, towards Carillon, and landed that night on the west-side of the lake, concealed our boat, and travelled by land to within a mile of the fort. I kept spies out the day after to improve any opportunity that might offer, and the next day sent them still nearer, but to no good purpose ; I at length discovered two men, centries to the piquet guard of the French army, one of which was posted on the road that leads from the fort to the woods ; I took five of my party, and marched directly down the road in the middle of the day, till we were challenged by the centry. I answered in French, signifying that we were friends ; the centinel was thereby deceived, till I came close to him, when perceiving his mistake, in great surprize he called, *Qui etes vous?* I answered, " Rogers," and led him from his post in great haste,

6

cutting his breeches and coat from him, that he might march with the greater ease and expedition. With this prisoner we arrived at Fort William Henry, Oct. 31, 1756. Upon examination, he reported, " That he belonged to the regiment of Languedoc ; that he left Brest last April was a twelve-month, and had served since at Lake Champlain, Crown Point, and Carillon, was last year with General Dieskaw in the battle at Fort William Henry : that they lost in that engagement of regulars, Canadians, and Indians, a great number : that at Carillon were at this time mounted thirty-six pieces of cannon, viz. twelve eighteen pounders, fifteen twelve pounders, and nine eight pounders : that at Crown Point were eighteen pieces, the largest of which were eighteen pounders : " that Mons. Montcalm's forces this year at Carillon were 3000 regulars, and 2000 Canadians and Indians : that Montcalm himself was drawn off with one battalion, and that the forces then in that neighborhood consisted of five battalions and about 800 Canadians : that the Indians were all gone off, 200 of whom talked of returning to spend the winter at Carillon : that the advanced guard on the west side above the falls were all drawn in, and that on the east consisted of 600 men, who were to decamp the 1st of November : that they had a camp of five battalions, and sixty Canadians, about half a league from Carillon, and that the rest of the army were under the fort : that they had barracks sufficient for 500 men, which he understood were to quarter there : that they had one schooner and 200 battoes on Lake Champlain, and but five or six on Lake George : that Mons. the Chevalier de Levi commanded in Mons. Moncalm's absence, and that the Canadians were commanded by Messieurs le Corn and Columbie : that when Monsieur Montcalm went off, he said he had done enough for this year, and would take Fort William Henry early in the spring: that the French had taken four of Captain Rogers's whale boats in Lake Champlain: that when he was taken prisoner, he imagined himself to be about a gun-shot and a half from the fort, and that the French camp was pretty healthy."

From this time we were constantly employed in patrolling the woods about Fort Edward till the 19th of November, 1756, when I had his Lordship's orders to take another excursion down the Lake. Captain Abercrombie, Aid-de-camp and nephew to General Abercrombie, did me the honour to accompany me; but nothing material being in our power to effect, except taking a view of the fort and works of the enemy at Ticonderoga, we returned safe to Fort Edward the 25th in the evening.

About this time his Lordship drew off the main body of the troops from Fort Edward to be quartered at Albany and New York.

Both armies being now retired to winter-quarters, nothing material happened to the end of this year. The rangers were stationed at the Forts William. Henry and Edward, to which also two new companies of rangers were sent this fall, commanded by Captain Spikeman and Captain Hobbs, in one of which my brother James Rogers was appointed an Ensign.*

These two companies were stationed at Fort William Henry, mine and my brother Richard's at Fort Edward.

Captain Richard Rogers had leave to go into New

---

* Capt. Spikeman and Lieut. Kennedy were killed on this expedition. The former was succeeded in command by Lieut. John Stark, Major General in the Revolution.

England for recruits to complete our two companies. He this winter waited upon the government of Boston, to obtain pay for our services in the winter 1755 before mentioned, but could obtain none, notwithstanding Lord Loudoun, who was then at Boston, generously supported and enforced our solicitations with his interest.

January 15, 1757. Agreeable to orders from the commanding officer at Fort Edward, I this day marched with my own Lieutenant Mr. Stark, Ensign Page of Captain Richard Roger's company, and fifty privates of said companies, to Fort William Henry, where we were employed in providing provisions, snow-shoes, &c., till the 17th, when being joined by Captain Spikeman, Lieutenant Kennedy and Ensign Brewer of his company, and fourteen of their men, together with Ensign James Rogers and fourteen men of Captain Hobbs's company, and Mr. Baker,* a volunteer of the 44th regiment of foot, we began our march on the ice down Lake George, and at night encamped on the east-side of the First Narrows. The next morning, finding that some of the detachment had hurt themselves in the march the day before, as many were dismissed to return to the fort, as reduced our party to seventy-four men, officers included.

The 18th we marched twelve miles down the lake, and encamped on the west side of it.

The 19th we marched three miles from our encampment further down the lake, and then took the land, and, upon snow-shoes, travelled north-west about eight miles from our landing, and three from the lake, where we encamped.

The 20th we marched north-by-east the whole day, and at night encamped on the western side, op-

---

* Mr. Baker was killed on this expedition.

posite to and about three miles distant from Lake Champlain.

The 21st we marched east, till we came to the lake, about mid-way between Crown Point and Ticonderoga, and immediately discovered a sled going from the latter to the former. I ordered Lieutenant Stark, with twenty men, to head the sled, while I, with a party, marched the other way to prevent its retreating back again, leaving Captain Spikeman in the center with the remainder. I soon discovered eight or ten sleds more following down the lake, and endeavored to give Mr. Stark intelligence of it before he sallied on the lake and discovered himself to them, but could not. They all hastily returned towards Ticonderoga. We pursued them, and took seven prisoners, three sleds and six horses; the remainder made their escape. We examined the captives separately, who reported: "That 200 Cana-"dians and 45 Indians were just arrived at Ticonde-"roga, and were to be reinforced that evening, or "next morning, by fifty Indians more from Crown "Point; that there were 600 regular troops at that "fortress, and 350 at Ticonderoga, where they soon "expected a large number of troops, who in the "spring were ' to besiege our forts; that they had "large magazines of provisions in their forts, and "that the above mentioned party were well equipped, "and in a condition to march upon any emergency at "the least notice, and were designed soon to way-lay "and distress our convoys between the forts."

From this account of things, and knowing that those who escaped would give early notice of us at Ticonderoga, I concluded it best to return; and ordered the party, with the utmost expedition, to march to the fires we had kindled the night before, and prepare for a battle, if it should be offered, by trying our guns, it being a rainy day, which we effected; and then marched in a single file, myself and Lieutenant Kennedy in the front, Lieutenant Stark in the rear, and Captain Spikeman in the center. Ensigns Page and Rogers were between the front and center, and Ensign Brewer between the center and rear, Serjeant Walker having the command of a rear guard. In this manner we advanced half a mile, or therabouts, over broken ground, when passing a valley of about fifteen rods breadth, the front having reached the summit of a hill on the west side of it; the enemy, who had here drawn up in the form of a half-moon, with a design, as we supposed, to surround us, saluted us with a volley of about 200 shot, at the distance of about five yards from the nearest, or front, and thirty from the rear of their party. This fire was about two o'clock in the afternoon, and proved fatal to Lieutenant Kennedy, and Mr. Gardner, a volunteer in my company, and wounded me and several others; myself, however, but slightly in the head. We immediately returned their fire. I then ordered my men to the opposite hill, where I supposed Lieutenant Stark and Ensign Brewer had made a stand with forty men to cover us, in case we were obliged to retreat. We were closely pursued, and Capt. Spikeman, with several of the party, were killed, and others made prisoners. My people, however, beat them back by a brisk fire from the hill, which gave us an opportunity to ascend and post ourselves to advantage. After which I ordered Lieutenant Stark and Mr. Baker in the center, with Ensign Rogers; Serjeants Walter and Phillips, with a party, being a reserve, to prevent our being flanked, and watch the motions of the enemy. Soon after we had thus formed ourselves for battle, the enemy attempted to flank us on the right, but the above re-

serve bravely attacked them, and giving them the
first fire very briskly, it stopped several from retreating to the main body. The enemy then pushed us
closely in the front ; but having the advantage of the
ground, and being sheltered by large trees, we maintained a continual fire upon them, which killed several, and obliged the rest to retire to their main body.
They then attempted to flank us again, but were
again met by our reserved party, and repulsed. Mr.
Baker about this time was killed. We maintained a
pretty constant fire on both sides, till the darkness
prevented our seeing each other, and about sun-set I
received a ball thro' my hand and wrist, which dis-
abled me from loading my gun. I however found
means to keep my people•from being intimidated by
this accident ; they gallantly kept their advantageous
situation, till the fire ceased on both sides. The
enemy, during the action, used many arts and stratagems to induce us to submit, sometimes threatening
us with severity if we refused, assuring us that they
every moment expected a large reinforcement, which
should cut us to pieces without mercy ; at other
times flattering and cajolling us, declaring it was a
pity so many brave men should be lost ; that we
should, upon our surrender, be treated with the greatest compassion and kindness ; calling me by name,
they gave me the strongest assurances of their esteem
and friendship that words could do ; but no one being dismayed by their menances, or flattered by fair
promises, we told them our numbers were sufficient,
and that we were determined to keep our ground as
long as there were two left to stand by each other.

After the action, in which we had a great number
so severely wounded that they could not travel without assistance, and our ammunition being nearly expended, and considering that we were near to Ticon-

deroga, from whence the enemy might easily make a descent, and overpower us by numbers, I thought it expedient to take the advantage of the night to retreat, and gave orders accordingly; and the next morning arrived at Lake George, about six miles south of the French advanced guard, from whence I dispatched Lieutenant Stark with two men to Fort William Henry, to procure conveyances for our wounded men thither; and the next morning we were met by a party of fifteen men and a sled, under the command of Lieutenant Buckley, of Hobbs's company of Rangers, at the first narrows at Lake George. Our whole party, which now consisted of only forty-eight effective, and six wounded men, arrived at Fort William Henry the same evening, being the 23d of January, 1757.*

---

* This engagement is located by Mr. Watson in his history of Essex Co., (p. 64,) as near the residence of M. B. Townsend, in the town of Crown Point.

In Mr. Stark's edition of Rogers' Journals, the following note is given:

"In regard to the battle of January 21, 1757, the late venerable Mr. Shute, of Concord, remarked that Rogers did not act with his usual prudence. He states that after taking the sleds, a council of war advised to return by a different route from that by which the party came, which was the usual practice of the Rangers, and on this occasion, would have enabled them to escape the hazards of a battle. Rogers however, said in regard to the enemy, that they would not *dare* to pursue him, and took the same route back. The first notice the Rangers had of the enemy was the noise in cocking their guns, which Shute supposed was one of the rangers preparing to kill a partridge. He was himself struck senseless by a shot, which ploughed the top of his head; on coming to himself, the first sight which met his eyes, was one of the Rangers cutting off Rogers' cue to stop the hole in his wrist, through which a shot had passed. On the night of their retreat, the Rangers made a circuit, to avoid a large fire in the woods, supposing the Indians were there. This caused them to lose time so that Joshua Morton, who had kindled the fire to warm himself, was enabled to follow, and get in sight of them, on the lake; otherwise he must have perished."

Stark's Reminiscences of the French War. (p. 36.)

The nearest computation we could make of the number which attacked us, was, that it consisted of about 250 French and Indians; and we afterwards had an account from the enemy, that their loss in this action, of those killed, and who afterwards died of their wounds, amounted to 116 men.

Both the officers and soldiers I had the honour to command, who survived the first onset, behaved with the most undaunted bravery and resolution, and seemed to vie with each other in their respective stations who should excel.[1]

Having laid this return before Major Sparks, commanding officer at Fort Edward, he transmitted the same to the General; and the 30th of January following, I wrote to Capt. James Abercrombie, then at Albany, recommending such officers as I thought most deserving, to fill up the vacancies occasioned by our late action, among whom were Lieutenant Stark to be Captain of Spikeman's company, and Serjeant Joshua Martin to be Ensign in Captain Richard Roger's company; and I also mentioned several things in favour of the Rangers. In consequence whereof, I received the following answer:

Albany Feb. 6, 1757.

DEAR SIR:

"The General received your letter that was sent by Major Sparks, and returns you and your men thanks for their behaviour, and has recommended both you and them strongly to my Lord Loudoun, as also that they have payment for the prisoners they

---

[1] A detailed account of this expedition is given by Dr. Asa Fitch, in his survey of Washington County.
—*Transactions of N. Y. State Agricultural Society*—1848. (P. 917.)

The following is the RETURN which was made of the Killed, Wounded and Missing, in the above action, *viz.* :

Company	Name	Killed	Missing	Wounded
Captain Roger's Company.	Capt. Robert Rogers			Wounded
	Mr. Baker, Volunteer	Killed		
	Mr. Gardner, ditto	ditto		
	Thomas Henson,	ditto		
	Serjeant Martin -			ditto
	Thomas Burnside -			ditto
	Sarjeant Henry -		Missing.	
	William Morris -		ditto	
	John Morrison -		ditto	
C. Rd. Roger's do.	Joseph Stephens -	ditto		
	Benjamin Woodall		ditto	
	David Kemble -		ditto	
	Ensign Caleb Page	ditto		
	David Page -			ditto
Capt. Hobbs's ditto.	Serjeant Jon. Howard	ditto		
	Phineas Kemp -	ditto		
	John Edmonds -	ditto		
	Thomas Farmer -	ditto		
	Emanuel Lapara -	ditto		
Capt. Spikeman's ditto.	Capt Spikeman -	ditto		
	Lieut. Kennedy -	ditto		
	Robert Avery - -	ditto		
	Thomas Brown - -		ditto	
	Samuel Fisk - -	ditto		
	Serjeant Moore - -			ditto
	John Cahill - -			ditto
	Total,	14	6	6

N. B. Those returned as Missing, we afterwards found, had been taken prisoners by the enemy.

— *Note by the Author.*

took. Upon receiving an account of your skirmish we sent an express to Boston, and, by the said opportunity, recommended, for Spikeman's company, your brother,* for a Lieutenant. We expect the express back in a day or two, by whom, I dare say, we shall have my Lord's approbation of the Rangers. Please to send me the names of the officers you would recommend for your own company, and also to fill up the vacancies in the others ; as I am certain you have the good of the service at heart, your recommendation will be paid great regard to. I yesterday received your's of the 30th of January. You cannot imagine how all ranks of the people here are pleased with your conduct, and your mens behaviour; for my part, it is no more than I expected ; I was so pleased with their appearance when I was out with them, that I took it for granted they would behave well whenever they met the enemy. When I returned I reported them as such, and am glad they have answered my expectation.

"I am heartily sorry for Spikeman and Kennedy, who I imagined would have turned out well, as likewise for the men you have lost ; but it is impossible to play at bowls without meeting with rubs. We must try to revenge the loss of them. There is few people that will believe it ; but, upon honour, I could be glad to have been with you, that I might have learned the manner of fighting in this country. The chance of being shot is all stuff, and King William's opinion and principle is much the best for a soldier, viz. : " That every bullet has it's billet,' and that it is " alloted how every man shall die ; " so that I am certain that every one will agree, that it is better to die with the reputation of a brave man,

---

* James Rogers. *(Note in the Original.)*

fighting for his country in a good cause, than either shamefully running away to preserve one's life, or lingering out an old age, and dying in one's bed, without having done his country or his King any service.

"The histories of this country, particularly, are full of the unheard-of cruelties committed by the French, and the Indians, by their instigation, which I think every brave man ought to do his utmost to humble that haughty nation, or reduce their bounds of conquest in this country to a narrow limit. As soon as General Abercrombie receives my Lord's instructions in regard to the Rangers, I shall send you notice of it; in the interim, I hope you'll get the better of your wound. If I can be of any service to you or your men as long as they continue to behave so well, you may command.

Your most humble servant,

To Capt.   JAMES ABERCROMBIE,
Robert Rogers.   Aid de Camp."

My wound growing worse, I was obliged to repair to Albany for better assistance, and there received the following instructions from General Abercrombie, viz.

Instructions for Capt. ROBERT ROGERS.

" His Excellency the Earl of Loudoun having given authority to me to augment the company of Rangers under your command, to 100 men each, viz.

One Captain, ⎫
Two Lieutenants, ⎬ upon an English pay;
One Ensign, ⎭

Four Serjeants at 4s. each, New York currency;

100 private men, at 2s. and 6d. each ditto per day;

" And whereas there are some private men of your company serving at present upon higher pay than the above establishment, you are at liberty to discharge them, in case they refuse to serve at the said establishment, as soon as you have other men to replace them. If your men agree to remain with you and serve upon the above establishment, you may assure them they will be taken notice of, and will be first provided for; each man to be allowed ten dollars bounty-money, and to find their own cloaths, arms, and blankets, and to sign a paper subjecting themselves to the rules and articles of war, and to serve during the war. You are to enlist no vagrants, but such as you and your officers are acquainted with, and who are every way qualified for the duty of Rangers; and you and your officers are to use your best endeavors to complete your companies as soon as possible, and bring them to Fort Edward.

JAMES ABERCROMBIE,
Major General."

About this time I again wrote to his Lordship, earnestly soliciting his friendly interposition and assistance, to obtain from the government here, an order for payment of what was due to me and my men, for our respective services during the winter 1755; but if that could not be obtained, that he would be pleased to direct me what method to take for recovery thereof. Whitherto his Lordship replied, that as these services were antecedent to his command here, it was not in his power to reward them. General Amherst, afterwards, on a like application, gave me much the same answer.

These applications not being attended with any

success, and suits of law being afterwards commenced against me, by, and on the behalf of those who served under me in that campaign, and verdicts obtained in their favour, I was not only obliged to answer their several demands, to the amount of £. 828 : 3 : 3 sterling, which I paid out of my private fortune, but also a considerable sum for law charges, exclusive of what I ought to have received for my own services during that severe season. But for all which I have not at any time since received one shilling consideration.

In the same letter I likewise informed his Lordship of the death of Capt. Hobbs of the Rangers who died a few days before, and recommended Lieutenant Bulkley of the same company, as a proper person to succeed him in that command.

March 5, I was taken ill with the small-pox, and not able to leave my room till the 15th of April following, during which time my officers were recruiting, agreeable to his Lordship's instructions. Not long after I received the following letter from Capt. Abercrombie.

New York, April 22, 1757.

Sir,

"As there is another ranging company sent up to Albany, with orders to proceed to the forts, you will acquaint Colonel Gage, that it is my Lord Loudoun's orders, that the two companies at Fort William Henry, and your own from Fort Edward, come down immediately to Albany, to be ready to embark for this place. Show this letter to Colonel Gage, that he may aquaint Colonel Monro of his Lordship's orders, and that quarters may be provided for your companions in the houses about Albany. You will take particular care that the companies have provided themselves with all necessaries, and see that they are complete and good men. Since his Lordship has put it in your charge, I hope you will be very diligent in executing the trust, for, upon a review of the men, if any are found insufficient for the service, the blame will be laid upon you. If the officers of this ranging company that is gone up, are not acquainted with the woods about Fort William Henry, your brother must send some officers and men of his company along with them, to let them know the different scouts. I am Sir,

Your most humble servant,

To Capt.   JAMES ABERCROMBIE,
Robert Rogers,   Aid de Camp."
at Albany.

Capt. Richard Rogers, with his own, and the new company of Rangers before mentioned, which was raised in the Jersies, and commanded by Capt. Burgin, being left at Fort William Henry, my own company from Fort Edward, and Capt. Stark's and Capt. Bulkley's from Fort William Henry, agreeable to the above instructions, marched down to Albany, and from thence embarked for New York, where we were joined by another new raised company of Rangers, under the command of Capt. Shephard from New Hampshire, and after some small stay there, re-embarked on board a transport, and left Sandy Hook on the 20th of June, with a fleet of near an hundred sail, bound for Halifax, where we soon arrived, and, according to orders, I encamped on the Dartmouth side of the harbour,* while the

---

* Dartmouth lies on the east side of Chibucto Harbor, opposite the town of Halifax.

army lay encamped on the Halifax side. The Rangers were here employed in various services.

On July 3d, by orders, I commanded a party to Lawrence Town, and from thence to Schitzcook; some were left there to cut and make up hay in the meadows, for the horses intended to be used in an expedition to Louisburg; others covered the haymakers, and others were dispatched on scouts, to make discoveries; in one of which two deserters from the 45th regiment were seized and brought in.

About the latter end of this month forty Rangers were sent across the Isthmus of Nova Scotia, to the settlements on the Bay of Fundy, and a party down to the north-west arm, to scour the woods for deserters, &c., and brought in several, both from the army and navy.

About this time Admiral Holbourn arrived with a fleet from England, with several regiments of regular troops on board, which were landed, and likewise encamped at Halifax, upon which all scouting parties were called in; but certain intelligence being received that a French fleet of superior force had actually arrived at Louisburg, the intended expedition against that place was laid aside, and thereupon the Rangers were remanded back to the western frontiers.

Great numbers of the Rangers having been carried off this summer by the small-pox, I sent several of my officers, by his Lordship's command, to recruit in New Hampshire, and the Massachuset's provinces, with orders to join me at Albany. I afterwards embarked with the Rangers under my command, on board the fleet which carried the regular troops to New York, and from thence proceeded in small vessels up Hudson's River to Albany, where I was soon after joined by the new-raised recruits.

I then proceeded to Fort Edward, which was the only remaining cover to the northern frontiers of New York, and the more eastern provinces, Fort William Henry * having been taken by the French, under the command of Monsieur Montcalm, the August before.† General Webb was then command-

---

* My brother Captain Richard Rogers died with the small-pox a few days before this fort was besieged; but such was the cruelty and rage of the enemy after their conquest, that they dug him up out of his grave, and scalped him. In consequence of the articles of capitulation at the surrender of this fort, the two companies of Rangers there were disbanded, and dismissed the service.

—*Note by the Author.*

In Stark's edition of Rogers Journal, the following note is added:

"When the French took Fort William Henry, they were rather more favorable with Samuel Blodget, the suttler of the garrison, whom they found concealed under a battoe, than they were with the remains of Capt. Rogers. They suffered him to go about his business, after plundering him of everything but his scalp. He was never partial to the military service afterwards; but became a considerable Merchant, a Judge, and was the first projector of the canal at Amoskeag Falls, on Merrimack River. He lived to a great age, and died at the Falls, universally respected, as an enterprising and public spirited citizen."

Pouchot, in his Memoirs of the war of 1756—60, mentions an instance of disinterment of the dead — perhaps the same as that of Richard Rogers, above noticed by the author, and relates the consequences as follows:

"The Indians as they set out to return to their country, carried with them a disease of which many died. Some of them seeing new graves, disinterred the dead to take their scalps, but unfortunately found that they had died of the small-pox, and the infection was thus given to the Indians. The Poutéotame's Nation, one of the bravest and most strongly attached to the French, almost entirely perished of this epidemic. We especially regretted some of the Chiefs, whom the French highly esteemed."

—*Hough's Translation of Pouchot's Memoirs,* ii, 91.

† In Stark's edition of Rogers' Journals, a statement is here introduced as text not found in the original. It is as follows:

"The capture of William Henry was more than once attempted by the French. Longee, a famous French Partisan, endeavored to effect a surprise on the night of March 17, 1757, while the Irish portion of the garrison were engaged in a drunken carousal. It was, however,

ing officer at Fort Edward, and by his orders we were continually employed in patrolling the woods between this fort and Ticonderoga. In one of these parties, my Lord How did us the honour to accompany us, being fond, as he expressed himself, to learn our method of marching, ambushing, retreating, &c., and, upon our return expressed his good opinion of us very generously.)

About this time Lord Loudoun sent the following volunteers in the regular troops, to be trained to the anging, or wood-service, under my command and inspection; with particular orders to me to instruct them to the utmost of my power in the ranging discipline, our methods of marching, retreating, ambushing, fighting, &c., that they might be the better qualified for any future services against the enemy we had to contend with, desiring me to take particular notice of each one's behaviour, and recommend them according to their several deserts,) *viz.* :

Walter Crofton Mr. Lyshat Mr. Roberts	of the 4th regiment of foot.
Charles Humbles Richard Edlington Andrew Crawley Thomas Millet	of the 22d ditto.

---

defeated by the vigilence of the Rangers, who repulsed the French, while the other troops were coming to their senses."
Reminiscenses of the French War, p. 43.

He also gives as "text," an account of the siege and capture of Fort William Henry, with reflections upon that event, which, perhaps should have occurred, or did occur to Major Rogers, but were ommitted in his own edition of the Journals.

A more detailed account of the St. Patrick's affair, is given by Mr. Caleb Stark, in his *Memoirs* and *Official Correspondence of Gen. John Stark.* p. 20.

John Wilcox John Wrightson Michael Kent Mr. Monsel Francis Creed	of the 27th ditto.
Alexander Robertson William Frazier John Graham Andrew Ross William Frazier, Jun. Archibald Campbell Arch. Campbell, Jun. Augus. Campbell Charles Menzies John Robertson	of the 42d ditto.
Will. Ervin, or Irwin Thomas Drought William Drought Francis Carruthers John Clarke	of the 44th ditto.
Walter Paterson Mr. Nicholson Richard Boyce Charles Perry	of the 48th ditto.
Mr. Christopher Mr. Still Mr. Hamilton Mr. Young	of the 55th ditto.
Allen Grant Jonathan McDougal Mr. Frisborough	of the second battalion of Royal Americans.
Nicholas Ward James Hill	of the 3d ditto.

John Schloser
Geor ge Wardoman
Francis Barnard
Engelbertus Horst
Ericke Reinhault
Andrew Wackerberg ⎬ of the 4th ditto.
Luhainfans Dekesar
Donald M'Bean
Henry Ven Bebber
John Boujour

Edward Crafton
James Pottinger
Simon Stephens
Archibald McDonald ⎬ Rangers.
Hugh Sterling
Mr. Bridge

These volunteers I formed into a company by themselves, and took the more immediate command and management of them to myself; and for their benefit and instruction reduced into writing the following rules or plan of discipline, which, on various occasions, I had found by experience to be necessary and advantageous, *viz.*:

I. All Rangers are to be subject to the rules and articles of war; to appear at roll-call every evening on their own parade, equipped, each with a fire-lock, sixty rounds of powder and ball, and a hatchet, at which time an officer from each company is to inspect the same, to see they are in order, so as to be ready on any emergency to march at a minute's warning; and before they are dismissed the necessary guards are to be draughted, and scouts for the next day appointed.

II Whenever you are ordered out to the enemies forts or frontiers for discoveries, if your number be small, march in a single file, keeping at such a distance from each other as to prevent one shot from killing two men, sending one man, or more, forward, and the like on each side, at the distance of twenty yards from the main body, if the ground you march over will admit of it, to give the signal to the officer of the approach of an enemy, and of their number, &c.

III. If you march over marshes or soft ground, change your position, and march abreast of each other, to prevent the enemy from tracking you, (as they would do if you marched in a single file) till you get over such ground, and then resume your former order, and march till it is quite dark before you encamp, which do, if possible, on a piece of ground that may afford your centries the advantage of seeing or hearing the enemy at some considerable distance, keeping one half of your whole party awake alternately through the night.

IV. Some time before you come to the place you would reconnoitre, make a stand, and send one or two men, in whom you can confide, to look out the best ground for making your observations.

V. If you have the good fortune to take any prisoners, keep them separate, till they are examined, and in your return take a different rout from that in which you went out, that you may the better discover any party in your rear, and have an opportunity, if their strength be superior to yours, to alter your course, or disperse, as circumstances may require.

VI. If you march in a large body of three or four hundred, with a design to attack the enemy, divide your party into three columns, each headed by a proper officer, and let these columns march in single files, the columns to the right and left keeping at twenty yards distance or more from that of the center, if the ground will admit, and let proper guards be kept in the front and rear, and suitable flanking parties at a due distance as before directed, with orders to halt on all eminences, to take a view of the surrounding ground, to prevent your being ambuscaded, and to notify the approach or retreat of the enemy, that proper dispositions may be made for attacking, defending, &c. And if the enemy approach in your front on level grouud, form a front of your three columns or main body with the advanced guard, keeping out your flanking parties, as if you were marching under the command of trusty officers, to prevent the enemy from pressing hard on either of your wings, or surrounding you, which is the usual method of the savages, if their number will admit of it, and be careful likewise to support and strengthen your rear guard.

VII. If you are obliged to receive the enemy's fire, fall, or squat down, till it is over, then rise and discharge at them. If their main body is equal to yours, extend yourselves occasionally; but if superior, be careful to support and strengthen your flanking parties, to make them equal with theirs, that if possible you may repulse them to their main body, in which case push upon them with the greatest resolution, with equal force in each flank and in the centre, observing to keep at a due distance from each other, and advance from tree to tree, with one half of the party before the other ten or twelve yards. If the enemy push upon you, let your front fire and fall down, and then let your rear advance thro' them and do the like, by which time those who before were in front will be ready to discharge again, and repeat the same alternately, as occasion shall require; by this means you will keep up such a constant fire, that the enemy will not be able easily to break your order, or gain your ground.

VIII. If you oblige the enemy to retreat, be careful, in your pursuit of them, to keep out your flanking parties, and prevent them from gaining eminences, or rising grounds, in which case they would perhaps be able to rally and repulse you in their turn.

IX. If you are obliged to retreat, let the front of your whole party fire and fall back, till the rear hath done the same, making for the best ground you can; by this means you will oblige the enemy to pursue you, if they do it at all, in the face of a constant fire.

X. If the enemy is so superior that you are in danger of being surrounded by them, let the whole body disperse, and every one take a different road to the place of rendezvous appointed for that evening, which must every morning be altered and fixed for the evening ensuing, in order to bring the whole party, or as many of them as possible together, after any separation that may happen in the day; but if you should happen to be actually surrounded, form yourselves into a square, or, if in the woods, a circle is best, and, if possible, make a stand till the darkness of night favours your escape.

XI. If your rear is attacked, the main body and flankers must face about to the right or left, as occasion shall require, and form themselves to oppose the enemy, as before directed; and the same method must be observed, if attacked in either of your flanks, by which means you will always make a rear of one of your flank guards.

XII. If you determine to rally after a retreat, in order to make a fresh stand against the enemy, by all means endeavor to do it on the most rising ground you can come at, which will give you greatly the advantage in point of situation, and enable you to repulse superior numbers.

XIII. In general, when pushed upon by the enemy, reserve your fire till they approach very near, which will then put them into the greater surprise and consternation, and give you an opportunity of rushing upon them with your hatchets and cutlasses to the better advantage.

XIV. When you encamp at night, fix your centries in such a manner as not to be relieved from the main body till morning, profound secrecy and silence being often of the last importance in these cases. Each centry, therefore, should consist of six men, two of whom must be constantly alert, and when relieved by their fellows, it should be done without noise; and in case those on duty see or hear any thing which alarms them, they are not to speak, but one of them is silently to retreat, and acquaint the commanding officer thereof, that proper dispositions may be made; and all occasional centries should be fixed in like manner.

XV. At the first dawn of day, awake your whole detachment; that being the time when the savages chuse to fall upon their enemies, you should by all means be in readiness to receive them.

XVI. If the enemy should be discovered by your detachments in the morning, and their numbers are superior to yours, and victory doubtful, you should not attack them till the evening, as then they will not

know your numbers, and if you are repulsed, your retreat will be favoured by the darkness of the night.

XVII. Before you leave your encampment, send out small parties
to scout round it, to see if there be any appearance or track of an
enemy that might have been near you during the night.

XVIII. When you stop for refreshment, chuse some spring or rivulet
if you can, and dispose your party so as not to be surprised, posting
proper guards and centries at a due distance, and let a small party way-
lay the path you came in, lest the enemy should be pursuing.

XIX. If, in your return, you have to cross rivers, avoid the usual
fords as much as possible, lest the enemy should have discovered, and
be there expecting you.

XX. If you have to pass by lakes, keep at some distance from the
edge of the water, lest, in case of an ambuscade or an attack from
the enemy, when in that situation, your retreat should be cut off.

XXI. If the enemy pursue your rear, take a circle till you come to
your own tracks, and there form an ambush to receive them, and give
them the first fire.

XXII. When you return from a scout, and come near our forts,
avoid the usual roads, and avenues thereto, lest the enemy should have
headed you, and lay in ambush to receive you, when almost exhausted
with fatigues.

XXIII. When you pursue any party that has been near our forts
or encampments, follow not directly in their tracks, lest you should be
discovered by their rear-guards, who, at such a time, would be most
alert; but endeavor, by a different route to head and meet them in
some narrow pass, or lay in ambush to receive them when and where
they least expect it.

XXIV. If you are to embark in canoes, battoes, or otherwise, by
water, chuse the evening for the time of your embarkation, as you will
then have the whole night before you, to pass undiscovered by any
parties of the enemy, on hills or other places, which command a prospect of the lake or river you are upon.

XXV. In padling or rowing, give orders that the boat or canoe
next the sternmost, wait for her, and the third for the second, and
the fourth for the third, and so on, to prevent separation, and that
you may be ready to assist each other on any emergency.

XXVI. Appoint one man in each boat to look out for fires, on the
adjacent shores, from the numbers and size of which you may form
some judgment of the number that kindled them, and whether you
are able to attack them or not.

XXII. If you find the enemy encamped near the banks of a river,
or lake, which you imagine they will attempt to cross for their security upon being attacked, leave a detachment of your party on the
opposite shore to receive them, while, with the remainder, you surprise them, having them between you and the lake or river.

XXVIII. If you cannot satisfy yourself as to the enemy's number and strength, from their fire, &c., conceal your boats at some distance, and ascertain their number by a reconnoitering party, when they embark, or march, in the morning, marking the course they steer, &c., when you may pursue, ambush, and attack them, or let them pass, as prudence shall direct you. In general, however, that you may not be discovered by the enemy on the lakes and rivers at a great distance, it is safest to lay by, with your boats and party concealed all day, without noise or shew, and to pursue your intended route by night; and whether you go by land or water, give out parole and countersigns, in order to know one another in the dark, and likewise appoint a station for every man to repair to, in case of any accident that may separate you.

Such in general are the rules to be observed in the Ranging service ; there are, however, a thousand occurrences and circumstances which may happen, that will make it necessary, in some measure, to depart from them, and to put other arts and stratagems in practice ; in which cases every man's reason and judgment must be his guide, according to the particular situation and nature of things ; and that he may do this to advantage, he should keep in mind a maxim never to be departed from by a commander, *viz.* : to preserve a firmness and presence of mind on every occasion.)

My Lord Loudoun about this time made a visit to Fort Edward, and after giving directions for quartering the army the approaching winter, left a strong garrison there under the command of Colonel Haviland, and returned to Albany. The, Rangers,* with the before mentioned volunteers, were encamped and quartered in huts on an adjacent island in Hudson's River, and were sent out on various scouts, in which my ill state of health at this time would not permit

---

* Several of them were dismissed with an allowance of thirteen days pay to carry them home, being rendered unfit for immediate service by their past fatigues, and several officers were sent recruiting in order to have the companies complete by the opening of the Spring.
    Note by the Author.

me to accompany them, till December 17, 1757, when, pursuant to orders from Lieutenant Colonel Haviland, commanding officer at Fort Edward, I marched from thence with a party of 150 men to reconnoitre Carillon, alias Ticonderoga, and if possible to take a prisoner. We marched six miles and encamped, the snow being then about three inches deep, and before morning it was fifteen; we however pursued our route.

On the 18th in the morning, eight of my party being tired, returned to the fort; with the remainder, I marched nine miles further, and encamped on the east side of Lake George, near the place where Mons. Montcalm landed his troops when he besieged and took Fort William Henry, where I found some cannon ball and shells, which had been hid by the French, and made a mark by which I might find them again.

The 19th we continued our march on the west side of the lake nine miles further, near the head of the north-west bay.

The 21st, so many of my party tired and returned as reduced our number to 123, officers included, with whom I proceeded ten miles further, and encamped at night, ordering each man to leave a day's provisions there till our return.

The next day we marched ten miles further, and en-camped near the great brook that runs into Lake George, eight miles from the French advanced guard.

The 23d we marched eight miles, and the 24th six more, and then halted within 600 yards of Carillon fort. Near the mills we discovered five Indian's tracks, that had marched that way the day before, as we supposed, on a hunting party. On my march this day between the advanced guard and the fort, I appointed three places of rendezvous to repair to, in case of being broke in an action, and acquainted every officer and soldier that I should rally the party at the nearest post to the fort, and if broke there to retreat to the second, and at the third to make a stand till the darkness of the night would give us an opportunity to get off. Soon after I halted, I formed an ambush on a road leading from the fort to the woods, with an advanced party of twenty men and a rear-guard of fifteen. About eleven o'clock a sergeant of marines came from the fort up the road to my advanced party, who let him pass to the main body, where I made him prisoner. Upon examination, he reported, " that there were in the garrison 350 regulars, about fifty " workmen, and but five Indians; that they had plenty of " provisions, &c., and that twelve masons were constantly " employed in blowing up rocks in the entrenchment, " and a number of soldiers to assist them ; that at Crown " Point there were 150 soldiers and fourteen Indians ; " that Mons. Montcalm was at Montreal ; that 500 " Ottawawas Indians wintered in Canada, and that 500 " Rangers were lately raised in Canada, each man having " a double-barrelled fuzee, and put under an experienced " officer, well acquainted with the country ; that he did not " know whether the French intended to attack any of " the English forts this winter or not ; but that they ex- " pected a great number of Indians as soon as the ice would " bear them, in order to go down to the English forts ; and " that all the bakers in Carillon were employed in baking " biscuit for the scouts above-mentioned."

About noon, a Frenchman, who had been hunting, came near my party in his return, when I ordered a party to pursue him to the edge of the cleared ground, and take him prisoner, with this caution, to shoot off a gun or two, and then retreat to the main body, in order to intice the enemy from their fort ; which orders were punctually obeyed, but not one of them ventured out.

The last prisoner, on examination, gave much the same account as the other, but with this addition, " that he had

" heard the English intended to attack Ticonderoga, as
" soon as the lake was froze so as to bear them."

When I found the French would not come out of the
fort, we went about killing their cattle, and destroyed seventeen head, and set fire to the wood, which they had collected
for the use of the garrison, and consumed five large piles;
the French shot off some cannon at the fires, but did us
no harm.* At eight o'clock at night I began my march
homewards, and arrived at Fort Edward with my prisoners
the 27th. In my return, I found at the north end of Lake
George, where the French had hid the boats they had taken
at Fort William Henry, with a great number of cannon-
balls ; but as the boats were under water we could not
destroy them. Upon my return to Fort Edward, I received a letter from Captain Abercrombie, informing me
that the Earl of Loudoun, who was then at New York,
had thoughts of augmenting the Rangers, and had desired
General Abercrombie to command me down to receive his
directions. I accordingly prepared for my journey, and
upon my arrival was received by his lordship in a very
friendly manner ; and, after much conversation upon the

---

* See *Pouchot's Memoirs*, i, 99, which closely agrees as to the number of
men in the attacking party and the extent of damage done.

In a document entitled " *Journal of Occurrences in Canada, 1757–1758*,"
printed with the *Paris Documents*, under date of January 2, 1758, we find the
following entry : " A courier from Carillon reports, that the English shewed
themselves there on Christmas eve, to the number of 150, with the design or
setting fire to the houses under the curtain of the fort ; that the cannon prevented them from doing so ; that they killed some fifteen beeves to the horns
of one of which the commander had affixed a letter couched in these words :

' I am obliged to you sir, for the repose you have allowed me to take. I
thank you for the fresh meat you have sent me. I will take care of my
prisoners. I request you to present my compliments to the Marquis de Montcalm.

(Signed)   ROGERS,
                    Commander of the Independent Companies.' "
                                    — *N. Y. Colonial History.*

subject, he was pleased to inform me of his intentions or levying five additional companies of Rangers, desiring me to name the persons whom I thought fit for officers, and such as might be depended upon, to levy the men his lordship desired ; which I accordingly did, and then received from him the following instructions.

" By his Excellency John Earl of Loudoun, Lord Machline and Tairenseen &c., &c., &c., one of the sixteen peers of Scotland, Governor and Captain General of Virginia, and Vice Admiral of the same, Colonel of the 13th Regiment of foot, Colonel in chief of the Royal American regiment, Major General and Commander in Chief of all his Majesty's forces, raised or to be raised in North America :

" Whereas I have this day thought proper to augment the Rangers with five additional companies, that is, four New England and one Indian company, to be forthwith raised and employed in his Majesty's service ; and whereas I have an entire confidence in your skill and knowledge, of the men most fit for that service ; I do therefore, by these presents, appoint you to raise such a number of non-commission officers and private men as will be necessary to compleat the said five companies, upon the following establishment, viz.: each company to consist of one Captain, two Lieutenants, one Ensign, four Serjeants, and 100 privates. The officers to have British pay, that is, the same as an officer of the like rank in his Majesty's regular forces ; the Serjeants 4*s.* New York currency per day, and the private men 2*s.* 6*d.* currency per day. And the better to enable you to make this levy of men, you shall have one month's pay for each of the said five companies advanced to you ; upon these conditions, that, out of the first warrants that shall hereafter be granted for the subsistence of these companies, shall be deducted the said month's pay now advanced. Your men to find their own arms, which must be such as upon examination, shall be found fit, and be approved of. They are likewise to provide themselves with good warm cloathing, which must be uniform in every company, and likewise with good warm blankets. And the company of Indians to be dressed in all respects in the true Indian fashion, and they are all to be subject to the rules and articles of war. You will forthwith acquaint the officers appointed to these companies, that they are immediately to set out on the recruiting service, and you will not fail to instruct them that they are not to inlist any man for a less term than one year, nor any but what are able-bodied, well acquainted with the woods, used to hunting, and every way qualified for the Rangeing service. You are also to observe that the number of men requisite to compleat the said five companies, are all to be at Fort Edward on or before the 15th day of March next ensuing, and those that shall come by the way of Albany are to be mustered there by the officer commanding, as shall those who go strait to Fort Edward by the officer commanding there. Given under my hand, at New York, the 11th day of January, 1758.

LOUDOUN.

By his Excellency's command,
  To Capt.   J. APPY."
  Robert Rogers.

In pursuance of the above instructions, I immediately sent officers into the New England provinces, where, by the assistance of my friends, the requested augmentation of Rangers was quickly compleated, the whole five companies being ready for service by the 4th day of March.

Four of these companies were sent to Louisburg to join General Amherst, and one joined the corps under my command; and tho' I was at the whole expence of raising the five companies, I never got the least allowance for it,

and one of the captains dying, to whom I had delivered a
thousand dollars as advance pay for his company, which,
agreeable to the instructions I received, I had a right to
do ; yet was I obliged to account with the government for
this money, and entirely lost every penny of it.*

It has already been mentioned, that the garrison at Fort
Edward was this winter under the command of Lieut. Col.
Haviland.†   This gentleman, about the 28th of February,
ordered out a scout under the direction of one Putnam,
captain of a company of one of the Connecticut provincial
regiments, with some of my men, giving out publicly at the
same time, that, upon Putnam's return, I should be sent to
the French forts with a strong party of 400 Rangers.   This
was known not only to all the officers, but soldiers also, at
Fort Edward before Putnam's departure.

While this party was out, a servant of Mr. Best, a sutler
to the Rangers, was captivated by a flying party of the enemy
from Ticonderoga ; unfortunately too, one of Putnam's
men had left him at Lake George, and deserted to the

---

* In Rev. Caleb Stark's edition of Roger's journals, the following note is
given at this place :

"Speaking of his financial concerns, puts us in mind of the following
anecdote of Rogers.   While in garrison at Fort Edward, in the winter of 1758,
two British officers half seas over, or sufficiently so to be very affectionate and
patriotic, were one evening lamenting the misfortunes of their country, occasioned by her enormous debt.   Rogers coming in and learning the cause of
their trouble, told them to give themselves no more uneasiness about the
matter, as he would pay half the debt and a friend of his the remainder, and
thus clear the nation at once of her difficulties.   The officers treated the
captain and pronounced him the nation's benefactor.   Hence the saying — 'to
pay one's debts as Rogers did that of the nation.'" — *Stark's History of Dunbarton, N. H.,* p. 180.

† William Haviland was appointed lieutenant colonel of the 27th regiment,
Dec. 16, 1752, and arrived with his regiment at Halifax, July 1, 1757.   He
was with the army on the northern frontier in February, 1758–60, became a
brigadier general in 1762.   General in the army in February, 1783, and died
n September, 1788.

enemy. Upon Captain Putnam's return, we were informed
he had ventured within eight miles of the French fort at
Ticonderoga, and that a party he had sent to make discoveries had reported to him, that there were near 600
Indians not far from the enemy's quarters.
March 10, 1758. Soon after the said Captain Putnam's
return, in consequence of positive orders from Col. Haviland, I this day began a march from Fort Edward for the
neighbourhood of Carillon, not with a party of 400 men,
as at first given out, but of 180 men only, officers included,
one Captain, one Lieutenant, and one Ensign, and three
volunteers, viz : Mess. Creed,* Kent and Wrightson, one
sergeant, and one private, all volunteers of the 27th regiment; and a detachment from the four companies of
Rangers, quartered on the island near Fort Edward, viz.
Capt. Bulkley, Lieutenants Philips, Moore, Crafton, Campbell, and Pottinger ; Ensigns Ross, Wait, M'Donald, and
White, and 162 private men. I acknowledge I entered
upon this service, and viewed this small detachment of
brave men march out, with no little concern and uneasiness
of mind ; for as there was the greatest reason to suspect,
that the French were, by the prisoner and deserter ·above
mentioned, fully informed of the design of sending me out
upon Putnam's return ; what could I think ! to see my
party, instead of being strengthened and augmented, reduced
to less than one half of the number at first proposed. I
must confess it appeared to me (ignorant and unskilled as I
then was in politicks and the arts of war) incomprehen-
sible ; *but my commander doubtless has his reasons, and is able
to vindicate his own conduct.* We marched to the half-way

* Francis Creed, Michael Kent and John Wrightson, were three of the
volunteers from the regular troops already mentioned on another page, as having
been sent by Lord Loudon, to be trained in the Ranging service under Roger's
command and inspection.

brook, in the road leading to Lake George, and there encamped the first night.*

The 11th we proceeded as far as the first Narrows on
Lake George, and encamped that evening on the east side
of the lake; and after dark, I sent a party three miles
further down, to see if the enemy might be coming towards
our forts, but they returned without discovering any. We
were however on our guard, and kept parties walking on
the lake all night, besides centries at all necessary places
on the land.

The 12th we marched from our encampment at sun rise,
and having distanced it about three miles, I saw a dog
running across the lake, whereupon I sent a detachment to
reconnoitre the island, thinking the Indians might have laid
in ambush there for us; but no such could be discovered;
upon which I thought it expedient to put to shore, and lay
by till night, to prevent any party from descrying us on the
lake, from hills, or otherwise. We halted at a place called
Sabbath day Point, on the west side of the lake, and sent
out parties to look down the lake† with perspective glasses,

---

* The "First Narrows," opposite the point of Tongue Mountain and just
north of the entrance of the "North Arm," or *Cankusker Bay*, of Capt. Jackson's map of 1756,* are about a mile in width, the narrowness being caused by
the numerous islands in the lake at this point, rather than by a convergance of
the shores. This is perhaps the most picturesque part of the lake, the scenery
on all sides being most grand and beautiful. The whole of these islands in
this region, lie in the town of Bolton, Warren County.

The "Second Narrows" were very near the outlet of the lake, and ancient
carrying place.

* Known as "North-west Bay," upon modern maps.

† Sabbath Day Point, is a low level point of land, on the west side of the
lake, in the present town of Hague, Warren County. The lake here bends
more northerly, as we go toward the outlet, and the point commands an extensive view both up and down the lake. It affords a natural and convenient
landing place and camping ground, and was often used as such in the military
expeditions of the French and Revolutionary wars.

The origin of the name is uncertain; but the inviting opportunity which it
presents for quiet repose, justifies the belief, that it may have been first given
by some early travelers who rested here for a Sabbath, on their journey through
the lake.

which we had for that purpose. As soon as it was dark we proceeded down the lake. I sent Lieutenant Philips with fifteen men, as an advanced guard, some of whom went before him on scates, while Ensign Ross flanked us on the left under the west shore, near which we kept the main body, marching as close as possible, to prevent separation, it being a very dark night. In this manner we continued our march till within eight miles of the French advanced guards, when Lieutenant Philips sent a man on scates back to me, to desire me to halt; upon which I ordered my men to squat down upon the ice. Mr. Philips soon came to me himself, leaving his party to look out, and said, he imagined he had discovered a fire * on the east shore, but was not certain; upon which I sent with him Ensign White, to make further discovery. In about an hour they returned, fully persuaded that a party of the enemy was encamped there. I then called in the advanced guard, and flanking party, and marched on to the west shore, where, in a thicket, we hid our sleys and packs, leaving a small guard with them, and with the remainder I marched to attack the enemy's encampment, if there was any; but when we came near the place, no fires were to be seen, which made us conclude that we had mistaken some bleach patches of snow, or pieces of rotten wood, for fire (which in the night, at a distance resembles it), whereupon we returned to our packs, and there lay the remainder of the night without fire.

The 13th, in the morning, I deliberated with the officers how to proceed, who were unanimously of opinion, that it was best to go by land in snow shoes, lest the enemy should

---

* A small party of the French, as we have since heard, had a fire here at this time; but, discovering my advanced party, extinguished their fire, and carried the news of our approach to the French fort.

— *Note by the Author.*

discover us on the lake ; we accordingly continued our march on the west side, keeping on the back of the mountains that overlooked the French advanced guards. At twelve of the clock we halted two miles west of those guards, and there refreshed ourselves till three, that the day scout from the fort might be returned home before we advanced ; intending at night to ambuscade some of their roads, in order to trepan them in the morning. We then marched in two divisions, the one headed by Captain Bulkley, the other by myself ; Ensigns White and Wait had the rear guard, the other officers were posted properly in each division, having a rivulet at a small distance on our left, and a steep mountain on our right. We kept close to the mountain, that the advanced guard might better observe the rivulet, on the ice of which I imagined they would travel if out, as the snow was four feet deep, and very bad travelling on snow shoes. In this manner we marched a mile and an half, when our advanced guard informed me of the enemy being in their view ; and soon after, that they had ascertained their number to be ninety-six, chiefly Indians. We immediately laid down our packs, and prepared for battle, supposing these to be the whole number or main body of the enemy, who were marching on our left up the rivulet, upon the ice. I ordered Ensign M'Donald to the command of the advanced guard, which, as we faced to the left, made a flanking party to our right. We marched to within a few yards of the bank, which was higher than the ground we occupied ; and observing the ground gradually to descend from the bank of the rivulet to the foot of the mountain, we extended our party along the bank, far enough to command the whole of the enemy's at once ; we waited till their front was nearly opposite to our left wing, when I fired a gun, as a signal for a general discharge upon them ; whereupon we gave them the first fire, which killed above forty Indians ; the rest retreated, and were pursued by about one-half of our people. I now imagined the enemy totally defeated, and ordered Ensign M'Donald to head the flying remains of them, that none might escape ; but we soon found our mistake, and the party we had attacked were only their advanced guard, their main body coming up, consisting of 600 more, Canadians and Indians ; upon which I ordered our people to retreat to their own ground, which we gained at the expence of fifty men killed ; the remainder I rallied, and drew up in pretty good order, where they fought with such intrepidity and bravery as obliged the enemy (tho' seven to one in number) to retreat a second time ; but we not being in a condition to pursue them, they rallied again, and recovered their ground, and warmly pushed us in front and both wings, while the mountain defended our rear ; but they were so warmly received, that their flanking parties soon retreated to their main body with considerable loss. This threw the whole again into disorder, and they retreated a third time ; but our number being now too far reduced to take advantage of their disorder, they rallied again, and made a fresh attack upon us. About this time we discovered 200 Indians going up the mountain on our right, as we supposed, to get possession of the rising ground, and attack our rear ; to prevent which I sent Lieutenant Philips, with eighteen men, to gain the first possession, and beat them back ; which he did : and being suspicious that the enemy would go round on our left, and take possession of the other part of the hill, I sent Lieutenant Crafton, with fifteen men, to prevent them there ; and soon after desired two gentlemen, who were volunteers in the party,* with a few men, to go and support him, which they did with great bravery.

---

* I had before this desired these gentlemen to retire, offering them a serjeant to conduct them ; that as they were not used to snow shoes, and were quite - unacquainted with the woods, they would have no chance of escaping the

The enemy pushed us so close in front, that the parties were not more than twenty yards asunder in general, and sometimes intermixed wrth each other.   The fire continued almost constant for an hour and half from the beginning of the attack, in which time we lost eight officers, and more than 100 private men killed on the spot.   We were at last obliged to break, and I with about twenty men ran up the hill to Philips and Crafton, where we stopped and fired on the Indians, who were eagerly pushing us, with numbers that we could not withstand.   Lieutenant Philips being surrounded by 300 Indians, was at this time capitulating for himself and party, on the other part of the hill.   He spoke to me, and said if the enemy would give them good quarters, be thought it best to surrender, otherwise that he would fight while he had one man left to fire a gun.*

------

enemy, in case we should be broke and put to flight, which I very much suspected.   They at first seemed to accept the offer, and began to retire ; but seeing us so closely beset, they undauntedly returned to our assistance.   What hefel them after our flight, may be seen by a letter from one of the gentlemen to the commanding officer, which I have inserted next to this account of our scout.—*Note by the Author.*

*This unfortunate officer, and his whole party, after they surrendered, upon the strongest assurances of good treatment from the enemy, were inhumanly tied up to trees and hewn to pieces, in a most barbarous and shocking manner.
— *Note by the Author.*

There appears to have been an error in this statement as will appear in the subsequent part of this note.   It must have been overlooked by the author, because this same man Phillips is subsequently mentioned in the Journal.

Lieut. William Phillips was half Indian, his father being of Dutch or French origin, and at the time when the war began, he resided near Albany.   He enlisted in Roger's company in 1755, became a sergeant, and after the battle on Lake Champlain, January 21, 1757, he received a lieutenant's commission from the Earl of Loudon.   The following account of his adventures in the encounter on Lake George, is given by the Rev. Mr. Bouton, in his *History of Concord, N. H. :*

" In the bloody fight at Lake George, March 13, 1758, when Philips and his company of about twenty men were nearly surrounded by about three hundred Indians, he said to Rogers, if the enemy would give good quarters, he thought it best to surrender, otherwise he would fight while he had a man left

I now thought it most prudent to retreat, and bring off with me as many of my party as I possibly could, which I immediately did ; the Indians closely pursuing us at the same time, took several prisoners. We came to Lake George in the evening, where we found several wounded men, whom we took with us to the place where we had left our sleds, from whence I sent an express to Fort Edward, desiring Mr. Haviland to send a party to meet us, and assist in bringing in the wounded ; with the remainder I tarried there the whole night, without fire or blankets, and in the morning we proceeded up the lake, and met with Captain Stark at Hoop Island, six miles north from Fort William Henry, and encamped there that night ; the next day being the 15th, in the evening we arrived at Fort Edward.*

to fire a gun ! He and his party were all taken, and fastened to trees by the Indians, for the purpose of being shot or hewn to pieces. Philips got one hand loose, took a knife from his pocket, which he opened with his teeth, cut the string that bound him and escaped."
— *Bouton's History of Concord,* p. 200.

This account, based, it is true upon tradition, was generally accepted by those with whom he was acquainted in after life. After the war, Phillips familiarly known as " Bill Phillips," lived for some time in Rumford, [Concord] where he married Miss Eleanor Eastman, daughter of Ebenezer Eastman, Jr., by whom he had a son. About 1784, his wife joined the Shakers at Canterbury, but Phillips said he " could not dance, and would not join." He afterwards lived a roving, unsettled life — fishing, hunting and *stealing ;* sometimes working at the blacksmith's trade, of which he knew a little, and at other times working at day's labor. He lived a while with his wife's brother, Stitson Eastman, but at length became a pauper, and according to usage of the times was "bid off," to be supported at the town charge. He lived several years in the family of Richard Potter, of Anthony Potter, of Joseph Potter and Ebenezer Tenney, on the Loudon road. At length it was discovered that he had gained a residence in Northfield, where he died about the year 1819, aged, as was supposed, about a hundred years. His wife died at the Shaker settlement at Canterbury, November 17, 1816, aged 70 years.
—*Bouton's History of Concord,* p. 200.

* The account of this battle given by Pouchot, the French historian, is as follows :

" On the 1st of March, a party of two hundred of our domiciled Indians and

The number of the enemy was about 700, 600 of which were Indians. By the best accounts we could get, we killed 150 of them, and wounded as many more. I will not pretend to determine what we should have done had

---

forty Canadians left Montreal. These Indians coming to the fort, asked of M. d'Ilbecourt, the commandant, some provisions, and said they wished to rest a few days, before setting out on their march. He gave them some, and a little brandy, and the Indians returned to their camp, and began to drink. One of them who did not wish to join them, began a jugglery, and after some time he called the rest to a council, and told them that he had learned by this means that the English had out a party, who had come to Carillon and that they could not be far distant. He then exhorted his comrades to set out the next day, which they in fact did. The commandant was agreeably surprised at this prompt resolution of relieving him, and granted all they asked. Several officers and soldiers of the garrison wished to join the expedition. They proceeded along the lake shore, and at three leagues beyond, their scouts noticed the tracks of men in considerable numbers on the ice, and reported this fact. It was determined at once to retire into the woods near which the English would pass. Our scouts seeing the English troops descending a little hill, ran to notify their people that they were approaching. They arrived at a little elevation by the time that the English were at the bottom of the hill, and they at once attacked them, killing one hundred and forty-six upon the spot. They did not save more than the fifth part of the two hundred that they had. Robert Rogers who commanded them, left his clothes, his commission and his instructions, to enable him the better to flee. Eleven officers or volunteers had joined this detachment of whom four belonged to regiments that had lately arrived from England. Five were taken prisoners to Carillon, and others were lost in the woods, where they perished of hunger. We had in this affair, five Iroquois of the Sault. Killed one Meppissen of the lake, and three more Iroquois mortally wounded. This was the most vigorous action of the Indians. They afterwards formed a select detachment of v)lunteers, under the name of *Decouverues*.
　　—.*Pouchot's Memoirs* (Hough's Translation), 1, p. 101.
　　Substantially the same account is given by Adjutant Malartic, in his *Journal of Occurrences in Canada*, 1757, 1758, under date of March 19, 1758:
　　" A cadet detached from Carillon, came to inform the general that M. la Durantaye's party had arrived the 12th, on which day an old sorcerer had assured them that they would see the English before long ; on the morning of the 13th five or six Indian scouts came to say that they had discovered fresh tracks of two hundred men, whereupon the chiefs raised the muster-whoop and set out immediately with their warriors, some soldiers and Canadians, who travelled three leagues without meeting any one ; suspecting that the

we been 400 or more strong; but this I am obliged to say of those brave men who attended me (most of whom are now no more) both officers and soldiers in their respective stations behaved with uncommon resolution and courage;

English had taken the Falls road, they took the same course. M. la Durantaye, who had joined them at the Bald mountain, was with the Vanguard; he received the enemy's first fire which made him fall back a little, and gave them time to scalp two Indians whom they had killed. Meanwhile M. de Langy having turned them with a strong party of Indians, and having fallen on them when they felt sure of victory, had entirely defeated them. The Indians having discovered a chief's scalp in the breast of an officer's jacket, refused all quarter, and took one hundred and fourteen scalps. The opinion is, that only twelve or thirteen men escaped, and that this detachment was comprised of one hundred and seventy to one hundred and eighty, commanded by Captain Rogers, who is supposed to be among the killed."
— *N. Y. Colonial History*, x, 837.

The modern tourist in passing through Lake George, cannot fail of having his attention called to a rock just south of the Essex county line sloping from an elevation of some five hundred feet, by a steep angle down to the lake. It is on the west side, about six miles from the outlet, and is known in all maps and guide books as "Roger's Slide." According to the tradition, the intrepid ranger, in the winter of ———, in an encounter with an overwhelming force under the command of ———, here eluded his pursuers by gliding down the rock, and escaping across the ice. Had this incident actually occurred, it could scarcely have been overlooked by our author, and his complete silence upon the subject, appears to justify the belief that it has no foundation in truth. We notice that Mr. W. C. Watson in his *History of Essex County* (p. 83) regards the tradition as a myth. If it occurred, it must have been upon the expedition here noticed in the text, and if the romantic or the credulous insist upon having this incident believed, there is no point on the lake more suitable than this for the exploit, and no occasion more probable than that of this date for its occurrence.

Mr. B. C. Butler in his *Lake George and Lake Champlain* (p. 191), gives a more probable version of the origin of the name. He says:

"Rogers himself escaped by approaching Bald Mountain, at the place since called *Roger's Slide*, then reversing his snow shoes, and taking a back track for some distance, he swung himself by a convenient branch into the defile, and found his way thence down into the lake. The Indians followed, approached the slide, and were awestruck at the apparent feat of sliding down five or six hundred feet into the lake, and gave up the pursuit."

M. de Montcalm in a letter to M. de Paulmy, dated Montreal, April 10, 1758, in speaking of this encounter, says:

nor do I know an instance during the whole action in which I can justly impeach the prudence or good conduct of any one of them.*

The following is a List of the Killed, Missing, &c.

The Captain and Lieutenant of his Majesty's regular troops volunteers in this party, were taken prisoners ; the Ensign, another volunteer of the same corps, was killed, as were two volunteers, and a Serjeant of the said corps, and one private.

Of Capt. Rogers's Company,

Lieut. Moore	-	-	-	Killed.
Serjeant Parnell	-	-	-	Ditto.
Thirty-six privates	-	-	-	Ditto.

"The English detachment consisted of two hundred picked men, under the command of Major Rogers, their most famous partisan, and twelve officers He has been utterly defeated ; our Indians would give no quarter ; they have brought back one hundred and forty-six scalps ; they retained only three prisoners to furnish *live letters to their father.* About four or five days after, two officers and five English surrendered themselves prisoners, because they were wandering in the woods, dying of hunger. I am fully persuaded that the small number who escaped the fury of the Indians will perish of want and not have returned to Fort Lydius, we had two colonial cadets and one Canadian slightly wounded, but the Indians who are not accustomed to lose, have had eight killed and seventeen wounded, two of whom are dying. The Marquis de Vaudreuil takes great care of the sick, has made presents in the name of the great *Ononthio* (that is, the king), to the families of those who have been slain, and the dead on this occasion have been covered with great ceremony ; the Indians are content and very anxious to avenge the loss. Lieut. de Pouviet, of the la Sarre regiment, and Sieur d'Avenne proposed to be employed on the regiment of Languedoc, have distinguished themselves on this occasion."

— *N. Y. Colonial Hist.*, x, 693.

See also p. 697 of the same volume.

* John Ogilvie in writing to Sir William Johnson, March 28, 1758, says : "The late affair of Rogers was gallant and bloody, and a considerable proof of his bravery and conduct, but envy, that arch fiend, will not allow him much merit.

—*Johnson Mss.*, XXIII, 276.

Of Capt. Shepherd's Company,
   Two Serjeants
   Sixteen privates

Of Capt. James Rogers's Company,
   Ensign M'Donald -   -   -   Killed.

Of Capt. John Starks's Company,
   Two Serjeants -   -   -   -   Killed.
   Fourteen privates -   -   -   Ditto.

Of Capt. Bulkley's Company,
   Capt. Bulkley -   -   -   -   Killed.
   Lieut. Pottinger -   -   -   Ditto.
   Ensign White -   -   -   -   Ditto.
   Forty-seven privates -   -   K. and Miss.

Of Capt. William Starks's Company,
   Ensign Ross -   -   -   -   Killed.

Of Capt. Brewer's Company,
   Lieut. Campbell -   -   -   Killed.

A gentleman of the army, who was a volunteer on this party, and who with another fell into the hands of the French, wrote the following letter, some time after, to the officer commanding the regiment they belonged to at Fort Edward.*

Carillon, March 28, 1758.

" Dear Sir,

" As a flag of truce is daily expected here with an answer to Monsieur Vaudreuil, I sit down to write the moment I am able, in order to have a letter ready, as no doubt you and our friends at Fort Edward are anxious to be in-

---

* In Stark's edition, the authorship of the letter is ascribed to Captain Francis Reed, one of the volunteers from the 27th regiment, mentioned on another page.

formed about Mr. ———— and me, whom, probably
you have reckoned amongst the slain in our unfortunate
rencontre of the 13th concerning which at present I
shall not be particular ; only to do this justice to three
who lost their lives there, and to those who have
escaped, to assure you, Sir, that such dispositions were
formed by the enemy (who discovered us long enough
before), it was impossible for a party so weak as ours to
hope for even a retreat. Towards the conclusion of the
affair, it was cried from a rising ground on our right, to
retire there ; where, after scrambling with difficulty, as I
was unaccustomed to snow shoes, I found Capt. Rogers, and
told him, that I saw, to retire further was impossible, therefore earnestly begged we might collect all the men left,
and make a stand there. Mr. ————, who was with him,
was of my opinion, and Capt. Rogers also ; who therefore
desired me to maintain one side of the hill, whilst he defended the other. Our parties did not exceed above ten
or twelve in each, and mine was shifting towards the
mountain, leaving me unable to defend my post, or to
labour with them up the hill. In the mean time, Capt.
Rogers with his party came to me, and said (as did all those
with him) that a large body of Indians had ascended to our
right ; he likewise added, what was true, that the combat
was very unequal, that I must retire, and he would give
Mr. ———— and me a serjeant to conduct us thro' the
mountain. No doubt prudence required us to accept his
offer ; but besides one of my snow shoes being untied, I
knew myself unable to march as fast as was requisite to
avoid becoming a sacrifice to an enemy we could no longer
oppose ; I therefore begged of him to proceed, and then
leaned against a rock in the path, determined to submit to
a fate I thought unavoidable. Unfortunately for Mr.
———— · his snow shoes were loosened likewise, which
obliged him to determine. with me, not to labour in a flight

we were both unequal to. Every instant we expected the
savages ; but what induced them to quit this path, in which
we actually saw them, we are ignorant of, unless they
changed it for a shorter, to intercept those who had just
left us. By their noise, and making a fire, we imagined
they had got the rum in the Rangers packs. This thought
with the approach of night, gave us the first hopes of re-
tiring; and when the moon arose, we marched to the
southward along the monntains about three hours, which
brought us to ice, and gave us reason to hope our difficulties were almost past ; but we knew not we had enemies
yet to combat with, more cruel than the savages we had
escaped. We marched all night and on the morning of
the 14th found ourselves entirely unacquainted witn the ice.
Here we saw a man, who came towards us ; he was the
servant of Capt. Rogers, with whom he had been often-
times all over the country, and, without the least hesitation
whatsoever, he informed us we were upon South bay ; that
Wood creek, was just before us ; that he knew the way to
Fort Anne extremely well, and would take us to Fort
Edward the next day. Notwithstanding we were disappointed in our hopes of being upon Lake George, we
thought ourselves fortunate in meeting such a guide to
whom we gave entire confidence, and which he in fact confirmed, by bringing us to a creek, where he shewed the
tracks of Indians, and the path he said they had taken to
Fort Anne. After struggling thro' the snow some hours,
we were obliged to halt to make snow shoes, as Mr. ——
and the guide had left theirs at arriving upon the ice.
Here we remained all night, without any blankets, no coat,
and but a single waistcoat each, for I gave one of mine to
Mr. ———, who had laid aside his green jacket in the
field, as I did likewise my furred cap, which became a
mark to the enemy, and probably was the cause of a slight
wound in my face ; so that I had but a silk handkerchief

on my head, and our fire could not be large, as we had nothing to cut wood with. Before morning we contrived, with forked sticks and strings of leather, a sort of snow shoes to prevent sinking entirely; and on the 15th, followed our guide west all day, but he did not fulfil his promise; however the next day it was impossible to fail; but even then, the 16th, he was unsuccessful; yet still we were patient, because he seemed well acquainted with the way, for he gave every mountain a name, and shewed us several places, where he said his master had either killed deer or encamped. The ground, or rather the want of sunshine, made us incline to the southward, from whence by accident we saw ice, at several miles distance, to the south-east. I was very certain, that, after marching two days west of South bay, Lake George could not lie south-east from us, and therefore concluded this to be the upper end of the bay we had left. For this reason, together with the assurances of our guide, I advised continuing our course to the west, which must shortly strike Fort Anne, or some other place that we knew. But Mr. ———— wished to be upon the ice at any rate; he was unable to continue in the snow, for the difficulties of our march had overcome him. And really, sir, was I to be minute in those we had experienced already and afterwards, they would almost be as tiresome to you to read, as they were to us to suffer.

Our snow shoes breaking, and sinking to our middle every fifty paces, the scrambling up mountains, and across fallen timber, our nights without sleep or covering, and but little fire, gathered with great fatigue, our sustenance mostly water, and the bark and berries of trees; for all our provisions from the beginning was only a small bologna sausage, and a little ginger, I happened to have, and which even now was very much decreased; so that I knew not how to oppose Mr. ————'s intreaties; but as our guide

still persisted Fort Anne was near, we concluded to search
a little longer, and if we made no discovery to proceed next
day towards the ice; but we fought in vain, as did our
guide the next morning, tho' he returned, confidently as-
serting he had discovered fresh proofs, that the fort could
not be far off. I confess I was still inclined to follow him,
for I was almost certain the best we could hope from descending upon this ice to our left, was to throw ourselves
into the hands of the French, and perhaps not be able to
effect even that ; but, from the circumstances I have mentioned, it was a point I must yield to, which I did with
great reluctancy. The whole day of the 17th we marched
a dreadful road, between the mountains, with but one good
snow shoe each, the other of our own making being almost
useless. The 18th brought us to the ice, which tho' we
we longed to arrive at, yet I still dreaded the consequence,
and with reason, for the first sight informed us, it was the
very place we had left five days before. Here I must own
my resolution almost failed me ; when fatigue, cold, hunger,
and even the prospect of perishing in the woods attended
us, I still had hopes, and still gave encouragement, but now
I wanted it myself ; we had no resource but to throw ourselves into the enemy's hands, or perish. We had nothing
to eat, our slender stock had been equally shared amongst
us three, and we were not so fortunate as ever to see either
bird or beast to shoot at. When our first thoughts were
a little calmed we conceived hopes, that, if we appeared
before the French fort, with a white flag, the commanding officer wonld relieve and return us to Fort Edward.
This served to palliate our nearest approach to despair, and
determined a resolution, where, in fact, we had no choice.
I knew Carillon had an extensive view up South bay, therefore we concluded to halt during the evening, and march
in the night, that we might approach it in the morning, besides the wind pierced us like a sword ; but instead of its

abating it increased, together with a freezing rain, that
incrusted us entirely with ice, and obliged us to remain
until morning, the 19th, when we fortunately got some
juniper berries, which revived, gave us spirits, and I thought
strength.   We were both so firmly of that opinion, that
we proposed taking the advantage of its being a dark snowy
day, to approach Carillon, to pass it in the night, and get
upon Lake George.   With difficulty we persuaded the
guide to be of our opinion, we promised large rewards in
vain, until I assured him of provisions hid upon the lake ;
but we little considered how much nature was exhausted,
and how unequal we were to the task ; however, a few
miles convinced us, we were soon midway up our legs in
the new fallen snow ; it drove full in our faces, and was
as dark as the fogs upon the banks of Newfoundland.   Our
strength and our hopes sunk together, nay, even those of
reaching Carillon were doubtful, but we must proceed or
perish.   As it cleared up a little, we laboured to see the
fort, which at every turn we expected, until we came to
where the ice was gone. and the water narrow.   This did
not agree with my idea of South Bay, but it was no time
for reflection ; we quitted the ice to the left, and after
marching two miles, our guide assured us we ought to be
on the other side of the water.   This was a very distressing
circumstance, yet we returned to the ice and passed to the
right, where, after struggling through the snow, about four
miles, and breaking in every step, as we had no snow shoes,
we were stopped by a large waterfall.   Here I was again
astonished with appearances, but nothing now was to be
thought of only reaching the fort before night ; yet to pass
this place seemed impracticable : however, I attempted to
ford it a little higher, and had almost gained the opposite
shore, where the depth of the water which was up to my
breast, and the rapidity of the stream, hurried me off the
slippery rocks, and plunged me entirely in the waters.   I

was obliged to quit my fuzee, and with great difficulty
escaped being carried down the fall. Mr. ———, who
followed me, and the guide, though they held by one
another, suffered the same fate; but the hopes of soon
reaching a fire made us think lightly of this; as night
approached, we laboured excessively through the snow;
we were certain the fort was not far from us, but our guide
confessed, for the first time, that he was at a loss. Here
we plainly observed that his brain was affected; he saw
Indians all around him, and though we have since learned
we had every thing to fear from them, yet it was a danger
we did not now attend to; nay, we shouted aloud several
times to give information we were there; but we could
neither hear nor see anybody to lead us right, or more
likely to destroy us, and if we halted a minute we became
pillars of ice; so that we resolved, as it froze so hard, to
make a fire, although the danger was apparent. Accidentally we had one dry cartridge, and in trying with my pistol
if it would flash a little of the powder Mr. ——— unfortunately held the cartridge too near, by which it took fire,
blew up in our faces, almost blinded him, and gave excessive
pain. This indeed promised to be the last stroke of fortune,
as our hopes of a fire were now no more; but although
we were not anxious about life, we knew it was more becoming to oppose than yield to this last misfortune. We
made a path round a tree, and there exercsied all the night,
though scarcely able to stand, or prevent each other from
sleeping. Our guide, notwithstanding repeated cautions,
straggled from us, where he sat down and died immediately.
On the morning of the 2rth, we saw the fort, which we
approached with a white flag; the officers run violently
towards us, and saved us from a danger we did not then
apprehend; for we are informed, that if the Indians, who
were close after them, had seized us first, it would not have
been in the power of the French to have prevented our

being hurried to tneir camp, and perhaps to Montreal the next day, or killed for not being able to march. Mons. Debecourt and all his officers treat us with humanity and politeness and are solicitous in our recovery, which returns slowly, as you may imagine, from all thsee difficulties ; and though I have omitted many, yet I am afraid you will think me too prolix ; but we wish, Sir, to persuade you of a truth, that nothing but the situation I have faithtfully described could determine us in a resolution which appeared only one degree preferable to perishing in the woods.

" I shall make no comments upon these distresses ; the malicious perhaps will say, which is very true, we brought them upon ourselves ; but let them not wantonly add, we deserved them because we were unsuccessful. They must allow we could not be led abroad, at such a season of snow aud ice, for amusement, or by an idle curiosity. I gave you, Sir, my reasons for asking leave, which you were pleased to approve, and I hope will defend them ; and the same would make me again, as a volunteer, experience the chance of war to-morrow, had I an opportunity. These are Mr. ———'s sentiments as well as mine ; and we both know you, Sir, too well, to harbour the least doubt of receiving justice with regard to our conduct in this affair, or our promotion in the regiment ; the prospect of not joining that so soon as we flattered ourselves, has depressed our spirits to the lowest degree, so that we earnestly beg you will be solicitous with the General to have us restored as soon as possible, or at least to prevent our being sent to France, and separated from you, perhaps, during the war.

I have but one thing more to add, which we learned here, and which perhaps you have already observed from what I have said, that we were upon no other ice than that of Lake George ; but by the day overtaking us, the morning of the 14th, in the very place we had, in coming, marched during the night, we were entirely unacquainted with it, and obliged to put a confidence in this guide, whose head must have been astray from the beginning, or he could not so grossly have mistaken a place where he had so often been. This information but added to our distress, until we reflected that our not being entirely lost was the more wonderful. That we had parted from South Bay on the 14th, was a point with us beyond all doubt, and about which we never once hesitated, so that we acted entirely contrary to what we had established as a truth; for if, according to that, we had continued our course to the west, we must inevitably have perished; but the hand of Providence led us back contrary to our judgment; and though even then, and often afterwards, we thought it severe, yet in the end it saved us, and obliged us to rest satisfied that we construed many things unfortunate, which tended to our preservation.   I am, &c.'

Upon my return from the late unfortunate scout, I was ordered to Albany to recruit my companies, where I met with a very friendly reception from my Lord How, who advanced me cash to recruit the Rangers, and gave me leave to wait upon General Abercrombie at New York, who had now succeeded my Lord Loudoun in the chief command, my Lord being at this time about to embark for England. I here received a commission from the General, of which the following is a copy:

" By his Excellency James Abercromby, Esq; Colonel of his Majesty's 44th Regiment of Foot, Colonel in Chief of the 60th or Royal American Regiment, Major General and Commander in Chief of all his Majesty's Forces raised or to be raised in North America, &c.

" Whereas it may be of great use to his Majesty's service in the operations now carrying on for recovering his rights in America, to have a number of men employed in obtaining intelligence of the strength, situation, and

11

motions of the enemy, as well as other services, for which
Rangers, or men acquainted with the woods, only are fit :
Having the greatest confidence in your loyalty, courage
and skill in this kind of service, I do, by virtue of the power
and authority to me given by his Majesty, hereby consti-
tute and appoint you to be Major of the Rangers in his
Majesty's service, and likewise Captain of a company of
said Rangers.   You are therefore to take the said Rangers
as Major, and the said Company as Captain, into your
care and charge, and duly exercise and instruct, as well
the officers as the soldiers thereof, in arms, and to use
your best endeavors to keep them in good order and discipline ; and I do hereby command them to obey you as
their Major and Captain respectively, and you are to follow
and observe such orders and directions from time to time
as you shall receive from his Majesty, myself, or any other
superior officer, according to the rules and discipline of
war.

   Given at New York, this 6th Day of April 1758, in
the thirty-first Year of the reign of our Sovereign Lord
George the Second, by the Grace of God, King of Great
Britain, France and Ireland, Defender of the Faith, &c.

JAMES ABERCROMBY.

By his Excellency's command,

J. APPY."

   I left New York April 8, and according to orders attended Lord How at Albany, for his directions, on the
12th, with whom I had a most agreeable interview, and a
long conversation concerning the methods of distressing
the enemy, and prosecuting the war with vigor the ensuing
campaign.   I parted with him, having the strongest assurances of his friendship and influence in my behalf, to
wait upon Colonel Grant, commanding officer at Fort

Edward, to assist him in conducting the Rangers, and scouting parties, in such a manner as might best serve the common cause, having a letter from my Lord to him. Capt. Stark was immediately dispatched to Ticonderoga on the west-side of Lake George. Capt. Jacob, whose Indian name was *Nawnawapeteoonks*, on the east-side, and Capt. Shepherd betwixt the lakes, with directions to take if possible some prisoners near Carillon. About the same time I marched myself with eighteen men for Crown Point. Capt. Burbank was likewise dispatched in quest of prisoners. These scouts, being often relieved, were kept out pretty constantly, in order to discover any parties of the enemy that might sally out towards our forts or frontiers, and to reconnoitre their situation and motions from time to time. The success of my own scout was as follows:

April 29, 1758, I marched from Fort Edward with a party of eighteen men, up the road that leads to Fort William Henry four miles, then north four miles, and encamped at Schoon Creek, it having been a very rainy day.

On the 30th we marched north-and-by-east all day, and encamped near South-Bay.

The 1st of May we continued the same course, and at night encamped near the narrows, north of South-Bay.

The 2d, in the morning, made a raft, and crossed the bay over to the east-side, and having distanced the lake about four miles we encamped.

The 3d we steered our course north, and lay at night about three miles from Carillon.

The 4th we marched north-by-east all day, and encamped at night three miles from Crown Point Fort.

The 5th we killed one Frenchman, and took three prisoners.

The 6th, in the morning, began our return homeward, and arrived with our prisoners at Fort Edward the 9th.

One of the prisoners, who appeared to be the most intelligible, reported, " that he was born at Lorrain in France ; that he had been in Canada eight years, viz. two at Quebec, one at Montreal, and five at Crown Point ; that at the latter were but 200 soldiers, of which Mons. le Janong was commander in chief; that at Ticonderoga there were 400 of the Queen's regiment, 150 marines, 200 Canadians, and about 700 Indians ; and that they daily expected 300 Indians more; that they did not intend to attack our forts this summer, but were preparing to receive us at Ticonderoga ; that they had heard that I, with most of my party, was killed in the conflict last March ; but afterwards, by some prisoners which a small party of their Indians had taken from Dutch Hoosyk, they were informed that Rogers was yet alive, and was going to attack them again, being fully resolved to revenge the inhumanity and barbarity with which they had used his men, in particular Lieut. Philips and his party, who were butchered by them, after they had promised them quarters ; that this was talked of among the Indians, who greatly blamed the French for encouraging them so to do."

Captains Stark and Jacob returned the day before me ; the former brought in with him six prisoners, four of which he took near Ticonderoga ; they having escaped from New York and Albany, were in their flight to the French forts. The latter, who had but one white man with him, and eighteen Indians, took ten prisoners, and seven scalps, out of a party of fifty French. An account of these scouts, and the intelligence thereby gained, was transmitted to my Lord How, and by him to the General.

About the middle of May, the flag of truce was sent to Ticonderoga, on Col. Schyler's account, which put a stop to all offensive scouts, till its return.

May 28, 1758, I received positive orders from the General, to order all officers and men, belonging to the Rangers, and the two Indian companies, who were on furlow, or recruiting parties, to join their respective companies as soon as possible, and that every man of the corps under my command should be at his post at or before the 10th of next month. These orders were obeyed, and parties kept out on various scouts till the 8th of June, when my Lord How arrived at Fort Edward with one-half of the army.

His Lordship immediately ordered me out with fifty men in whale-boats, which were carried over in waggons to Lake George, and directed me at all events to take a plan of the landing-place at the north-end with all possible accuracy, and also of the ground from the landing-place to the French fort at Carillon, and of Lake Champlain for three miles beyond it, and to discover the enemy's number in that quarter. Agreeable to these orders, on the 12th in the morning, I marched with a party of fifty men, and encamped in the evening at the place where Fort William-Henry stood.

On the 30th we proceeded down the lake in five whale-boats to the first narrows, and so on to the west-end of the the lake, where I took the plan his Lordship desired. Part of my party then proceeded to reconnoitre Ticonderoga, and discovered a large encampment there, and a great number of Indians. While I was, with two or three others, taking a plan of the fort, encampment, &c. I left the remainder of my party at some considerable distance ; when I was returning to them, at the distance of about 300 yards, they were fallen upon by a superior number of the enemy

who had got between me and them.   Capt. Jacobs, with the
Mohegon Indians, run off at the first onset, calling to our
people to run likewise; but they stood their ground, and discharged their pieces several times at last broke through the
enemy, by whom they were surrounded on all sides except
their rear, where a river covered them; they killed three
of the enemy, but lost eight of their own party in this
skirmish.   My party rallied at the boats, where I joined
them, and having collected all but the slain together, we
returned homewards.   On the 20th, at Half Way brook,
we met my Lord Howe advanced with three thousand men,
to whom I gave an account of my scout, together with a
plan of the landing-place, the fort at Carillon, and the
situation of the lakes.

I obtained leave of my Lord to go to Fort Edward where
his Excellency Major General Abercrombie was then
posted, who ordered me to join my Lord Howe the next
day with all the Rangers, being 600, in order to proceed
with his Lordship to the lake.

On the 22d his Lordship encamped at the lake where
formerly stood Fort William-Henry,[1] and ordered the
Rangers to advance 400 yards on the west side, and encamp there; from which place, by his Lordship's orders,
I sent off next morning three small parties of Rangers, viz.
one to the narrows of South Bay, another to the west-side
of Lake George, and a third to Ticonderoga Fort, all three

---

[1] Fort William Henry was captured by General Montcalm, August 7, 1757,
through the cowardice of General Daniel Wells then stationed at Fort Edward,
who with a large army at hand, refused to send succor to Colonel Munro. The
horrible massacre that followed this surrender, presents the blackest page of
our colonial history.   It was estimated by Carver, the traveller, who was
present, that fifteen hundred persons were killed upon this occasion, or carried
into a captivity scarcely preferable to death.

Fort William Henry was named by Gen. Johnson in honor of William
Henry, Duke of Cumberland, brother of the heir apparent, George the Third.

received directions from Capt. Abercrombie, one of his Aids de Camp, to gain the top of a mountain that bore north about a mile from the landing-place, and from thence to steer east to the river that runs into the falls betwixt the landing and the saw-mill, to take possession of some rising ground on the enemy's side, and there to wait the army's coming. I immediately marched, ascended the top of the hill, and from thence marched to the place I was ordered, where I arrived in about an hour, and posted my party to as good advantage as I could, being within one quarter of a mile of where Mons. Montcalm was posted with 1500 men, whom I had discovered by some small reconnoitring parties sent out for that purpose. About twelve o'clock 'Colonels Lyman and Fitch of the Provincials came to my rear, whom I informed of the enemy's being so very near and inquiring concerning the army, they told me they were coming along. While this conversation passed, a sharp fire began in the rear of Col. Lyman's regiment, on which he said he would make his front immediately, and desired me to fall on their left flank, which I. accordingly did, having first ordered Capt. Burbanks[1] with 150 men to remain at the place where I was posted, to observe the motions of the French at the saw-mills, and went with the remainder of the Rangers on the left flank of the enemy, the river being on their right, and killed several. By this time my Lord Howe, with a detachment from his front, had broke the enemy, and hemmed them in on every side; but advancing himself with great eagerness and intrepidity

---

[1] Capt. Jonathan Burbank was scalped by an Indian, who held up the trophy, thinking it to be that of Major Rogers. When told of his mistake by the other prisoners, he appeared to be sorry, saying that he was a good man. He had some time previously shown some of them a kindness.—*Stark's Memoirs*, 444; *Farmer's Moore's Hist. Coll.*, 1, 286; *Drake's Five Years' French and Indian War*, 8, 92.

parties by land. Another party, consisting of two Lieutenants and seventeen men, proceeded down the lake for
discoveries, and were all made prisoners by about 300
French and Indians. This party embarked in whale-boats.
About the 28th of June his Excellency Major General
Abercrombie arrived at the lake with the remainder of the
army, where he tarried till the morning of the 5th of July,
and then the whole army, consisting of near 16,000, embarked in battoes for Ticonderoga.

The order of march was a most agreeable sight ; the
regular troops were in the center, provincials on each wing,
the light infantry on the right of the advanced guard, the
Rangers on the left with Colonel Broadstreet's battoemen
in the center. In this manner we proceeded, till dusk,
down Lake George, to Sabbath Day Point, where the army
halted and refreshed. About ten o'clock the army moved
again, when my Lord How went in the front with his
whale-boat, Lieutenant Col. Broadstreet's and mine, with
Lieutenant Holmes, in another, whom he sent forward
to go near the landing-place, and observe if any enemy was
posted there.

Holmes returned about day-break, met the army near
the Blue Mountains within four miles of the landing-place,
and reported that there was a party of the enemy at the
landing-place, which he discovered by their fires.

As soon as it was light his Lordship, with Col. Broadstreet and myself, went down to observe the landing-place
before the army, and when within about a quarter of a mile,
plainly discerned that it was but a small detachment of the
enemy that was there ; whereupon his Lordship said he
would return to the General, that the army might land and
march to Ticonderoga. About twelve o'clock the whole
army landed, the Rangers on the left wing. I immediately
sent an officer to wait upon the General for his orders, and

received directions from Capt. Abercombie one of his
Aids de Camp, to gain the top of a mountain that bore
north about a mile from the landing place, and from thence
to steer east to the river that runs into the falls betwixt the
landing and the saw mill, to take possession of some rising
ground on the enemy's side, and there wait the army's
coming. I immediately marched to the place I was ordered, where I arrived in about an hour, and posted my
party to as good advantage as I could, being within, one-
quarter of a mile of where Mons. Montcalm was posted
with .1.500 men, whom I had discovered, by some small
reconnoitering parties sent out for that purpose. About
twelve o'clock, Colonels Lyman and Fitch of the Provincials came to my rear, whom I informed of the enemy's
being so very near, and inquiring concerning the army,
they told me were coming along. While this conversation
passed, a sharp fire began in the rear of Col. Lyman's
Regiment, on which he said he would make his front immediately, and desired me to fall on his left flank, which I
accordingly did, having first ordered Capt. Burbanks with
one hundred and fifty men to remain at the place where
I was posted, to observe the movement of the French at
the Saw Mills, and went with the remainder of the
Rangers on the left flank of the enemy, the river being
on their right, and killed several.* By this time my

----

* The map in Mante's History, showing the plan of attack at Ticonderoga
represents the position of the Rangers as described in the text. They were on
the extreme left of the English line, and in front of the French regiments of
Béarn and La Reine. The firing in the rear, was probably by the party of

Lord Howe, with a detachment from his front, had broke the enemy and hemmed them on every side; but advancing himself with great eagerness and intrepidity

---

M. de Trépesec, which got separated from their main body, and were nearly all killed or captured.

The French had stationed three regiments under M. de Boulamarque at the foot of Lake George, to prevent if possible the English from landing; but finding it impossible to do this, they hastily destroyed their camp and retreated.

M. de Montcalm in reporting an account of the battle, after speaking of this withdrawal of the French from the portage, says:

" This retreat would have been effected without the loss of a man, had not M. de Trépesec's detachment gone astray; abandoned by the small number of Indians which acted as guides, it lost itself in the mountains covered with trees and after a march of twelve hours, fell into an English Column which was marching towards the river of the Falls. Six officers, and about a hundred and fifty soldiers belonging to that detachment, have been taken; they fought for a long time but were obliged to yield to numbers. The English on that occasion, suffered a considerable loss in the person of Brigadier General Lord Howe of their army, the colonel of one of the regiments from Old England."—
N. Y. Colonial Hist. Vol. x. p. 737.

The line of French breastworks defended by the French in this battle can still be traced without difficulty.

upon them, was unfortunately shot and died immediately.* There were taken prisoners of the enemy in this action, five officers, two volunteers, and one hundred and sixty men, who were sent to the landing-place. Nothing more material was done this day. The next morning, at six o'clock, I was ordered to march to the river that runs into the falls, the place where I was the day before, and there to halt on the west side till further orders, with four hundred Rangers, while Captain Stark, with the remainder of the Rangers, marched with Capt. Abercrombie and Mr. Clerk the Engineer to observe the position of the enemy at the fort, from whence they returned again that evening. The whole army lay the ensuing night under arms. By sunrise next morning, Sir William Johnson joined the army with four hundred and forty Indians. At seven o'clock I received orders to march with my Rangers. A Lieutenant of Captain Stark's led the advance guard. I was within about three hundred yards of the breast-work, when my advance guard was ambushed and fired upon by about 200 Frenchmen. I immediately formed a front and marched up to the advanced guard, who maintained their ground, and the enemy immediately retreated ; soon after the battoe-men formed on my left and light infantry on my

---

* This noble and brave officer being universally beloved by both officers and soldiers of the army, his fall was not only most sincerely lamented, but seemed to produce an almost general consternation and languor through the whole.

The remains of Lord Howe were taken to Albany and buried under the English church, In 1802 the church was rebuilt, and it is probable that they were then removed to England, as no traces of them were found in a second rebuilding of St. Peter's church in 1859. A monument was erected to his memory in Westminster Hall at the expense of the province of Massachusetts. Lord Viscount George Augustus Howe was a brother of Major General Sir William Howe, and Admiral Richard Howe, of the British army and navy engaged in America during the Revolutionary war.

—*Note by the Author.*

right. This fire of the enemy did not kill a single man. Soon after, three regiments of Provincials came up and formed in my rear, at two hundred yards distance. While the army was thus forming, a scattering fire was kept up between our flying parties and those of the enemy without the breast-work. About half an hour past ten, the greatest part of the army being drawn up, a smart fire began on the left wing, where Col. De Lancey's, (the New Yorkers,) and the battoe-men were posted, upon which I was ordered forward to endeavour to beat the enemy within the breast-work, and then to fall down, that the pickets and grenadiers might march through. The enemy soon retired within their works ; Major Proby marched through with his pickets within a few yards of the breast-work, where he unhappily fell, and the enemy keeping up a heavy fire, the soldiers hastened to the right about, when Col. Haldiman came up with the grenadiers to support them, being followed by the battalions in brigades for their support. Col. Haldiman advanced very near the breast-work, which was at least eight feet high ; some of the Provincials with the Mohocks came up also.*

We toiled with repeated attacks for four hours, being greatly embarrassed by trees that were felled by the enemy without their breast-work, when the General thought proper to order a retreat, directing me to bring up the rear, which I did in the dusk of the evening. On the ninth in the evening, we arrived at our encampment at the south-end of Lake George, where the army received the thanks of the General for their good behaviour, and were ordered to en-

---

* This attack was begun before the General intended it should be, and as it were by accident, from the fire of the New Yorkers in the left wing ; upon which Col. Haviland being in or near the center, ordered the troops to advance.
—*Note by the Author.*

trench themselves; the wounded were sent to Fort Edward and Albany. Our loss both in the regular and provincial troops, was somewhat considerable. The enemy's loss was about five hundred, besides those who were taken prisoners.

July 8, 1758. By order of the General, I this day began a scout to South Bay, from which I returned the 16th, having effected nothing considerable, except discovering a large party of the enemy, supposed to be near a thousand, on the east-side of the lake. This party the next day, viz. the 17th, fell upon a detachment of Col. Nicholls's Regiment at the half-way brook, killed three Captains, and upwards of twenty private men.

The 27th another party of the enemy fell upon a convoy of waggoners between Fort Edward and Half-Way Brook, and killed 116 men, sixteen of which were Rangers. In pursuit of this party, with a design to intercept their retreat, I was ordered to embark the 18th with 700 men; the enemy however escaped me, and in my return home on the 31st, I was met by an express from the General, with orders to march with 700 men to South and East Bay, and return by way of Fort Edward,* in the prosecution of which orders nothing very material happened till the 8th of August; in our return, early in the morning of which day we decamped from the place where Fort Anne stood, and began our march, Major Putnam with a party of Pro-

---

* Pouchots' account of this affair is as follows:

"The English on their part, labored to form an entrenched camp. A party under M. Marin, a Colonial Captain, encountered a body of their troops composed of seven or eight hundred men, and commanded by Rogers, M. Marin took prisoner a major of militia from Old England, with some others, and took only two scalps. The loss of the English was estimated at one hundred men, while the French had four Indians killed and four wounded, and six Canadians killed and six wounded, among whom was an officer and a cadet."

—*Memoirs*, i, 123.

vincials marching in the front, my Rangers in the rear,
Capt. Dalyell* with the regulars in the center, the other
officers suitably disposed among the men, being in number
530, exclusive of officers (a number having by leave returned home the day before).   After marching about three-
quarters of a mile, a fire begun with five hundred of the
enemy in the front; I brought my people into as good
order as possible, Capt. Dalyell in the center, and the
Rangers on the right, with Col. Partridge's light infantry;
on the left was Capt. Gidding's of the Boston troops with
his people, and Major Putnam being in the front of his
men when the fire began, the enemy rushing in, took him,
one Lieutenant, and two others, prisoners, and considerably
disordered others of the party, who afterwards rallied and
did good service, particularly Lieutenant Durkee,† who
notwithstanding two wounds, one in his thigh, the other
in his wrist, kept in the action the whole time, encouraging
his men with great earnestness and resolution.   Capt.
Dalyell with Gage's light infantry, and Lieut. Eyers of the

---

*James Dalyell (sometimes written *Dalzell*, served as a lieutenant in the
60th Regiment, and afterwards as a captain in the 2d Battalion of the Royals,
or 1st Regiment of foot.   He perished in a brave but indiscreet attack upon
the Indian enemy near Detroit, in 1763.

—See Carver's Travels, p. 163.

M. De Courgne, in writing from Niagara, Aug. 24, says, in speaking of the
sortie in which Major Rogers was engaged :

"About fifteen men, with Major Rogers, got in a house, who was to bring
up the rear and cover the retreat, which soon was surrounded by the Indians,
and had no other way to get clear of them but by showing them a clean pair
of heels, which he and a corporal of the 55th had a fair tryal for, and got safe
into the fort.

—Johnson MSS., VII, 126.

† Lieut. Robert Durkee, served with distinction through the war, and afterwards settled in the Valley of Wyoming, where he was slain in battle, July
3, 1778.

44th regiment, behaved with great bravery, they being in the center, where was at first the hottest fire, which afterwards fell to the right where the Rangers were, and where the enemy made four different attacks; in short, officers and soldiers throughout the detachment behaved with such vigour and resolution, as in one hour's time broke the enemy, and obliged them to retreat, which they did with such caution in small scattering parties, as gave us no opportunity to distress them by a pursuit; we kept the field and buried our dead.* When the action was over, we had missing fifty-four men, twenty-one of which afterwards came in, being separated from us while the action continued. The enemy's loss was 199 killed on the spot, several of which were Indians.† We arrived at Fort Edward on the 9th, being met at some distance from it by Col. Provost, with a party of 300, and refreshments for the wounded, which I had desired by an express sent before.

I remained at Fort Edward till the 11th of the month, when I received orders from Col. Provost, who now ranked as Brigadier, and commanded at Fort Edward, to march and pursue the tracks of a large party of Indians, of which he had received intelligence, down the east-side of Hudson's River, in order to secure our convoys from them, and intercept their retreat; but this report which the Colonel had heard being groundless, my scout was ineffectual. I returned to Fort Edward on the 14th, and went with my detachment directly to the encampment at Lake George.

---

*A French account of this engagement is given in a letter from M. Doreil to Marshal de Belle Isle, dated Quebec, August 31, 1758.
— *N.Y. Colonial History*, x, 818.

† By a detachment that went out afterwards, fifty more of the enemy were found dead near the place of action.
—*Note by the Author.*

Aug. 20, 1758. By orders from the General I embarked with five men in a whale-boat, to visit and reconnoitre Ticonderoga, in which excursion I obtained several articles of intelligence concerning the enemy, their situation and numbers at different posts, and returned the 24th to the encampment at Lake George.

I was employed in various other excursions towards the enemy's forts and frontiers, and in pursuit of their flying parties till the campaign for this year ended, and our army retired to winter-quarters.

Notwithstanding little was effected by our late campaign to Ticonderoga ; yet the British arms in America were not everywhere unsuccessful : for Col. Broadstreet with a detachment of 2000 men, reduced the French fort at Cataraqua, called Fort Frontenac,* and General Amherst, who commanded the British troops at Cape Breton, had succeeded in the reduction of that important fortress, and now returned from his conquest, with a part of the troops that had been employed there, and was appointed commander in chief of his Majesty's forces in North America (General Abercrombie embarking for England). The head quarters were now fixed at New York, and I had now new commanders to obey, new companions to converse with, and, as it were, a new apprenticeship to serve. From Albany, where I was settling some accounts with the Pay-

---

* This fort was square faced, had four bastions built with stone, and was near three-quarters of a mile in circumferance. Its situation was very beautiful, the banks of the river presenting on every side an agreeable landscape, with a fine prospect of the Lake Ontario, which was distant about a league, interspersed with many islands that were well wooded, and seemingly fruitful. The French had formerly a great trade at this fort with the Indians, it being erected on purpose to prevent their trading with the English ; but it is now totally destroyed.
— *Note by the Author.*

master, I began my acquaintance by the following letter to Col. Townsend, Deputy Adjutant General to his Excellency.

" Sir, *Albany, Jan.* 28, 1759.

" Inclosed I send you the present state of his Majesty's companies of Rangers at Fort Edward, together with a list of the officers, now recruiting in the different parts of New England, who have lately advised me, that they have already inlisted near 400 men, which recruits are much wanted at Fort Edward, as it may be expected that the enemy will soon send their Indians, to endeavour to intercept our convoys between here and Fort Edward.

" To be seasonably strong to prevent their playing their old pranks, I would humbly propose, were it consistent with the service and agreeable to General Amherst, my setting out for New England, in order to despatch such Rangers as are there with all possible speed to Fort Edward, or otherwise, as his Excellency shall direct. If it should be agreeable to the General that I should go to New England, I should be glad it might be by way of New York, that I might have an opportunity to wait upon the General myself, and represent to him the necessity of an augmentation of the Rangers now at Fort Edward, and the desire of the Stockbridge Indians to re-enter the service.

" The arms of the Rangers are in the hands of Mr. Cunningham at New York, which will be soon wanted at Fort Edward ; I should therefore be glad they might be forwarded as soon as may be. I have wrote to Mr. Cunningham, to make application to you for convenient carriages for the same, which I should be glad you would furnish him with. And till the time I have an opportunity of paying you my respects in person, I beg leave to subscribe myself, Sir, Your most obedient humble servant,

Robert Rogers."

" *P. S.* General Stanwix informs me, that a subaltern officer, and about twenty Rangers, are to be stationed at No. 4 ; the officer I would recommend for that post, is Lieut. Stephans who is well acquainted with the country thereabout. He is now recruiting."

To Col. Townsend.

Soon after this I returned to Fort Edward, where I received the Colonel's answer, as follows :

" Sir,   *Feb.* 5, 1759.

" I received your letter with the enclosed return. The General commands me to inform you, he can by no means approve of your leaving Fort Edward.

" Your recruiting officers are all ordered to send up their recruits to Fort Edward. They are not only wrote to, but an advertisement is put in all the papers, which was the only method the General had of conveying his intentions to them, as you had not sent me any return of the officers names, and places where they were to recruit at. In obedience to that order, the recruits will be up sooner than if they waited your coming down. I have likewise repeated the order to every officer according to your return, by this post, and if you are complete by the returns they make, I shall order up every individual officer to their posts.

" Any proposals for the augmentation of the Rangers, or proposals from the Stockbridge Indians, you would chuse to offer to the General, he desires may be immediately sent down to him.

" The arms for the Rangers, which you mention are in the hands of Mr. Cunningham, shall be sent up to you immediately.

" I have wrote to Lieut. Samuel Stephans, to acquaint him with the General's intentions of leaving him at No. 4.

" If the enemy send out any scouting parties this year to

pick up intelligence, or attack our convoys, the season of the year is now coming on that we may expect them; you therefore must see the necessity of your remaining at Fort Edward. Your officers and men should join you as fast as possible. The General would at another time comply with your request.

Your obedient, humble servant,

R. Townshend, D. A. G."

Feb. 15, 1759.

To Major Rogers.

I wrote to the Colonel, proposing an addition of two new companies of Rangers, upon the same footing as those already in the service, and the raising of three companies of Indians to serve the ensuing campaign; and left the Indians should be gone out on their hunting parties, and so be prevented from joining us, 'I wrote to three of their Sachems, or chiefs; one of which to King Uncus, head Sachem of the Mohegan Indians (which in substance is like the others) I will here insert, as a specimen of the method in which we are obliged to address these savages.

" Brother Uncus,

" As it is for the advantage of his Majesty King George, to have a large body of Rangers employed in his service the ensuing campaign, and as I am well convinced of the sincere attachment you have to him, I therefore carefully obey General Amherst's orders to me, to engage your assistance here early in the spring.

" I hope you'll continue to shew that ardent zeal you have all along expressed for the English, ever since you have been allied to them, by raising a company of your men with the utmost expedition.

" Should you chuse to come out a Captain, General Amherst will readily give you the commission for it; if

13

not, I shall expect Doquipe and Nunnipad. I leave to you the choice of an Ensign and two serjeants ; but I hope you'll engage the fittest men for their stations. I would have the company consist of fifty private men, or more, if you can get them ; and if those men that deserted from Capt. Brewer will join you, the General will pardon them. You may employ a Clerk for the company, to whom General Amherst will allow the usual pay.

"I heartily wish you success in raising your men, and shall be exceeding glad that you join me with all the expedition you possibly can. I am,

Brother Uncus,

Your most obedient humble servant,

To King Uncus.   *Robert Rogers."*

With this letter, or any other wrote to them, in order to give it any credit or influence, must go a belt of wampum, suitable to the matter and occasion of it, and upon which the bearer, after having read the letter, interprets it, and then delivers both to the Sachem, or person they are directed to.

The latter end of February, about fifty Mohocks, commanded by Captain Lotridge, came from Sir William Johnson to join me, and proceed to Ticonderoga on a scout.

March 3, 1759, I received the following orders from Col. Haldiman : "An officer being chosen by the General to make observations upon the enemy's situation, and the strength of their forts upon Lake Champlain, you are ordered to march with your Rangers, and the Mohock Indians, under the command of Capt. Lotridge, and take all the measures and precautions possible, that he may execute his intentions, and perform the service, which the General has much at heart ; and to effect this with more security, a body of regulars is likewise ordered to join with you, and you are to have command of the whole. Lieut. Brheem* is to communicate his orders to you; and the service being performed, you will endeavour to take a prisoner, or prisoners, or strike such a stroke on the enemy, and try to bring us intelligence.

" He recommends it in the strongest manner, that if some of the enemy should fall into your hands, to prevent the Indians from exercising their cruelty upon them, as he desires prisoners may be treated with humanity.

Fred Haldiman,
Commander at
Fort Edward."

Fort Edward,
March 3, 1759.

Pursuant to the above orders, I marched the same day with a party of 358 men, officers included, and encamped the first night at Half-Way Brook. One Indian, being hurt by accident, returned to Fort Edward. The 4th, marched to within one mile and a half of Lake George, and halted till evening, that we might the better pass undiscovered by the enemy, if any were on the hill reconnoitering. We continued our march till two o'clock in the morning, and halted at the first narrows. It being excessive cold, and several of our party being frost-bitten, I sent back twenty-three, under the charge of a careful serjeant, to Fort Edward. We continued here till the evening of the 5th, then marched to Sabbath-day Point, where we arrived about eleven o'clock, almost overcome with the cold. At two o'clock we continued our march, and reached the landing place about eight. I sent out a small

---

* Diedrick Brehm was a German, and was commissioned as lieutenant in the 2d Battalion of the 60th or Royal American Regiment. Feb. 21, 1756. He accompanied Major Rogers to Detroit; obtained the command of a company in the 60th Regiment, November 16, 1774, and became major in the army March 19, 1783. See *Wilson's Orderly Book*, p. 46, and authorities there cited.

party to observe if any of the enemy's parties went out. They returned and reported, that none were to be seen on the west-side of the lake, but on the east were two working parties. It now appeared to be a suitable time for the engineer to make his observations. I left Capt. Williams to remain at this place with the Regulars, and thirty Rangers, while I, with the engineer, forty-nine Rangers, and Capt. Lotridge, with forty-five Indians, went to the isthmus that overlooks the fort, where he made his observations. We returned to our party, leaving five Indians and one Ranger to observe what numbers crossed the lake in the evening from the east-side to the fort, that I might know the better how to attack them next morning. At dark the engineer went again, with Lieut. Tute, and a guard of ten men, to the entrenchments, and returned at midnight without opposition, having done his business to his satisfaction. On which I ordered Capt. Williams with the Regulars back to Sabbath-day Point; the party being extremely distressed with the cold, it appeared to me imprudent to march his men any further, especially as they had no snow shoes. I sent with him Lieut. Tute and thirty Rangers, with directions to kindle fires on the aforesaid point. At three o'clock I marched with three Lieutenants and forty Rangers, one Regular, and Capt. Lotridge with forty-six Indians, in order to be ready to attack the enemy's working parties on the east-side of the lake early in the morning. We crossed South-Bay about eight miles south of the fort ;* from thence, it being about six o'clock, bore down right opposite the fort, and within half a mile of where the French parties, agreeable to our expectations, were cutting of wood. Here I halted, and

---

* Here we found that a party of Indians had gone up the bay towards our forts.—*Note in the original.*

sent two Indians and two Rangers to observe their situation. They returned in a few minutes, and brought intelligence, that the working parties were close to the banks of the lake, and opposite the fort, and were about forty in number; upon which we stripped off our blankets, and ran down upon them, took several prisoners, and destroyed most of the party as they were retreating to the fort, from whence being discovered, about eighty Canadians and Indians pursued us closely, being backed by about 150 French regulars, and in a mile's march they began a fire in our rear; and as we marched in a line abreast, our front was easily made; I halted on a rising ground, resolving to make a stand against the enemy, who appeared at first very resolute : but we repulsed them before their reinforcement came up, and began our march again in a line abreast; having advanced about half a mile further, they came in sight again. As soon as we could obtain an advantageous post, which was a long ridge, we again made a stand on the side opposite the enemy. The Canadians and Indians came very close, but were soon stopped by a warm fire from the Rangers and Mohocks. They broke immediately, and the Mohocks with some Rangers pursued, and entirely routed them before their Regulars could come up. After this we marched without any opposition. In these several skirmishes we had two Rangers and one Regular killed, and one Indian wounded, and killed about thirty of the enemy. We continued our march till twelve o'clock at night, and came to Capt. Williams at Sabbath-day Point (fifty miles distant from the place we set out from in the morning). The Captain received us with good fires, than which scarce any thing could be more acceptable to my party, several of which had their feet froze. it being excessive cold, and the snow four feet deep. Next morning marched the whole de-

as far as Long Island* in Lake George, and there encamped that night. On our march from Sabbath-day
Point to this island, I gave leave to some of the Rangers
and Indians to hunt near the side of the lake, who brought
us in great plenty of venison for our refreshment.

I sent Lieut. Tute, with the following letter, to Col
Haldiman, fearing lest a party of Indians we had some
notice of might have gone up South Bay, and get an opportunity of doing mischief before I could reach Fort Edward
with the whole detachment.

Camp at Sabbath-day Point, Friday,
eight o'clock in the morning.

" Sir,

" I send this to let you know that sixty Indians, in two
parties, are gone towards Fort Edward and Saratoga, and I
fear will strike some blow before this reaches you. Mr.
Brheem is satisfied he has done his business agreeable to
his orders; since which I have taken some prisoners from
Ticonderoga, and destroyed others of the enemy, of the
particulars of which the bearer will inform you.

 "The Mohocks behaved with great bravery; some have
been within pistol-shot of the French fort.

" Two-thirds of my detachment have froze their feet
(the weather being so severe, that it is almost impossible to
describe it) some of which we are obliged to carry.

I am, &c.,

R. Rogers."

---

* Long Island, about six miles from the head of the lake, is the largest
island in the lake and lies opposite the entrance of the " South Arm," or
Takundawide Bay. There are in fact three bays or divisions of this water,
variously named as " Van Wormer's Bay," Sandy Bay," " Middle Bay," etc.,
on modern maps. As named on Capt. Jackson's map of 1756. It at the
present day has a farm upon it in the town of Queensbury, Warren Co., and
has a steamboat dock on the east side.

Fort Edward, March 10, 1759.

"Dear Sir,

" I congratulate you heartily on your good success, and send you twenty-two sleys to transport your sick. You will, by this opportunity, take as many boards as you can conveniently.* My best compliments to Capt. Williams, and to all the gentlemen, I am, Sir,

Your most humble servant,
Fred Haldimand.

" *P. S.* I had the signal-guns fired to give notice to the different posts. Nothing has appeared as yet. † "

We were met by the sleys, and a detachment of 100 men at Lake George, and all arrived safe at Fort Edward, where I received the following letters upon my arrival.

" SIR,

" I yesterday received your letter by Mr. Stark. The General approves of raising the Indian companies ; but as he has not heard the Rangers are complete, he cannot agree to the raising more companies, till the present ones are complete at Fort Edward. Mr. Stark sets out to-morrow for New England. I have ordered him to hurry up the recruits of your corps, and repeat my orders to the officers, to join their companies if they are complete. Your arms have been tried and proved by the artillery ; they answer very well, and are ordered to be sent to you as fast as possible : the General has sent to you by Capt. Jacobs. We have chose out one hundred men from

---

* Boards left at the place where Fort William-Henry stood, and now wanted at Fort Edward.

† The explosion of these signal-guns (as we afterwards heard) was heard by the party of the enemy, then near Fort Millar, eight miles below Fort Edward, who thereupon supposing themselves discovered, retreated with precipitation.—*Note in the original.*

each regiment, and pitched upon the officers to act this year
as light infantry ; they are cloathed and accoutred as light as
possible, and, in my opinion, are a kind of troops that has
been much wanted in this country.   They have what ammunition they want, so that I don't doubt but they will be
excellent marksmen.   You may depend upon General
Amherst's intentions to have you ; I heard Brigadier Gage
mention you to him.   From what knowledge I have of the
General, I can only say that merit is sure to be rewarded ;
nor does he favour any recommendation, without the
person recommended really deserves, his promotion.   You
will return your companies to me as soon as complete.

Your obedient humble servant,
R. *Townshend.*"

New York,
Feb. 26, 1759,
To Major Rogers.

"Sir,   *New York, Feb.* 13, 1759.
" This will be delivered to you by Capt. Jacob Naw-
nawampeteoonk, who last campaign commanded a company
of Stockbridge Indians, and who, upon hearing that you
had wrote to me concerning him, came to offer me his
service for the ensuing campaign : But as you have not
mentioned to me the terms and conditions on which he
was to engage, I have referred him to you to give in his
proposals, that you may report to me thereupon, and inform
me if you think his service adequate to them ; after which
I shall give you my answer.   I am, Sir,

Your very humble servant,
Jeff. Amherst."

To Major Rogers.
Before I received this letter from his Excellency, I had
wrote to him, recommending several officers to the vacancies in the ranging companies, and inclosed a journal of

my late scout; soon after my return from which I went to Albany, to settle my accompts with the government, where I waited upon his Excellency the General, by whom I was very kindly received, and assured that I should have the rank of Major in the army from the date of my commission under General Abercrombie.

I returned to Fort Edward the fifteenth of May, where I received the melancholy news, that Capt. Burbank, with a party of thirty men, had in my absence been sent out on a scout, and were all cut off. This gave me great uneasiness, as Mr. Burbank was a gentleman I very highly esteemed, and one of the best officers among the Rangers, and more especially as I judged the scout he was sent out upon by the commanding officer at the fort was needless, and unadvisedly undertaken.

Preparations for the campaign were hastened by his Excellency the General in every quarter; the levies from the several provinces forwarded, the companies of Rangers compleated, and disciplined in the best manner I was capable of, and of which the General was pleased greatly to approve.

In the month of June, part of the army marched with General Gage* for the lake. I was ordered to send three companies there with Capt. Stark, and to remain with the General myself with the other three companies, till such time as he marched thither. In this interval, pursuant to his Excellency's orders, I sent out several parties to the French forts, who from time to time discovered the situation of the enemy, and brought satisfactory intelligence.

---

* Gen. Thomas Gage, after the conquest of Canada, was appointed Governor of Montreal, and in 1763 succeeded Lord Amherst as Commander-in-Chief of the British forces in America, and in 1774 was appointed Governor of Massachusetts. He returned to England in October, 1775, and died in April, 1787.

14

About the 20th of June, the General with the remainder of the army marched to the lake, the Rangers being in the advanced guard; and here his Excellency was pleased to fulfil his promise to me, by declaring in public orders, my rank of Major in the army, from the date of my commission, as Major of the Rangers. We continued here collecting our strength together, and making necessary preparations, and getting what intelligence we could of the strength and situation of the enemy, till July 21, 1759, when the army embarked for Ticonderoga. I was in the front with the Rangers on the right wing, and was the first body that landed on July 22, at the north end of Lake George, followed by the grenadiers and light infantry, which Colonel Haviland commanded.

I marched, agreeable to orders from the General, across the mountains in the isthmus; from thence, in a by-way, athwart the woods to the bridge at the Saw-mills; where finding the bridge standing, I immediately crossed it with my Rangers, and took possession of the rising ground on the other side, and beat from thence a party of the enemy, and took several prisoners, killed others, and put the remainder to flight, before Col. Haviland with his grenadiers and light infantry got over. The army took possession that night of the heights near the Saw-mills, where they lay all this evening.

The enemy kept out a scouting-party, with a body of Canadians and Indians, which killed several of our men, and galled us prodigiously.

July 23, the General, early in the morning, put the army in motion; at the same time ordered me in the front, with directions to proceed across the Chestnut Plain the nighest and best way I could, to Lake Champlain, and do my endeavour to strike it near the edge of the cleared ground, between that and the breastwork, where I was to halt till I received further orders. Having pursued my orders, and halted at the lake, I informed the General of my situation, and that nothing extraordinary had happened in our march.

The General by this time had appointed and formed a a detachment to attack their main breast-work on the hill, and had got possession of it. I was ordered to send two hundred men to take possession of a small entrenchment next to Lake Champlain ; and Captain Brewer, whom I had sent to take possession of this post, happily succeeded.

From the time the army came in sight the enemy kept up a constant fire of cannon from their walls and batteries at our people. The General at this time had left several Provincial regiments to bring the cannon and ammunition across the Carrying Place, together with provisions, which they did with great expedition *.

July 24. All this day the engineers were employed in raising batteries, as was likewise a great part of the army in that work and in making and fetching fascines, till the 26th at night ; all which time I had parties out to Crown Point to watch the motions of the enemy there ; by which means the General had not only daily, but hourly intelligence from those posts.

I this day received orders from the General to attempt to cut away a boom which the French had thrown across the lake opposite the fort, which prevented our boats from from passing by, and cutting off their retreat. For the completion of this order I had sixty Rangers in one

---

* About this time some of the Provincial regiments were sent to Oswego' to assist in building a fort there.
—*Note by the Author.*

English flat-bottomed boat, and two whale boats*, in which, after night came on, I embarked, and passed over to the other side of Lake Champlain, opposite to the Rangers encampment, and from that intended to steer my course along the east-shore, and privately saw off their boom, for which end I had taken saws with me, the boom being made with logs of timber.

About nine o'clock, when I had got about half way from the place where I had embarked, the enemy, who had undermined their fort, sprung their mines, which blew up with a loud explosion, the enemy being all ready to embark on board their boats, and make a retreat. This gave me an opportunity to attack them with such success as to drive several of them ashore; so that next morning we took from the east-shore ten boats, with a considerable quantity of baggage, and upwards of fifty barrels of powder and large quantities of ball. About ten o'clock I returned, and made my report to the General.

The 27th I was ordered with my party to the Saw-mills (to wait the flying parties of the enemy which were expected that way) where I lay till the 11th of August†, on which day I received the following orders from General Amherst.

---

* These boats were carried across the land from Lake George to Lake Champlain, on which day the brave and worthy Col. Townshend was killed by a cannon ball from the enemy, whose fall was much lamented by the General.—*Note by the Author.*

Roger Townshend, fourth son of Viscount Townshend was commissioned as Lieutenant Colonel Feb. 1, 1756, and served as Adjutant General in the expedition against Louisburgh, and as Deputy Adjutant General in the Campaign of 1759, with the rank of Colonel. His remains were taken to Albany for burial.—*Wilson's Orderly Book.*

† About this time a party of my people discovered that the enemy's Fort at Crown Point was likewise blown up, and the enemy fled.
—*Note by the Author.*

" SIR,

" You are this night to send a Captain, with a proper proportion of subalterns, and two hundred men, to Crown Point, where the officer is to post himself in such a manner as not to be surprised, and to seize on the best ground for defending himself ; and if he should be attacked by the enemy, he is not to retreat with his party, but keep his ground till he is reinforced from the army. I am, Sir,

Your most obedient,

To Major Rogers.   *Jeff. Amherst.*"

Capt. Brewer went with a party, and the General followed the 12th with the whole army, and the same day arrived at Crown Point, where it was found that Capt. Brewer had executed his orders extremely well.

This evening I had orders for encamping, and the grounds for each corps being laid out, my camp was fixed in the front of the army. Immediately after the General had got the disposition of his camp settled, he began to clear ground, and prepare a place for erecting a new fort, in which service great part of the army was employed. I had orders to send Capt. Stark, with two hundred Rangers, to cut a road to No. 4. which party was immediately sent.

During these transactions I sent out (by the General's approbation) several scouting parties against the enemy*, which brought in prisoners from St. John's Fort, and others penetrated into the back country, the better to learn the nature and situation of it.

Thus were we employed till the 12th of September, when the General, exasperated at the treatment which Capt. Kennedy had met with, who had been sent with a

---

* Capt. Tute, and Lieutenant Fletcher, in two different scouting parties, were taken and carried to Canada.
—*Note by the Author.*

party as a flag of truce to the St. Francis Indians, with proposals of peace to them, and was by them made a prisoner with his whole party ; this ungenerous, inhumane treatment determined the General to chastize these savages with some severity, and, in order to it, I received from him the following orders, viz.

* " You are this night to set out with the detachment as ordered yesterday, viz. of 200 men, which you will take under your command, and proceed to Misisquey Bay, from whence you will march and attack the enemy's settlements on the south-side of the river St. Lawrence, in such a manner as you shall judge most effectual to disgrace the enemy, and for the success and honour of his Majesty's arms.

" Remember the barbarities that have been committed by the enemy's Indian scoundrels on every occasion, where they had an opportunity of shewing their infamous cruelties on the King's subjects, which they have done without mercy. Take your revenge, but don't forget that tho' those villains have dastardly and promiscuously murdered the women and children of all ages, it is my orders that no women or children are killed or hurt.

" When you have executed your intended service, you will return with your detachment to camp, or to join me wherever the army may be.

Yours, &c.

Camp at Crown Point,　　　　　　　*Jeff. Amherst."*
　Sept. 13, 1759.
To Major Rogers.

---

* That this expedition might be carried on with the utmost secresy after the plan of it was concerted the day before my march, it was put into public orders, that I was to march a different way, at the same time I had private instructions to proceed directly to St. Francis.

—*Note by the Author.*

In pursuance of the above orders, I set out the same evening with a detachment; and as to the particulars of my proceedings, and the great difficulties we met with in effecting our design, the reader is referred to the letter I wrote to General Amherst upon my return, and the remarks following it.

Copy of my letter to the General upon my return from St. Francis.

"Sir,

"The twenty-second day after my departure from Crown Point, I came in sight of the Indian town St. Francis in the evening, which I discovered from a tree that I climbed, at about three miles distance. Here I halted my party, which now consisted of 142 men, officers included, being reduced to that number by the unhappy accident which hefel Capt. Williams*, and several since tiring, whom I was obliged to send back. At eight o'clock this evening I left the detachment, and took with me Lieut. Turner, and Ensign Avery, and went to reconnoitre the town, which I did to my satisfaction, and I found the Indians in a high frolic or dance. I returned to my party at two o'clock, and at three marched it to within five hundred yards of the town, where I lightened the men of their packs, and formed them for the attack.

" At half an hour before sun-rise I surprised the town when they were all fast asleep, on the right, left, and center, which was done with so much alacrity by both the officers and men, that the enemy had not time to recover themselves, or take arms for their own defence, till they were chiefly

---

* Capt. Williams of the Royal Regiment was, the fifth day of our march accidentally burnt with gun-powder, and several men hurt, which, together with some sick, returned back to Crown Point, to the number of forty, under the care of Capt. Williams, who returned with great reluctance.
—*Note by the Author.*

destroyed, except some few of them who took to the water.
About forty of my people pursued them, who destroyed
such as attempted to make their escape that way, and sunk
both them and their boats. A little after sun-rise I set fire
to all their houses, except three, in which there was corn,
that I reserved for the use of the party.

"The fire consumed many of the Indians who had concealed themselves in the cellars and lofts of their houses.
About seven o'clock in the morning the affair was com-
pletely over, in which time we had killed at least two hundred Indians, and taken twenty of their women and children
prisoners,* fifteen of whom I let go their own way, and
five I brought with me, viz. two Indian boys, and three
Indian girls. I likewise retook five English captives, which
I also took under my care.

---

* These prisoners, when brought to Number Four, claimed Mrs. Johnson
as an old acquaintance, she having been with their tribe as a prisoner, some
time before. One of them was called Sebattis. The bell of the Catholic
chapel was also brought away, and a quantity of silver brooches taken from
the savages who were slain.—*Stark's Memoirs*, 449.

A French account of the burning of St. Francis, is given in a journal kept
in the army of the late M. de Montcalm, as follows :

"Towards the fore part of October, a detachment of about 200 men of Mr.
Amherst's army, headed by Captain Rogers, having had the boldness to traverse
a pretty extensive tract of country covered with timber, succeeded, under cover
of the surprise, in burning the Indian village of St. Francis. M. de Bourla-
mayne was fully advised of his march; he had caused the removal of the
canoes which Rogers had been obliged to abandon beyond Isle aux Noix, and
expecting him to return by the same route, had him watched, at the passage,
by a strong detachment of Canadians and Indians; but Rogers had anticipated
all that, and had, in consequence, resolved to reach Orange by another way. He
could not however escape the pursuit of a party of 200 Indians who rushed to
vengeance. Want of provisions rendered it necessary for him to divide his force
in small platoons, in order more easily to find subsistence. They massacred
some forty, and carried off ten prisoners to their village, where one of them
fell a victim to the fury of the women, notwithstanding the efforts the Canadian could make to save them.—*N. Y. Colonial History*, x, 1042.

"When I had paraded my detachment, I found I had Capt. Ogden badly wounded in his body, but not so as to hinder him from doing his duty. I had also six men slightly wounded, and one Stockbridge Indian killed.

"I ordered my people to take corn out of the reserved houses for their subsistence home, there being no other provision there ; and whilst they were loading themselves I examined the prisoners and captives, who gave the following intelligence : ' That a party of 300 French, and some Indians, were about four miles down the river below us ; and that our boats were way-laid, which I had reason to believe was true, as they told the exact number, and the place where I left them at ; that a party of 200 French and fifteen Indians had, three days before I attacked the town, gone up the river Wigwam Martinic, supposing that was the place I intended to attack ;' whereupon I called the officers together, to consult the safety of our return, who were of opinion there was no other way for us to return with safety, but by No. 4 on Connecticut River. I marched the detachment eight days in a body that way ; and when provisions grew scarce, near Ampara Magog Lake,* I divided the detachment into small companies, putting proper guides to each, who were to assemble at the mouth of Amonsook River,† as I expected provisions would be brought there for our relief,‡ not knowing which way I should return.

---

*Lake Memphremagog on the line between the present state of Vermont and the Province of Quebec. Rogers afterwards endeavored to obtain a grant of land near this lake.

† Amonsook river falls into Connecticut river about sixty miles above Number Four.—*Note by the Author.*

‡ An officer, upon some intelligence that I had when going out, was sent back to Crown Point from Misisquey bay, to desire that provisions might be conveyed to this place, as I had reason to believe we should be deprived of our boats, and consequently be obliged to return this way.—*Note by the Author.*

" Two days after we parted, Ensign Avery, of Fitche's, fell in on my track, and followed in my rear ; and a party of the enemy came upon them, and took seven of his party prisoners, two of whom that night made their escape, and came in to me next morning. Avery, with the remainder of his party joined mine, and came with me to the Cohase Intervales, where I left them with Lieut. Grant, from which place, I, with Capt. Ogden, and one man more, put down the river on a small raft to this place, where I arrived yesterday ; and in half an hour after my arrival dispatched provisions up the river to Lieut. Grant in a canoe, which I am pretty certain will reach him this night, and next morning sent two other canoes up the river for the relief of the other parties, loaded with provisions, to the mouth of Amonsook River.

" I shall set off to go up the river myself to-morrow, to seek and bring in as many of our men as I can find, and expect to be back in about eight days, when I shall, with all expedition, return to Crown Point. As to other par-'iculars relative to this scout, which your Excellency may think proper to inquire after, I refer you to Capt. Ogden, who bears this, and has accompanied me all the time I have been out, behaving very well. I am, Sir, with the greatest respect,

Your Excellency's most obedient servant,

No. 4.   *R. Rogers.*"

Nov. 5, 1759.

To General Amherst.

I cannot forbear here making some remarks on the difficulties and distresses which attended us, in effecting this enterprize upon St. Francis, which is situated within three miles of the river St. Lawrence, in the middle of Canada, about half way between Montreal and Quebec. It hath already been mentioned, how our party was reduced by the accident which befell Capt. Williams, the fifth day after our departure, and still farther by numbers tiring and falling sick afterwards. It was extremely difficult while we kept the water (and which retarded our progress very much) to pass undiscovered by the enemy, who were then cruizing in great numbers upon the lake; and had prepared certain vessels, on purpose to decoy any party of ours, that might come that way, armed with all manner of machines and implements for their destruction; but we happily escaped their snares of this kind, and landed (as hath been mentioned) the tenth day at Misisquey Bay. Here, that I might with more certainty know whether my boats (with which I left provision sufficient to carry us back to Crown Point) were discovered by the enemy, I left two trusty Indians to lie at a distance in sight of the boats, and there to stay till I came back, except the enemy found them; in which latter case they were with all possible speed to follow on my track, and give me intelligence. It happened the second day after I left them, that these two Indians came up to me in the evening, and informed me that about 400 French had discovered and taken my boats, and that about one half of them were hotly pursuing on my track. This unlucky circumstance (it may well be supposed) put us into some consternation. Should the enemy overtake us, and we get the better of them in an encounter; yet being so far advanced into their country, where no reinforcement could possibly relieve us, and where they could be supported by any number they pleased, afforded us little hopes of escaping their hands. Our boats being taken, cut off all hope of a retreat by them; besides, the loss of our provisions left with them, of which we knew we should have great need at any rate, in case we survived, was a melancholly consideration. It was, however, resolved to prosecute our design at all adventures, and, when we had accomplished it, to attempt a retreat (the only possible way we could think of) by way of No. 4; and that we might not be destroyed by famine in our return, I dispatched Lieut. M'Mullen by land to Crown Point, to desire of the General to relieve me with provision at Amonsook River, at the end of Cohase Intervales* on Connecticut River, that being the way I should return, if at all, and the place appointed being about sixty miles from No. 4, then the most northerly English settlement. This being done, we determined if possible to outmarch our pursuers, and effect our design upon St. Francis before they could overtake us. We marched nine days through wet, sunken ground; the water most of the way near a foot deep, it being a spruce bog. When we encamped at night, we had no way to secure ourselves from the water, but by cutting the bows of trees, and with them erecting a kind of hammocks. We commonly began our march a little before day, and continued it till after dark at night.

The tenth day after leaving Misisquey Bay, we came to a river about fifteen miles above the town of St. Francis to the south of it; and the town being on the opposite or east side of it, we were obliged to ford it, which was attended with no small difficulty, the water being five feet deep, and the current swift. I put the tallest men up stream, and then holding by each other, we got over with the loss of several of our guns, some of which we recovered by diving to the bottom for them. We had now good dry ground to march upon, and discovered and destroyed the town as before related, which in all probability would have been effected with the loss of no man but the Indian who was killed in the action, had not my boats been discovered, and our retreat that way cut off.

---

* Variously writtien as *Cohase, Cohos, Coos,* etc., referring to the meadows along the Upper Connecticut Valley in the present county of Coos, New Hampshire.

This nation of Indians was notoriously attached to the French, and had for near a century past harrassed the frontiers of New England, killing people of all ages and sexes in a most barbarous manner, at a time when they did not in the least expect them; and to my own knowledge, in six years' time, carried into captivity, and killed, on the before mentioned frontiers, 400 persons. We found in the town hanging on poles over their doors, &c., about 600 scalps, mostly English.

The circumstances of our return are chiefly related in the preceding letter; however, it is hardly possible to describe the grief and consternation of those of us who came to Cohase Intervales. Upon our arrival there (after so many days' tedious march over steep, rocky mountains, or through wet, dirty swamps, with the terrible attendants of fatigue and hunger) to find that here was no relief for us, where we had encouraged ourselves that we should find it, and have our distresses alleviated; for notwithstanding the officer I dispatched to the General discharged his trust with great expedition, and in nine days arrived at Crown Point, which was an hundred miles through the woods, and the General, without delay, sent Lieut. Stephens to No. 4. with orders to take provisions up the river to the place I had appointed, and there wait as long as there was any hopes of my returning; yet the officer that was sent being an indolent fellow, tarried at the place but two days, when he returned, taking all the provisions back with him, about two hours before our arrival. Finding a fresh fire burning in his camp, I fired guns to bring him back, which guns he heard, but would not return, supposing we were an enemy.*

---

* This Gentleman, for this piece of conduct, was broke by a general court-martial, and rendered incapable of sustaining any office in his Majesty's service for the future : a poor reward, however, for the distresses and anguish thereby occasioned to so many brave men, to some of which it proved fatal, they actually dying with hunger.—*Note by the Author.*

Our distress upon this occasion was truly inexpressible ; our spirits greatly depressed by the hunger and fatigues we had already suffered, now almost entirely sunk within us, seeing no resource left, nor any reasonable ground to hope that we should escape a most miserable death by famine. At length I came to a resolution to push as fast as possible towards No. 4, leaving the remains of my party, now unable to march further, to get such wretched subsistence as the barren wilderness could afford,* till I could get relief to them, which I engaged to do within ten days. I, with Capt. Ogden, one Ranger, and a captive Indian boy, embarked upon a raft we had made of dry pine-trees. The current carried us down the stream in the middle of the river; where we endeavoured to keep our wretched vessel by such paddles as we had made out of small trees or spires split and hewed. The second day we reached White River Falls, and very narrowly escaped being carried over them by the current. Our little remains of strength however enabled us to land, and to march by them. At the bottom of these falls, while Capt. Ogden and the Ranger hunted for red squirrels for a refreshment, who had the good fortune likewise to kill a partridge, I attempted the forming a new raft for our further conveyance. Being not able to cut down trees. I burnt them down, and then burnt them off at proper lengths. This was our third day's work after leaving our companions. The next day we got our materials together, and compleated our raft, and floated with the stream again till we came to Wattockquitchey Falls, which are about fifty yards in length ; here we landed, and by a weath made of hazel bushes, Capt. Ogden

---

* This was ground-nuts and lilly roots, which being cleaned and boiled will serve to preserve life, and the use and method of preparing which I taught to Lieut. Grant, commander of the party.
—*Note by the Author.*

held the raft, till I went to the bottom, prepared to swim in and board it when it came down, and if possible paddle it ashore, this being our only resource for life, as we were not able to make a third raft in case we had lost this. I had the good fortune to succeed, and the next morning we embarked and floated down the stream to within a small distance of No. 4, where we found some men cutting of timber, who gave us the first relief, and assisted us to the fort, from whence I despatched a canoe with provisions, which reached the men at Cohase four days after, which (agreeable to my engagement) was the tenth after I left them.

Two days after my arrival at No. 4, I went with other canoes, loaded with provisions, up the river myself, for for the relief of others of my party that might be coming in that way,* having hired some of the inhabitants to assist me in this affair. I likewise sent expresses to Suncook and Pennecook upon Merrimack River, that any who should chance to straggle that way might be assisted ; and provisions were sent up said rivers accordingly.

On my return to No. 4, I waited a few days to refresh such of my party as I had been able to collect together, and during my stay there received the following letter from General Amherst, in answer to mine of Nov. 5.

" Sir,   *Crown Point, Nov.* 8, 1759.

" Captain Ogden delivered me your letter of the 5th instant, for which I am not only to thank you, but to

---

* I met several different parties ; as Lieut. Curgill, Lieut. Campbell, Lieut. Farrington, and Serjeant Evans, with their respective divisions, and sent canoes further up for the relief of such as might be still behind, and coming this way. Some I met who escaped from Dunbar's and Turner's party, who were overtaken (being upwards of twenty in number) and were mostly killed or taken by the enemy.
—*Note by the Author.*

assure you of the satisfaction I had on reading it ; as every step you inform me you have taken, has been very well judged, and deserves my full approbation.   I am sorry Lieut. Stephans judged so ill in coming away with the provisions from the place where I sent him to wait for you.

" An Indian is come in last night, and said he had left some of your party at Otter River, I sent for them ; they are come in.   This afternoon four Indians, two Rangers, a German woman, and three other prisoners ; they quitted four of your party some days since, and thought they had arrived here.*   I am in hopes all the rest will get in very safe.   I think there is no danger but they will, as you quitted them not till having marched eight days in a body ; the only risk after that will be meeting hunting parties. I am, Sir,

Your humble servant,

To Major Rogers.   *Jeff. Amherst.*

As soon as my party were refreshed, such as were able I marched to Crown Point, where I arrived Dec. 1, 1759, and upon examination found, that since our leaving the ruins of St. Francis, I had lost three officers, viz. Lieut. Dunbar of Gage's Light Infantry, Lieut Turner of the Rangers, and Lieut. Jenkins of the Provincials, and forty-six sergeants and privates.   The Rangers at that place were all dismissed before my return, excepting two companies, commanded by Captains Johnson and Tute †, with whom I found orders left by the General for me to continue at that garrison during the winter, but had leave, however to go down the country, and to wait upon his Excellency at New York.

---

* Upon our separation, some of the divisions were ordered to make for Crown Point, that being the best route for hunting.—*Note by the Author.*

† Capt. Tute, who had been taken prisoner, was returned by a flag of truce, while I was gone to St. Francis.

After giving in my return to the General, and what intelligence I could of the enemy's situation, he desired me, when I had leisure, to draw a plan of my march to St. Francis ; and then, by his order, I returned by the way of Albany ; which place I left the 6th of February, 1760, with thirteen recruits I had inlisted ; and the 13th, on my way between Ticonderoga and Crown Point, my party was attacked by about sixty Indians, who killed five, and took four prisoners. I, with the remainder, made my escape to Crown Point, from whence I would have pursued them immediately ; but Col. Haviland, the commanding officer there, judged it not prudent, by reason the garrison at that time was very sickly.* I continued at Crown Point the remainder of the winter.

On the 31st of March, Capt. James Tute, with two regular officers and six men, went out a scouting, and were all made prisoners ; the enemy was not pursued, on account of the sickness of the garrison.

The same day I received from General Amherst the following letter.

Sir, *New York, March 1, 1760.*

" The command I have received from his Majesty, to pursue the war in this country, has determined me, if pos-

---

* My own sley was taken with 1196*l.* York currency in cash, besides stores and others necessaries ; 800*l,* of this money belonged to the crown, which was afterwards allowed me, the remaining 396*l,* was my own, which I entirely lost.—*Note by the Author.*

Colonel Haviland was the same who had sent Rogers out in March, 1758, with a small force, when he knew a superior one awaited him. It is remarked by Mr. Stark that this officer was one of that sort of men who manage to escape public censure, let them do what they will. " He was one of the many British Officers who were meanly jealous of the daring achievements of their brave American comrades, but for whose intrepidity and arduous services all the British armies sent to America, during the Seven Years War, would have effected little towards the conquest of Canada."

— *Stark's Memoirs, p.* 454.

16

sible, to complete the companies of Rangers that were on foot last campaign; and as Capt. Wait called upon me yesterday, and represented that he could easily complete the one he commands in the colony of Connecticut and the Province of the Massachuset's Bay, I have furnished him with beating orders for that purpose, as also with a warrant for 800 dollars on account of that service.

" This day I have wrote to Capt. John Stark in New Hampshire, and Capt. David Brewer in the Massachuset's Bay, inclosing to each of them a beating order for the respective provinces; and I herewith send you a copy of the instructions that accompany the same, by which you will see they are ordered, as fast as they get any number of men, to send them to Albany. I am, Sir,

Your humble servant

To Major Rogers. *Jeff. Amherst.*"

My answer to the above.

" Sir, *Crown Point, March* 15, 1760.

" I received your Excellency's letter dated the 1st instant, together with a copy of your instructions to Capt. John Stark and Capt. David Brewer, whereby I learn that they are to be at Albany by the 1st of May next with their companies. Since I received intelligence from your Excellency that the Rangers are to be raised again, I have wrote to several of my friends in New England, who will assist them in compleating their companies; and as many of the men belonging to the two companies here were frost-bitten in the winter, and others sick, many of whom I judged would not be fit for service the ensuing campaign, I employed Lieut. M'Cormack, of Capt. William Stark's*

---

* William Stark was the elder brother of Gen. John Stark, of the revolution. He served as a provincial officer at Ticonderoga, Louisburgh and Quebec, and at the beginning of the revolution applied for a command in a New Hampshire

company (that was with Major Scott) Lieut. John Fletcher, and one Holmes, and sent them recruiting the 20th of February for my own and Captain Johnson's company, and advanced them 1100 dollars. These three recruiters I do not doubt will bring good men enough to complete us here ; so that those who are frost-bitten may be sent to hospitals, and those unfit for duty discharged or otherwise disposed of, as your Excellency shall direct.

There being so few Rangers fit for duty here, and those that are much wanted at this place, has prevented me from proposing any tour to the French and Indian settlements in pursuit of a prisoner, which may, I believe, be easily got at any time, if sent for. I am, SIR,

Your Excellency's

most obedient humble servant,

R. Rogers.

To General Amherst.

A letter from General Amherst.

"SIR, *New York,* 9th *March,* 1760.

" As I have not heard that either of the Jacobuses, who each commanded a company of Stockbridge Indians the last campaign, are returned from their captivity, I would have you write (if you think Lieut. Solomon capable of and fit for such a command) to him, to know if he chuses to accept of the same ; but it must be upon condition of bringing to the field none but good men, that are well in-clined, and that are hale and strong. Whatever number he or any of his friends can raise that will answer this description, I will readily employ this summer, and they

---

regiment. Disappointed in this he became disgusted with the cause, joined the enemy at New York, was appointed a colonel, and lost his life by being thrown from a horse. He was proscribed and his estates were confiscated by an act of the legislature of New Hampshire dated Nov. 28, 1778, and in another act dated June 25, 1779. His son John became an officer in the British army.

shall meet with all the encouragement their services shall merit. All others that are too old or too young, I shall reject, nor shall I make them any allowance of payment, altho' they should join the army; so that, in order to prevent his having any difference with these people, it will behove him to engage none but what shall be esteemed fit for the service ; he must also observe to be assembled with them at Albany by the 1st of May at furthest, from which day he and they shall be entitled to their pay, that is, for so many as shall be mustered there, and for no more ; he must likewise take care that every man comes provided with a good firelock, and that they be always ready to march at a moment's warning, wherever they are ordered to, in default of which they shall forfeit their pay that shall be due to them at that time. All this you will explain to him particularly, and so soon as you receive his answer, inform me thereof. As an encouragement to enter the service upon the foregoing conditions, you may assure him also, that if he conforms to them in every respect, and that he and his men prove useful, they shall be better rewarded than they have yet been.

Capt. Ogden having solicited me for a company of Rangers, assured me that he could raise and complete a very good one in the Jersies ; I have given him a beating order for that purpose, and instructions similar to those I sent you a copy of in my last for Captains Stark and Brewer, and have also granted him a warrant for five hundred dollars, on account of the bounty-money, to be as usual stopped out of the first warrant for the subsistence of that company. I am, SIR,

Your humble servant.

To Major Rogers.   *Jeff. Amherst."*

My Letter to the General.

" SIR, .   *Crown Point*, 20th *March*, 1760.

" I observe the contents of your Excellency's letter of

the 19th, and shall take particular care to let Lieut. Solomon know every circumstance relative to his being employed the next summer, and to advise your Excellency as soon as I hear from him. He has already informed me he would be glad to engage with some Indians.

"Mr. Stuart, the Adjutant of the Rangers, who is at Albany, I have desired to go to Stockbridge, to deliver Solomon his orders, and to explain them properly to him.

"I am heartily glad that your Excellency hath been pleased to give to Capt Ogden a company of the Rangers, who, from the good character he bears, I doubt not will answer your expectations.

"Inclosed is a sketch of my travels to and from St. Francis. I am, Sir,
   Your Excellency's most humble servant,
To General Amherst.   •   *R. Rogers.*"

   The General's Letter to me.

 "Sir,   *New York*, 6th *April*, 1760.

"I am to own the receipt of your letters of the 15th and 20th ultimo, and to approve what you therein mention to have done for completing your and Capt. Johnson's company; as also your having sent Adjutant Stuart to Stockbridge, to deliver Solomon his orders, and to explain them properly to him. This will avoid all mistakes, and enable you the sooner to inform me of Solomon's intentions, which I shall be glad to know as soon as possible.

"I thank you for your sketch of your travels to and from St. Francis, and am, Sir,
   Your very humble servant,
To Major Rogers.   *Jeff. Amherst.*"

Soon after this I had the pleasure of informing the General that the Stockbridge Indians determined to enter the service this year; but as many of them were out a hunting, that they could not be collected at Albany before the 10th of May; and that the recruits of the ranging companies began to assemble at Crown Point.

May 4, 1760. This day Serjeant Beverly, who had been taken prisoner, and made his escape, came in seven days from Montreal to Crown Point   He had lived at the Governor's (Monsieur de Vaudreuil) house, and brought the following intelligence, which I immediately transmitted to the General, viz:

" That about the 10th of April, the enemy withdrew all their troops from Nut Island, excepting 300, which they left there to garrison the place, under the command of Monsieur Bonville : that the enemy also brought from the island one half of the ammunition they had there, and half of the cannon : that the enemy had two frigates, one of 36 guns, the other of 20 guns, that lay all winter in the river St. Lawrence, and some other small vessels, such as rowgalleys, &c., that all the troops of France in Canada went down to Jecorty the 20th of April, except those left to garrison their fort, which was very slenderly done, together with all the militia that could be spared out of the country, leaving only one man to two females to sow their grain, where they were assembled by Monsieur Levy, their General, with an intent to retake Quebec * : that ninety-six men of the enemy were drowned going down to Jecorty : that he saw a man who was taken prisoner the 15th of April, belonging to our troops at Quebec : that this man told him our garrison there was healthy ; and that Brigadier General Murray had 4000 men fit for duty in the city, besides a post of 300 men at Point Levy, which the enemy attempted to take possession of in the month of February

---

* This place, the capital of all Canada, had been taken by the English troops last year, under the command of General Wolfe.—*Note by the Author.*

last, with a considerable body of troops, and began to fortify a church at or near the Point, but that General Murray
sent over a detachment of about 1000 men, which drove
the enemy from post, and took a Captain, with about thirty
French soldiers, prisoners, and fortified the church for his
own coveniency : that the General has another post on the
north-side of the river at Laurat* , a little distance from the
town, in which he keeps 300 men : that there is a line of
block-houses well fortified all around the land-side of the
town, under cover of the cannon : that a breast-work of
fraziers is extended from one block-house to another, as
far as those houses extend : that they heard at Quebec of
the enemy's coming, but were not in the least concerned :
that a detachment from Quebec surprised two of the
enemy's guards, at a place called Point de Treamble, each
guard consisting of fifty men, and killed or took the most
part of them. One of those guards were all granadiers."

He moreover reports, " That two more of our frigates
had got up the river, and that two more men of war were
near the Island of Orleans : that the French told him that
there was a fleet of ten sail of men of war seen at Gaspee
Bay, with some transports, but put back to sea again on
account of the ice ; but as they had up different colours,
they could not tell they were French or English : that the
beginning of May the enemy was to draw off 2000 of their
men to Nut Island, and as many more to Oswagotchy † :
he heard that they did not intend to attack Quebec, except
the French fleet gets up the river before ours : that 100
Indians were to come this way, and set out about the fifth
of May ; the remainder of the Indians were at present gone
to Jecorty : that Gen. Levy, the Attawawas, and Cold
Country Indians, will all be in Canada by the beginning .

---

* Lorette.
† Ogdensburgh, N. Y,

of June, ten Sachems being sent by the French last fall, to call those nations to their assistance : that a great number had deserted to the French from the battalion of Royal Americans at Quebec, which the French have engaged in their service ; but that they were to be sent off, under the care of Monsieur Boarbier, up to Attawawas River, to the French colony betwixt the lakes and the Mississippi River : that the most part of the enemy's Indians are intent on going there ; and that a great number of French, especially those who have money, think to save it by carrying it to New Orleans : that he saw at Montreal two Rangers, Reynolds and Hall, that were returned by Col. Haviland deserted last fall : that they were taken prisoners near River-head Block-house, when after catttle ; that two more Rangers are to be here in ten days with fresh intelligence from Montreal, if they can possibly make their escape : that Monsieur Longee, the famous partisan, was drowned in the River St. Laurence, a few days after he returned with the party that took Capt. Tute : that the Indians have a great eye to the No. 4 roads, as they say they can get sheep and oxen coming here from that place : that he heard Gen. Murray had hanged several Canadians lately, that were carrying ammunition out of Quebec to the enemy : that the two Captains Jacobs are still in Canada ; the one taken with Capt. Kennedy is on board a vessel in irons, the other ran away last fall, but returned, having froze his feet, and is at Montreal."

A few days after this, I went down the Lake Champlain, to reconnoitre Nut Island, and the garrison there, the landing places, &c. On my return from that service to Crown Point, I had an order from Gen. Amherst to repair to Albany, the head-quarters, as fast as possible.

I set out, in obedience to this order, the 18th of May, and waited upon the General at Albany the 23d, and gave him all the information I could, in regard to the passage into Canada by the Island de Noix, or Nut Island, and likewise that by Oswego and La Galette*.

The General being acquainted by an express that Quebec was then besieged by the French, informed me of his in-tentions of sending me with a party into Canada, and if the siege of Quebec was continued, to destroy their country as far as possible, and by constantly marching from one place to another, try to draw off the enemy's troops, and prolong the siege till our vessels got up the river. He strongly re-commended, and ordered me to govern myself according to the motions of the French army ; to retreat if they had raised the siege ; and in case, by prisoners or otherwise, I should find the siege still going on, to barrass the country, tho' it were at the expense of my party. I had at the same time the following instructions from him in writing:

" Major Rogers, you are to take under your command a party of 300 men, composed of 275 Rangers, with their proper officers, and a subaltern, two serjeants, and twenty-five men of the Light Infantry regiments ; with which de-tachment you will proceed down the lake, under convoy of the brig, where you will fix upon the safest and best place for laying up your boats, which I imagine one of the islands will best answer, while you are executing the follow-ing services.

" You will with 250 men land on the west-side, in such manner that you may get to St. John's (without the enemy at the Isle au Noix having any intelligence of it) where you will try to surprize the fort, and destroy the vessels,

---

* Galette, was an Indian settlement on the north bank of the St. Law-rence a little below the present town of Prescott. It was founded by the French, for the Indians of the Five Nations whom they had persuaded to emi-grate and settle under their protection in Canada.

boats, provisions, or whatever else may be there for the use of the troops at the Isle au Noix. You will then march to Fort Chamble, where you will do the same, and you destroy every magazine you can find in that part, so as to distress the enemy as much as you can. This will soon be known at the Isle au Noix, and you must take care not to be cut off in your retreat; for which reason, when you have done all you think practicable on the western side; I judge your best and safest retreat will be, to cross the river and march back the east-side of Isle aux Noix. When you land on the west-side, you will send such officer with the fifty Rangers, as you think will best answer their intended service, which is to march for Wigwam Martinique, to destroy what he may find there and on the east-side of the river, and afterwards to join you, or to retreat in such manner as you will direct him. You will take such provisions as you judge necessary with you, and fix with Capt. Grant (who shall have orders to wait for your return) the places where he may look out for you when you come back.

" You will take your men as light with you as possible, and give them all the necessary caution for the conduct, and their obedience to their officers; no firing without order, no unnecessary alarms, no retreating without an order; they are to stick by one another and nothing can hurt them; let every man whose firelock will carry it have a bayonet; you are not to suffer the Indians to destroy women or children, no plunder to be taken to load your men, who shall be rewarded at their return as they deserve. *May* 25, 1760.

Jeff. Amherst."

With the above instructions the General delivered me a letter directed to General Murray at Quebec, desiring me to convey it to him in such manner as I thought would be quickest and safest.

Having received these instructions I returned to Crown Point as fast as possible, and about the beginning of June set out from thence with a party of two hundred and fifty men * down Lake Champlain, having four vessels, on board of which this detachment embarked, putting our boats and provisions into them, that the enemy might have less opportunity of discovering our designs.

The 3d, I landed Lieut. Holmes with fifty men in Misisquey Bay, and gave him proper directions agreeable to my orders from the General, informing him that one of the sloops should cruise for him till his return, which upon signals that were given him would take him on board, upon which he was to join me or wait on board till my return, as the situation of affairs might direct him. Here likewise I sent the letter I had reserved from the General to Brigadier Murray, thro' the woods, and gave the following instructions to the officer I intrusted with it, viz.

Instructions for Serjeant Beverly of his Majesty's Rangers.

"You are hereby directed to take under your command, these three men, viz. John Shute†, Luxford Goodwin, and

---

* The Stockbridge Indians who had been mustered at, and now marched from Albany, and who were to be a part of the detachment of 300, agreeable to the General's orders, had not arrived at Crown Point at the time of my embarkation, but were ordered to follow after and join me.
— *Note by the Author.*

† Shute and Eastman were both from Rumford, N. H., and were messmates through the war, equally distinguished for enterprise, hardihood and valor. John Shute was the son of Jacob Shute, and Eastman born May 20, 1720, was probably nephew of Ebenezer, and son of Joseph of Salisbury.
On account of the danger and difficulty of the service, the distance of this journey through the woods being estimated at five hundred miles, a reward of £50 was offered for any four who would volunteer. Serjeant Beverly who had been a prisoner and escaped from Canada the preceding year, with the three persons named, volunteered for the service.
A detailed account of the journey, as taken down from Mr. Shute's lips about the year 1820, is given in *Bouton's History.*

Joseph Eastman, and march them from Misisquey Bay, to which place you will be convoyed by Lieut. Holmes with a party I have sent there for a particular purpose ; you are to land in the night-time, as otherwise you may be discovered by a party from the Isle au Noix ; you will steer your course about north-east, and make all the dispatch you possibly can with the letter in your charge to Quebec, or to the English army at or near that place, and deliver it to Brigadier Murray, or to the officer commanding his Majesty's forces in or upon the river St. Lawrence. A sketch of the country will be delivered you with these orders, that you may the better know the considerable rivers you have to cross, betwixt Misisquey Bay and Quebec. The distances are marked in the draught, as is the road I travelled in last fall, from Misisquey Bay to St. Francis, which road you will cross several times, if you keep the course I before directed. The rivers are so plainly described in the plan, that you will know them when you come to them. The river St. Francis is about half-way of your journey. and is very still water, and may be easily rafted where you cross it ; but lower down it is so swift and rapid that you must not attempt it. Shedoir River you will likewise be obliged to pass on a raft ; it is swift water for some miles from its mouth ; you had better examine it well before you attempt to cross it. As soon as you pass this river, steer your course about east, leaving Point Levy on your left hand, and fall in with the river St. Lawrence, near the lower end of the Island of Orleans, as it may be possible that Gen. Murray may have encamped the army either at the isle of Orleans or the isle of Quodoa ; therefore you are not to depend on finding at once the exact place of his encampment, but are postively ordered to look out for the English fleet, and the first line of battle ship you see, you are to venture on board, as I think it not possible the enemy should have any large ships there, and whatever English ship you get on board of, will convoy you directly to General Murray, when you will deliver him the verbal message I told you. You may apply to the General for fifty pounds, who will pay it to you, and also give you proper directions to join me as soon as you have rested yourself from your march. I wish you a good journey, and am,

Your's &c.

To Serjeant Beverley.   *Robert Rogers*."

As soon as I had dispatched the two parties beforementioned, I, with the remainder, crossed Lake Champlain to the west-side, and the 4th in the morning got into my boats, and landed with about 200 men, about twelve miles south of the island Noix, with an intent to put in execution the General's orders to me of May 5th with all speed. Capt. Grant sent the two sloops to attend, which I ordered to cruize further down the lake than where I landed, and nearer to their fort, to command the attention of the enemy till I could get into their country.* I lay still all the 5th, there being a heavy rain, and the bushes so wet that both we and our provisions would have been greatly exposed by a march.

In the afternoon of this day, several French boats appeared on the Lake, which were discovered by the two sloops, as well as by my party on the shore. These boats continued as near as they could to our vessels without endangering themselves, till after dark. Concluding their boats would cruize the whole night to watch the motions of our sloops, I imagined it would be a prudent step to send the sloops back to Capt. Grant, the commander of these vessels, who lay near Mott Island; I accordingly went to the sloops in a boat after dark, and ordered them to return. The enemy, who kept all night in their boats, having, by a strict look-out, discovered where I landed, sent a detachment from the island next morning to cut off my party. I discovered their intentions by my reconnoitering parties, who counted them as they crossed from the fort in the morning in their boats, to the west shore, and informed me that they were 350 in number. I had intelligence again when they were about a mile from us. Half after eleven they attacked me very briskly on my left, having on my right a bog, which they did not venture over, thro' which however, by the edge of the lake, I sent seventy of my party to get round and attack them in the rear. This party was commanded by Lieut. Farrington. As soon as he began his attack, I pushed them in front, which broke them immediately. I pursued them with the greatest part of my people about a mile, where they retired to a thick cedar swamp, and divided into small parties. By this time it rained again very hard. I called my party immediately together at the boats, where I found that Ensign Wood of the 17th regiment was killed, Capt. Johnson wounded through the body, a second shot thro' his left arm, and a third in-his head. I had two men of the Light Infantry, and eight Rangers, wounded, and sixteen Rangers killed. We killed forty of the enemy, and recovered about fifty firelocks. Their commanding officer, Monsieur la Force, was mortally hurt, and several of the party were likewise wounded. After the action I got the killed and maimed of my detachment together in battoes, returned with them to the Isle á Mot, near which the brig lay. I dispatched one of the vessels to Crown Point, on board of which was put the corpse of Mr. Wood, but Capt. Johnson died on his passage thither; this vessel I ordered to bring more provisions. I buried the rest of the dead on an island, and then began to prepare for a second landing; being joined about this time by the Stockbridge

Indian Company, I was determined at all adventures to pursue my orders, settled the plan of landing, and left the following instructions with Capt. Grant, viz :

"You will be so good as to fall down the lake with your vessels as soon as possible, as far as the Wind Mill Point, or near where you lay at anchor the last time I was with you, and cruize near it for two or three days, which will be the only method I can think of that has any appearance of attracting the attention of the enemy till I get into their country ; as soon as I observe or think you pretty near the Wind Mill Point, I shall land with my party on the west side opposite to the north end of the Isle á Mot, in the river that runs into the bay which forms itself there, and from thence proceed to execute the General's orders. If they do not attack me in my march till I compleat my design, you may be certain I shall come back on the east side, and endeavour to join you near the Wind Mill Point, or betwixt that and the Isle á Mot. When I arrive, the signal that I will make for your discovering me, will be a smoak and three guns, at a minute's interval each from the other, and repeated a second time, in half an hour after the first ; but if the enemy should attack me on my march before I get to the place I am ordered, which I believe they will do, in case I am worsted I shall be obliged to come back on the west side, and shall make the before mentioned signals betwixt the Isle a Mot and the place where I had the battle with the enemy the 6th instant. It is uncertain when I shall be at either shore so that I would recommend it to you not to come back south of the Isle á Mot till my return, as a contrary wind might prevent your getting in with your vessels to relieve me. I send you Serjeant Hacket and ten Rangers, to be with you in my absence, as we this day agreed. If Lieutenant Darcy comes down in season to go with me,

I shall leave Ensign Wilson with you ; but if Darcy should not come till after I land, you'll be pleased to take him under your direction, as well as all those that may come with him to join me ; tho' I would recommend it not to send any party to the island, to take a prisoner, till the fifth day after my landing, as the loss of a man from us may be of very bad consequence. Lieutenant Holmes has appointed between the eleventh and sixteenth day after his landing for his return to Misisquey Bay, and from the eleventh to the sixteenth, as before mentioned ; I should be glad the sloop might cruize for him at the place he appointed to meet her. I am, SIR,

Your humble servant,

R. Rogers."

I cannot but observe with pleasure, that Mr. Grant, like an able officer, very diligently did all that could be expected of him for the good of the service, carefully attending with his vessels till my return from this second excursion, on which I embarked with two hundred and twenty men, officers included, and landed the 9th of June, about midnight, on the west-shore opposite the Isle a Mot, from thence marched as fast as possible to St. John's, and came to the road that leads from it to Montreal, about two miles from the fort, the evening of the 15th. At eleven o'clock this night, I marched with an intent to surprise the fort, to within four hundred yards of it, where I halted to reconnoitre ; which I did, and found they had more men than I expected. The number of the centries within the fort were seventeen, and so well fixed, that I thought it was impossible for me to take the place by surprise, especially as they had seen me, and fired several guns accordingly. I left it at two o'clock, and marched down the river to St. d'Etrese; at break of day I reconnoitred this place, and found that the enemy had in it a stockaded fort, defensible against small arms. I observed two large store-houses in the inside, and that the enemy were carting hay into the fort. I waited for an opportunity when the cart had just entered the gate-way, run forward, and got into the fort before they could clear the way for shutting the gate. I had at this time sent different parties to the several houses, about fifteen in number, which were near the fort, and were all surprised at the same instant of time, and without firing a single gun. We took in the fort twenty-four soldiers, and in the houses seventy-eight prisoners, women and children included; some young men made their escape to Chamblee. I examined the prisoners, and found I could not proceed to Chamblee with any prospect of success; therefore concluded my best way was, to burn the fort and village, which I did, together with a considerable magazine of hay, and some provisions, with every battoe and canoe, except eight battoes which I kept to cross the river, and these we afterwards cut to pieces: we also killed their cattle, horses, &c. destroyed their waggons, and every other thing which we thought could ever be of service to the enemy. When this was done, I sent back the women and children, and gave them a pass to go to Montreal, directed to the several officers of the different detachments under my command. I continued my march on the east-side of Lake Champlain, and when passing by Misisquey Bay, opposite the Isle Noix, my advance-party, and the advance-party of about 800 French, that were out after me from their fort, engaged with each other; but the body of the enemy, being about a mile behind their advance-party, retreated, to my great satisfaction. I pursued my march with all possible speed: and the same day, being the 20th day of June, arrived at the lake opposite where the vessels lay; and as I had sent a few men forward to repeat the signals, the boats met us at the shore. We directly put on board, the enemy soon after appeared on the shore

17

where we embarked. I had not at this time any account from Lieutenant Holmes, either by prisoners or otherways.

Upon examination the prisoners reported, (some of them had been at the siege of Quebec) " that the French lost five hundred men there ; and that they retreated after twelve days bombarding and cannonading, and came to Jack's quarters,·where General Levy left five hundred men, being composed of a picquet of each battalion of the army, and that there were four hundred Canadians who staid voluntarily with them ; that the rest of the army was quartered by two's and three's on the inhabitants, from there to St. John's. In Montreal there are about a hundred and fifty troops, and the inhabitants do duty. That in Chamblee Fort are about one hundred and fifty men, including workmen ; and the remnant of the Queen's regiment are in the village. That there are twelve cannon at St. John's, and about three hundred men, including workmen, who are obliged to take arms on any alarm. That at the Isle au Noix are about eight hundred stationed, besides the scouts between that and Montreal. That there are about an hundred pieces of cannon there." This is the substance of their report, in which they all agree, and which, with an account of my proceedings, I transmitted to the General.

On the 21st I put the twenty-six prisoners on board one of the vessels, with fifty men of my detachment, and ordered her to proceed to Crown Point, and tarried with the other vessels to cover Mr. Holmes's retreat, who joined us the same evening, without having succeeded in his enterprise, missing his way by following down a river that falls into Sorrel, instead of that called Wigwam Martinic, which empties itself into St. Lawrence at Lake St. Francis. I arrived at Crown Point the 23d of June, and encamped my Rangers on the east-shore, opposite the fort.

The following letter I received from General Amherst *,
dated at Canijoharry, June 26, 1760.

"Sir,

"Colonel Haviland sent me your letter of June 21, which
I received last night, and saw with pleasure you was returned without the loss of a man of your party, and that
you had done every thing that was prudent for you to attempt with the number of men you had under your command. From the situation the enemy is now in, by being
forced back to their former quarters, on Governor Murray's
having obliged them to abandon their cannon, and raise the
siege of Quebec, I hope Lieutenant Holmes will return
with equal success as you have done. I am, Sir,

Your humble servant,

To Major Rogers. ⸱ *Jeff. Amherst.*"

I remained at Crown Point with my people, without effecting any thing considerable, more than in small parties
reconnoitring the country about the fort, while every thing
was got in readiness for embarking the army the 16th of
August; which was done accordingly, having one brig, three
sloops, and four rideaus, which latter were occupied by the
royal train of artillery, commanded by Lieut. Colonel Ord.
Our order of march was as follows, viz.

Six hundred Rangers and seventy Indians in whale-boats
in the front, commanded by Major Rogers, as an advance-
guard for the whole army, all in a line a-breast, about half
a mile a-head of the main body, followed by the light infantry and grenadiers in two columns, two boats a-breast in
each column, commanded by Col. Darby. The right wing
was composed of Provincials, commanded by Brigadier

---

* Gen. Amherst was at this time on his way to Canada, by way of Oswego,
to assist in finishing the conquest of the French in that province. Can-
ajoharie is about fifty-five miles west of Albany, on the Mohawk. ,

Ruggles, who was second in command of the whole army. The left was made up of New Hampshire and Boston troops, commanded by Col. Thomas. The seventeenth and twenty-seventh regiments, with some few of the Royals, that formed the center column, were commanded by Major Campbell of the 17th regiment. Col. Haviland was in the front of these divisions, between that and the light infantry, and grenadiers. The royal artillery followed the columns, and was commanded by Colonel Ord, who had, for his escort, one Rhode Island regiment of Provincials. The sutlers, &c. followed the artillery. In this manner we rowed down the lake forty miles the first day, putting ashore where there was good landing on the west-side, and there encamped.

The day following we lay by. The 18th, the wind blowing fresh at south, orders were given for embarking, and the same day reached a place on the west-shore, within ten miles of the Isle a Mot, where the army encamped. It having blown a fresh gale most part of the day, some of my boats split open by the violence of the waves, and ten of my Rangers were thereby drowned.

The 19th we set sail again early in the morning, and that night encamped on the north-end of the Isle a Mot.

The 20th, before day, the army was under way, with intention to land; having but twenty miles to go, and having the advantage of a fair wind, we soon came in sight of the French fort, and about ten in the morning Col. Darby, with the Grenadiers and Light Infantry, and myself with the Rangers, landed on the east-shore, and marched and took possession of the ground opposite the fort on that side, without the least opposition. Having done this, an officer was sent to acquaint Col. Haviland (who, with the remainder of the army, was at the place where we landed) that there was not the least danger to apprehend from the enemy. The next day we began to raise batteries, and soon after to throw some shells into the garrison. About the 24th proposal was made for taking the enemy's vessels, three of which were at anchor a little below the fort, and some of their rideaus likewise. It was introduced by Col. Darby, who was ordered to take the command of the party appointed for this service, which consisted of two companies of Regulars, and four companies of my Rangers, with the Indians. We carried with us two light howitzers and one six-pounder, and silently conveying them along thro' the trees, brought them opposite the vessels, and began a brisk fire upon them, before they were in the least apprised of our design, and, by good fortune, the first shot from the six-pounder cut the cable of the great rideau, and the wind being at west, blew her to the east shore, where we were, and the other vessels weighed anchor and made for St. John's, but got all aground, in turning a point about two miles below the fort. I was, by Col. Darby, ordered down the east shore with my Rangers, and crossed a river of about thirty yards wide, which falls into Lake Champlain from the east. I soon got opposite the vessels, and, by firing from the shore, gave an opportunity to some of my party to swim on board with their tomahawks, and took one of the vessels; in the mean time Col. Darby had got on board the rideau, and had her manned, and took the other two; of which success he immediately acquainted Col. Haviland, who sent down a sufficient number of men to take charge of and man the vessels; and ordered the remainder of the Rangers, Light Infantry and Grenadiers, to join the army that night, which was accordingly done; and about midnight the night following the French troops left the island, and landed safe on the main; so that next morning nothing of them was to be seen but a few sick, and Col. Haviland took posession of the fort.

The second day after the departure of Monsieur Bonville and his troops from the island, Mr. Haviland sent me with my Rangers to pursue him as far as St. John's Fort, which was about twenty miles further down the lake; and at that place I was to wait the coming of the army, but by no means to follow further than that fort, nor run any risk of advancing further towards Montreal. I went in boats, and about daylight got to St. John's, and found it just set on fire. I pursued, and took two prisoners, who reported, " That Monsieur Bonville was to encamp that night about half-way on the road to Montreal ; and that he went from St. John's about nine o'clock the night before ; but that many of their men were sick, and that they thought some of the troops would not reach the place appointed till the middle of the afternoon." It being now about seven in the morning, I set all hands to work, except proper guards, to fortify the log houses that stood near the lake side, in order that part of my people might cover the battoes, while I, with the remainder, followed Monsieur Bonville, and about eight o'clock I got so well fortified, that I ventured our boats and baggage under the care of 200 Rangers, and took with me 400, together with the two companies of Indians, and followed after the French army, which con-sisted of about 1500 men, and about 100 Indians they had to guard them. I was resolved to make his dance a little the merrier, and pursued with such haste, that I overtook his rear guard about two miles before they got to their en-camping ground. I immediately attacked them, who not being above 200, suddenly broke, and then stood for the main body, which I very eagerly pursued, but in good order, expecting Monsieur Bonville would have made a stand, which however he did not chuse, but pushed forward to get to the river, where they were to encamp, and having crossed it, pulled up the bridge, which put a stop to my march, not judging it prudent to cross at a disadvantage, inasmuch as the enemy had a good breast-work on the other side, of which they took possession ; in this pursuit, however, we considerably lessened their number, and returned in safety.

In the evening Mr. Haviland came in sight, and landed at St. John's. As soon as he came on shore, I waited upon him, and acquainted him with what I had done, &c., and that I had two prisoners for him ; he said it was very well, and ordered his troops to encamp there that night, and next day went down the river Sorriel, as far as St. d'Etrese, where he encamped, and made a strong breastwork, to defend his people from being surprised. I was sent down the river Sorriel, to bring the inhabitants under subjection to his Britannic Majesty, and went into their settled country in the night, took all their priests and militia officers, and sent some of them for the inhabitants. The first day I caused all the inhabitants near Chamblee to take the oaths of allegiance, &c., who appeared glad to have it in their power to take the oaths and keep their posessions, and were all extremely submissive. Having obliged them to bring in their arms, and fulfilled my instructions in the best manner I could, I joined Col. Darby at Chamblee, who came there to take the fort, and had brought with him some light cannon. It soon surrendered, as the garrison consisted only of about fifty men. This happened on the first of September.

On the 2d, our army having nothing to do, and having good intelligence both from Gen. Amherst and Gen. Murray, Mr. Haviland sent me to join the latter, while he marched with the rest of the army for La Pierre. The 5th in the morning I got to Longville, about four miles below Montreal, opposite to where Brigadier Murray lay, and gave him notice of my arrival, but not till the morning of the 6th, by reason of my arriving so late.

By the time I came to Longville, the army, under the command of Gen. Amherst, had landed about two miles from the town, where they encamped; and early this morning Monsieur de Vaudreuil, the governor and commander in chief of all Canada, sent out to capitulate with our General, which put a stop to all our movements till the 8th of September, when the articles of capitulation were agreed to, and signed, and our troops took possession of the town gates that night. Next morning the Light Infantry, and Granadiers of the whole army, under the command of Col. Haldiman, with a company of the royal artillery, with two pieces of cannon, and some hobitzers, entered the town, retaking the English colours belonging to Pepperel's and Shirley's regiments, which had been taken by the French at Oswego.

Thus, at length, at the end of the fifth campaign, Montreal and the whole country of Canada was given up, and became subject to the King of Great Britain; a conquest perhaps of the greatest importance that is to be met with in the British annals, whether we consider the prodigious extent of country we are hereby made masters of, the vast addition it must make to trade and navigation, or the security it must afford to the northern provinces of America, particularly those flourishing ones of New England and New York, the irretrievable loss France sustains hereby, and the importance it must give the British crown among the several states of Europe : all this, I say, duly considered, will, perhaps, in its consequences render the year 1760 more glorious than any preceding.

And to this acquisition, had we, during the late war, either by conquest or treaty, added the fertile and extensive country of Louisiana, we should have been possessed of perhaps the most valuable territory upon the face of the globe, attended with more real advantages than the so-much-boasted mines of Mexico and Peru, and would have for ever deprived the French, those treacherous rivals of

Britain's glory, of an opportunity of acting hereafter the same perfidious parts they have already so often repeated.

On the 9th Gen. Amherst informed me 'of his intention of sending me to Detroit, and on the 12th in the morning, when I waited upon him again, I received the following orders :

By his Excellency Jeffery Amherst, Esq.; Major General and Commander in Chief of all his Majesty's forces in North America, &c. &c. &c.

To Major Rogers, commanding his Majesty's independent companies of Rangers.

" You will, upon receipt thereof, with Capt. Waite's and Capt. Hazen's companies of Rangers under your command,* proceed in whale-boats from hence to Fort William Augustus, taking along with you one Joseph Poupao, alias La Fleur, an inhabitant of Detroit, and Lieut. Brehme, Assistant Engineer.

" From Fort William-Augustus† you will continue your voyage by the north-shore to Niagara, where you will land

---

* John Hazen was doubtless at this time a citizen of Plaistow, N. H., and in 1757, '8, '9, '60, was enrolled in the New Hampshire Militia under Col. Stevens. He subsequently settled at Haverhill, N. H., and afterwards at St. John's, Canada; but having joined the patriot cause, his house was burned during the Revolution and he was forced to leave the province. He finally settled in Albany, where he suffered from paralysis in 1785, and died some years after.— *Report of Adjutant General of New Hampshire*, 1866, 11, p. 211. The muster roll of his company for the season of 1758, is given at the report here cited.

† Fort William Augustus, had formerly been known as Fort Levis. It occupied the whole of Isle Royal, the *Oraconenton*, of the natives. It lies three miles below the present city of Ogdensburgh and is now known as "Chimney Island," from the ruins of its ancient works. The name was changed by General Amherst, after its conquest in August, 1760. A plan of this fort as it existed at the time of its surrender by the French, is given in Mante's History of the War of 1756–60, and a minute description by Pouchot, by whom it was built in 1759, and defended till its final surrender in 1760.

your whale-boats, and transport them across the Carrying-place into Lake Erie, applying to Major Walters, or the officer commanding at Niagara, for any assistance you may want on that or any other occasion, requesting of him at the same time to deliver up to you Monsieur Gamelin, who was made prisoner at the reduction of said fort, and has continued there ever since, in order to conduct him, with the above-mentioned Poupao, to their habitations at Detroit, where, upon taking the oath of allegiance to his most sacred Majesty, whose subjects they are become by the capitulation of the 8th inst; they shall be protected in the peaceable and quiet possession of their properties, and, so long as they behave as becometh good and faithful subjects, shall partake of all the other privileges and immunities granted unto them by the said capitulation.

" With these, and the detachment under your command, you will proceed in your whale-boats across Lake Erie to Presque Isle,* where, upon your arrival, you will make known the orders I have given to the officer commanding that post ; and you will leave said whale-boats and party, taking only a small detachment of your party, and marching by land, to join Brigadier General Monkton,† wherever he may be.

" Upon your arrival with him, you will deliver into his hands the dispatches you shall herewith receive for him, and follow and obey such orders as he shall give you for the relief of the garrisons of the French posts at Detroit, Michlimakana, or any others in that district, for gathering in the arms of the inhabitants thereof, and for administering to them the oath of allegiance already mentioned ; when

---

* Presque Isle is now Erie, Pa., a point early occupied and fortified by the French as a part of their chain of forts extending from Canada to Louisiana.

† General Robert Monkton was governor of New York in 1762-3, and afterwards of Portsmouth. He died in 1782.

you will likewise administer, or see administered, the same to the before-mentioned Gamelin and Poupao ; and when this is done, and that you have reconnoitered and explored the country as much as you can, without losing time unnecessarily, you are to bring away the French troops and arms, to such place as you shall be directed by General Monkton.

" And when the whole of this service is compleated, you will march back your detachment to Presque Isle, or Niagara, according to the orders you receive from Brigadier Monkton, where you will embark the whole, and in like manner, as before, transport your whale boats across the Carrying-place,* into Lake Ontario, where you will deliver over your whale-boats into the care of the commanding officer, marching your detachment by land to Albany, or wherever I may be, to receive what further orders I may have to give you.

" Given under my hand, at the headquarters in the camp of Montreal, 12th Sept. 1760.

Jeff. Amberst."

"By his Excellency's command,

J. Appy."

An additional order was given, which was to be shewn only to the commanding officers of the different posts I might touch at, the expedition being intended to be kept a profound secret, for fear the march should be impeded by the enemy Indians, through whose country I was obliged to march.

This order was as follows, viz :

" Major Walters, or the officer commanding at Niagara, will judge whether or not there is provision sufficient at

---

* The portage was on the east side of Niagara river, from the present village of Lewiston, to the foot of navigation about two miles above the Falls.

'Presque Isle; and Major Rogers will accordingly take provisions from Niagara. Eight days provision will take him from Montreal to Fort William-Augustus; there he will apply to the commanding officer for a sufficient quantity to proceed to Niagara. Major Rogers knows where he is going, and the provisions he will want; some should be in store likewise at Presque Isle, for the party Brigadier General Monkton will send.

Jeff. Amherst."

Montreal, 12th Sept., 1760.

In pursuance of these orders* I embarked at Montreal the 13th Sept., 1760 (with Captain Brewer, Captain Wait, Lieutenant Brheme, Assisstant Engineer, Lieut. Davis of the Royal train of artillery, and two hundred Rangers) about noon, in fifteen whale-boats; and that night we encamped at la Chine; next morning we reached Isle de Praires, and took a view of the two Indian settlements at Coyhavagu and Conesadagu.

On the 16th we got up to an island in the Lake of St. Francis, and the next night encamped on the western shore, at the lower end of the upper rifts. We ascended these rifts the day following, and continued all night on the north shore, opposite a number of islands.

---

* Mr. Francis Parkman in his *Conspiracy of Pontiac* (6th ed. 1, p. 163), in noticing Rogers' Journal of this expedition, says :

" Although Rogers, especially where his pecuniary interest was concerned, was far from scrupulous, I have no hesitation in following his account of the expedition up the lakes. The incidents of each day are minuted along in a dry, unambitious style, bearing the clear impress of truth. Extracts from the Orderly Book and other official papers are given, while portions of the narrative verified by contemporary documents, may stand as earnests for the truth of the whole.

In the evening of the 19th we came to the Isle de Gallettes,* and spent the 20th in repairing our whale-boats, which had received some damage in ascending the rifts.

This morning I sent off ten sick Rangers to Albany, by the way of Oswego, recommending them to the care of Col. Fitch, commanding at Oswego, who was to give them suitable directions.

We left Isle de Gallettes on the 21st; about twelve o'clock, the wind being unfavourable, we passed Oswegachi and encamped but three miles above it on the northern shore.

On the 22d we continued our course up the river, the wind blowing fresh at south, and halted in the evening at the narrow passes near the islands; but, upon the wind's abating at midnight, we embarked and rowed the remainder of that night and the whole day following, till we came to the place where formerly stood the old Fort of Frontiniac,† where we found some Indian hunters from Oswegachi. We were detained here all the next day by the tempestuousness of the weather, which was very windy, attended with snow and rain; we, however, improved the time in taking a plan of the old fort, situated at the bottom of a fine, safe harbour.

There were about five hundred acres of cleared ground about it, which, tho' covered with clover, seemed bad and rocky, and interspersed with some pine-trees. The Indians here seemed to be well pleased with the news we brought them of the surrender of all Canada, and supplied us with great plenty of venison and wild fowl.

---

* Isle de Gallettes, now Galloo Island, opposite Lisbon, in St. Lawrence Co., and near the head of the rapids of the St. Lawrence. There was formerly an Indian settlement and a mission church on the upper end of the island, the traces of which can still be seen.

† The site of Fort Frontenac is now the city of Kingston, Province of Ontario, Canada.

We left this place the 25th, about ten in the morning, steering a south-course two miles, then west six miles, which brought us to the mouth of a river thirty feet wide; then south four miles, where we halted to refresh the party.

About four in the afternoon we rowed for a mountain bearing south-west, which we did not come up to till some time in the night, and found it to be a steep rock, about one hundred feet high. It now grew foggy, and mistaking our way about six miles, we rowed all night, and till 8 o'clock next morning, before we put ashore; which we then did on a point, where we breakfasted, and then proceeded on our voyage, rowing till 8 o'clock at night (being about one hundred miles, as we imagined, from Frontiniac) we landed. This evening we passed two small islands at the end of a point extending far into the lake; the darkness and fog prevented us from taking such a survey of them as to be able to give a particular description of them.

The 27th of September, being very windy, we spent the time in deer-hunting, there being great plenty of them there, tho' the land is rocky, the timber bad, chiefly hemlock and pine; and I believe it is generally so on the north-side of Lake Ontario.

We embarked very early on the 28th, steering south-west, leaving a large bay on the right, about twenty miles wide; the western side of which terminates in a point, and a small island: having passed both, about fifteen miles on a course west by south, we entered the chops of a river, called by the Indians the *Grace of Man;* there we encamped, and found about 50 Mississagua Indians fishing for salmon. At our first appearance they ran down, both men and boys, to the edge of the lake, and continued firing their pieces, to express their joy at the sight of the English colours, till such time as we had landed.

They presented me with a deer just killed and split in halves, with the skin on, but the bowels taken out, which, with them, is a most elegant and polite present, and significant of the greatest respect. I told them of the success of their English brethren, against their fathers the French; at which they either were, or pretended to be, very well pleased.

Some of us fished with them in the evening, being invited by them, and filled a bark-canoe with salmon in about half an hour. Their method of catching the fish is very extraordinary. One person holds a lighted pine-torch, while a second strikes the fish with a spear. This is the season in which the salmon spawn in these parts, contrary to what they do in any other place I ever knew them before.

I found the soil near this river very good and level. The timber is chiefly oak and maple, or the sugar-tree.

At seven o'clock the next morning we took our departure from this river, the wind being a-head. About fifteen miles further, on a west-south-west course, we put into another river, called the Life of Man. The Messissaguas, who were hunting here, about thirty in number, paid us the same compliments with those we just before received from their countrymen, and, instead of a deer, split up a young bear, and presented me with it. Plenty of fish was catched here also. The land continued good and level, the soil of a blackish colour, and the banks of the lake were low.

The wind being fair the 30th, we embarked at the first dawn of day, and with the assistance of sails and oars, made great way on a south-west course, and in the evening reached the river Toronto, having run seventy miles. Many points extending far into the lake, occasioned a frequent alteration of our course. We passed a bank of twenty miles in length, but the land behind it seemed to be level, well-timbered with large oaks, hickories, maples, and some poplars. No mountains appeared in sight. There was a track of about 300 acres of cleared ground, round the place where formerly the French had a fort, that was called Fort Toronto. The soil here is principally clay. The deer are extremely plenty in this country. Some Indians were hunting at the mouth of the river, who run into the woods at our approach, very much frightened. They came in, however, in the morning, and testified their joy at the news of our success against the French. They told us " that we could easily accomplish our journey from thence to Detroit in eight days ; that when the French traded at that place, the Indians used to come with their poultry from Michlimakana, down the river Toronto : that the portage was but twenty miles from that to a river falling into Lake Huron, which had some falls, but none very considerable ; " they added, that there was a Carrying-place of fifteen miles from some westerly part of Lake Erie, to a river running without any falls, thro' several Indian towns into Lake St. Clair.

I think Toronto a most convenient place for a factory, and that from thence we may very easily settle the north-side of Lake Erie.

We left Toronto the 1st of October, steering south, right across the west-end of Lake Ontario. At dark we arrived at the south-shore, five miles west of Fort Niagara, some of our boats being now become exceeding leaky and dangerous.

This morning, before we set out, I directed the following order of march :

" The boats in a line. If the wind rose high, the red flag hoisted, and the boats to crowd nearer, that they might be ready to give mutual assistance in case of a leak or other accident ;" by which means we saved the crew and arms of the boat commanded by Lieut. M'Cormack, which sprung a leak and sunk, losing nothing except their packs.

We halted all the next day at Niagara, and provided ourselves with blankets, coats, shirts, shoes, magassins, &c.

I received from the commanding officer eighty barrels of provisions, and changed two whale-boats for as many battoes, which proved leaky.

In the evening some of my party proceeded with the provisions to the falls, and in the morning marched the rest there, and began the portage of the provisions and boats. Mess. Brheme and Davis took a survey of the great cataract of Niagara.

As the winter-season was now advancing very fast in this country, and I had orders to join Brig. Monkton from Presque Isle, wherever he might be, to receive his directions, I set out this evening, the 5th of October, in a bark-canoe, with Lieutenants Brheme and Holmes, and eight Rangers, leaving the command of my party to Capt. Brewer, with instructions to follow to Prefque Isle, and encamped eight miles up the stream issuing out of Lake Erie. The land appeared to be good on both sides the river.

Next morning embarked early, and steered a south-west course. About noon opened Lake Erie, and leaving a bay to the left, we arrived by sun-set at the southern shore of the lake; we then steered west till eight o'clock at night, and drew up our boats on a sandy beach, forty miles distant from where we embarked in the morning.

The wind was very fresh next day, which prevented our setting out till 11 o'clock; so that we made no further progress than about twenty-eight miles on a west-south-west course. A little after noon, on the 8th of October, we arrived at Presque Isle, having kept a southerly course all the morning; I tarried there till 3 o'clock, when having sent back my party to assist Capt. Brewer, Mr. Brheme, Lieutenant Holmes, and myself, took leave of Colonel Bouquet,* who commanded at Presque Isle, and with three other men, in a bark-canoe, proceeded to French Creek, and at night encamped on the road, half way to Fort du Bouf. We got to this fort about 10 o'clock next day, and after three hours rest launched our canoe into the river, and paddled down about ten miles below the fort.

On the 10th we encamped at the second crossings of the river, the land on both sides appeared to be good all the way. The 11th we reached the Mingo Cabbins, and the night of the 12th we lodged at Venango; from thence went down the River Ohio; and on the morning of the 17th I waited upon Brigadier Monkton at Pittsburgh, and delivered him General Amherst's dispatches, and my own instructions.

I left Pittsburgh the 20th, at the request of General Monkton, who promised to send his orders after me to Presque Isle, by Mr. Croghan, and to forward Capt. Campbell immediately with a company of the Royal Americans; I got back to Presque Isle the 30th of October, Captain Campbell arrived the day after; Captain Brewer was got there before us, with the Rangers from Niagara, having lost some of the boats, and part of the provisions.

We immediately began to repair the damaged boats; and, as there was an account that a vessel, expected with pro-

---

* Henry Bouquet, served in the British army with distinction through the French and Indian wars, and after the conquest of Canada was employed in expeditions against hostile Indian tribes in the west and south. He died at Pensacola in February, 1766, being at that time a brigadier general in the British army.

visions from Niagara, was lost, I dispatched Capt. Brewer by land to Detroit, with a drove of forty oxen, supplied by Col. Bouquet. Capt. Wait was about the same time sent back to Niagara for more provisions, and ordered to cruise along the north-coast of Lake Erie, and halt about twenty miles to the east of the streight between the Lakes Huron and Erie; till further orders. Brewer had a battoe to ferry his party over the Creeks, two horses, and Capt. Monter with twenty Indians, composed of the Six Nations, Delawares and Shawanese, to protect him from the insults of the enemy Indians.

My order of march over from Presque Isle was as follows:
"The boats to row two deep; first, Major Rogers's boat, abreast of him Capt. Croghan; Capt. Campbell follows with his company, the Rangers next; and lastly, Lieutenant Holmes, who commands the rear guard, with his own boat, and that of Ensign Wait's, so as to be ready to assist any boat that may be in distress. Boats in distress are to fire a gun, when Mr. Holmes with the other boats under his command are immediately to go to their relief, take them to the shore, or give such other assistance as he thinks may be best. When the wind blows hard, so that the boats cannot keep their order, a red flag will be hoisted in the Major's boat; then the boats are not to mind their order, but put after the flag as fast as possible to the place of landing, to which the flag-boat will always be a guide.

"It is recommended to the soldiers as well as officers, not to mind the waves of the lake; but when the surf is high to stick to their oars, and the men at helm to keep the boat quartering on the waves, and briskly follow, then no mischief will happen by any storm whatever. Ten of the best steersmen amongst the Rangers are to attend Captain Campbell and company in his boats. It is likewise recommended to the officers commanding in those boats, to hearken to the steersmen in a storm or bad weather, in

managing their boats. At evening, (if it is thought necessary to row in the night-time) a blue flag will be hoisted in
the Major's boat, which is the signal for the boats to dress,
and then proceed in the following manner: the boats next
the hindermost, are to wait for the two in the rear, the two
third boats for the second two; and so on to the boats
leading a-head, to prevent separation, which in the night
would be hazardous.

" Mr. Brheme is not to mind the order of march, but to
steer as is most convenient for him to make his observations: he is however desired never to go more than a league
a-head of the detachment, and is to join them at landing or
encamping.

" On landing, the Regulars are to encamp in the center,
and Lieutenant Holmes's division on the right wing with
Mr. Croghan's people, Lieutenant M'Cormick on the left
wing with his division; Mr. Jequipe to be always ready
with his Mohegan Indians, which are the picquet of the
detachment, part of which are always to encamp in the
front of the party; Capt. Campbell will mount a guard
consisting of one Subaltern, one Serjeant, and thirty privates,
immediately on landing, for the security of his own encampment and battoes; Lieutenant Holmes's division to keep a
guard of one Serjeant and ten Rangers on the right, and
Lieutenant M'Cormick the like number on the left, and
likewise to act as Adjutant to the detachment, and the
orderly drum to attend him, to be at the Serjeant's call.
The general to beat when ordered by the Major, at which
time the whole party is to prepare for embarking, the troops
half an hour after, when all the guards are to be called in,
and the party embark immediately after.

" There is to be no firing of guns in this detatchment
without permission from the commanding officer, except
when in distress on the lake. No man to go without the

centries, when in camp, unless he has orders so to do; great care to be taken of the arms, and the officers to review them daily. Captain Campbell will order a drum to beat, for the regulation of his company when landed, at any time he thinks proper for parading his men, or reviewing their arms, &c.

" It is not doubted but due attention will be paid to all orders given.

" Mr. Croghan will, at landing, always attend the Major for orders, and to give such intelligence as he may have ⚑ had from the Indians throughout the day."

We left Presque Isle the 4th of November, kept a western course, and by night had advanced twenty miles.

The badness of the weather obliged us to lie by all the next day; and as the wind continued very high, we did not advance more than ten or twelve miles the 6th, on a course west·south-west.

We set out very early on the 7th, and came to 'the mouth of Chogage* River, ; here we met with a party of Attawawa Indians, just arrived from Detroit. We in-

---

* Probably *Cuyahoga River*, at the modern city of Cleveland, O., Mr. Parkman thus describes the interview between Major Rogers and the Indians, on this occasion : ,

" Soon after the arrival of the Rangers, a party of Indian chiefs and warriors entered the eamp. They proclaimed themselves an embassy from Pontiac, ruler of all that country, and directed in his name, that the English should advance no farther until they had had an interview with the great chief who was close at hand. In truth, before the day had closed, Pontiac himself appeared ; and it it is here for the first time that this remarkable man stands forth distinctly on the page of history. He greeted Rogers with a haughty demand, what was his business in that country, and how he dared to enter it without permission. Rogers informed him that the French were defeated : that Canada had surrendered, and that he was on his way to take possession of Detroit, and restore a general peace, to white men and Indians alike. Pontiac listened with attention, but only replied that he should stand in the path of the English until morning. Having inquired if the strangers were in need of anything

formed them of our success in the total reduction of
Canada, and that we were going to bring off the French
garrison at Detroit, who were included in the capitulation.
I held out a belt, and told them I would take my brothers
by the hand, and carry them to Detroit, to see the truth of
what I had said. They retired, and held a council, and
promised an answer next morning. That evening we
smoaked the calamet, or pipe of peace, all the officers and
Indians smoaking by turns out of the same pipe. The
peace thus concluded, we went to rest, but kept good
guards, a little distrusting their sincerity.

The Indians gave their answer early in the morning, and
said their young warriors should go with me, while the old
ones staid to hunt for their wives and children.

I gave them ammunition at their request, and a string of
wampum in testimony of my approbation, and charged
them to send some of their sachems, or chiefs, with the
party who drove the oxen along the shore; and they promised to spread the news, and prevent any annoyance from
their hunters.

We were detained here by unfavourable weather till the
12th, during which time the Indians held a plentiful market
n our camp of venison and turkies.

From this place we steered one mile west, then a mile
south, then four miles west, then south-west ten miles,

---

which the country could afford, he withdrew with his chiefs, at nightfall, to
his own encampment; while the English ill at ease, and suspecting treachery,
stood well on their guard throughout the night.

In the morning, Pontiac returned to the camp with his attendant chiefs,
and made his reply to Roger's speech of the previous day. He was willing,
he said, to live at peace with the English and suffer them to remain in his
country, as long as they treated him with due respect and deference. The Indian chiefs and provincial officers smoked the calumet together, and perfect
harmony seemed established between them."

—*Parkman's Conspiracy of Pontiac*, 6th ed. 1, 165.

then five miles west-and-by-south, then south-west eight miles, then west-and-by-south seven miles, then four miles west, and then south-west six miles, which brought us to Elk River, as the Indians call it, where we halted two days on account of bad weather and contrary winds.

On the 15th we embarked, and kept the following courses; west-south-west two miles, west north-west three miles, west-by-north one mile, west two miles; here we passed the mouth of a river, and then steered west one mile, west-by south two miles, west-by-north four miles, north-west three miles, west-north-west two miles, west-by-north ten miles, where we encamped at the mouth of a river twenty-five yards wide.

The weather did not permit us to depart till the 18th, when our course was west-by-south six miles; west by-north four miles, west two miles; here we found a river about fifteen yards over, then proceeded west half a mile, west-south-west six miles and a half, west two miles and an half, north-west two miles, where we encamped, and discovered a river sixteen yards broad at the entrance.

We left this place the next day, steering north-west four miles, north-north-west six miles, which brought us to Sandusky Lake; we continued the same course two miles, then north-north-east half a mile, north-west a quarter of a mile, north the same distance, north-west half a mile, north-by-east one furlong, north-west-by-north one quarter of a mile, north-west-by-west one mile, west-north-west one mile, then west half a mile, where we encamped near a small river, on the east side.

From this place I detached Mr. Brheme with a letter to Monsieur Beleter, the French commandant at Detroit, in these words:

To Capt. Beleter, *or the Officer commanding at* Detroit.

SIR :

"That you may not be alarmed at the approach of the English troops under my command, when they come to Detroit, I send forward this by Lieut. Brheme, to acquaint you, that I have Gen. Amherst's orders to take possession of Detroit, and such other posts as are in that district, which, by capitulation, agreed to and signed by the Marquis de Vaudreuil, and his Excellency Major Gen. Amherst, the 8th of September last, now belong to the King of Great Britain.

" I have with me the Marquis de Vaudreil's letters to you directed, for your guidance on this occasion, which letters I shall deliver you when I arrive at or near your post, and shall encamp the troops I have with me at some distance from the fort, till you have reasonable time to be made acquainted with the Marquis de Vaudreuil's instructions, and the capitulation, a copy of which I have with me likewise. I am,

SIR,

Your humble servant,

Robert Rogers."

The land on the south-side of Lake Erie, from Presque Isle, puts on a very fine appearance ; the country level, the timber tall, and of the best sort such as oak, hickerie and locust ; and for game, both for plenty and variety, perhaps exceeded by no part of the world.

I followed Mr. Brheme on the 20th, and took a course north-west four miles and an half, south-west two, and west three, to the mouth of a river in breadth 300 feet.

Here we found several Huron sachems, who told me, " that a body of 400 Indian warriors was collected at the entrance into the great streight, in order to obstruct our passage ; and that Monsieur Beleter had excited them to defend their country; that they were messengers to know my business, and whether the person I had sent forward had reported the truth, that Canada was reduced." I confirmed this account, and that the fort at Detroit was given up by the French Governor. I presented them a large belt, and spoke to this effect :

" Brothers,

" With this belt I take you by the hand. You are to go directly to your brothers assembled at the mouth of the river, and tell them to go to their towns till I arrive at the fort. I shall call you there as soon as Monsieur Beleter is sent away, which shall be in two days after my arrival. We will then settle all matters. You live happily in your own country. Your brothers have long desired to bring this about. Tell your warriors to mind their fathers (the French) no more, for they are all prisoners to your brothers (the English), who pitied them, and left them their houses and goods, on their swearing by the Great One who made the world, to become as Englishmen forever. They are now your brothers; if you abuse them, you affront me, unless they behave ill. Tell this to your brothers the Indians. What I say is truth. When we meet at Detroit I will convince you it is all true."

These sachems set out in good temper the next morning, being the 21st; but as the wind was very high, we did not move from this place.

On the 22d we encamped on a beach, after having steered that day north-west six miles, north-north-west four, to a river of the breadth of twenty yards, then north-west-by-west two miles, north-west one, west four, and west-north-west five; it was with great difficulty we could procure any fuel here, the west-side of the Lake Erie abounding with swamps.

We rowed ten miles the next day, on a course north-west and by west, to Point Cedar, and then formed a camp; here we met some of the Indian messengers, to whom we had spoken two days before : they told us, their warriors were gone up to Monsieur Beleter, who, they said, is a strong man, and intends to fight you ; a sachem of Attawawas was amongst them. All their Indians set out with us. The 24th we went north-west and by north ten miles, and fourteen miles north-east, to a long point ; . this night sixty of the Indian party came to our camp, who congratulated us on our arrival in their country, and offered themselves as an escort to Detroit, from whence they came the day before. They informed me, that Mr. Bbreme and his party were confined ; and that Monsieur Beleter had set up an high flag-staff, with a wooden effigy of a man's head on the top, and upon that a crow ; that the crow was to represent himself, the man's head mine, and the meaning of the whole, that he would scratch out my brains. This artifice, however, had no effect ; for the Indians told him (as they said) that the reverse would be the true explanation of the sign.

After we had proceeded six miles north-east, we halted at the request of the Indians, who desired me to call in the chief Captains of the party at the Streight's mouth. I did so, and spent the 26th at the same place, in conciliating their savage minds to peace and friendship.

The morning of the 27, Monsieur Beleter sent me the following letter by Monsieur Babee.

" Monsieur,

" J'ai reçu la lettre que vous m'avez écrite par un de vos Officiers ; comme je n'ai point d'interprete, je ne puis faire la reponse amplement.

L'Officier qui m'a remise la votre, me fait favoir qu'il étoit détaché afin de m'anoncer votre arrivé, pour prendre possession de cette garison, selon la capitulation fait en Canada, que vous avez conjointement avec un lettre de

Monsieur de Vaudreuil à mon addresse. Je vous prie, Monsieur, d'arrêter vos troupes à l'entrance de la riviere, jusques à cc que vous m'envoyés la capitulation & la lettre de Monseigneur le Marquis de Vaudreuil, afin de pouvoir y conformer.

Je suis bien surpris qu'on ne m'a pas envoyé un Officier François avec vous, selon la coûtume.

J'ai l'honneur d'étre, &c. &c.

De Beleter."

" A Monsieur Monsieur *Rogers,*
   Major, & commandant le
   detachment Anglois."

In English thus,

" SIR,

" I received the letter you wrote me by one of your Officers; but, as I have no interpreter, cannot fully answer it.

The Officer that delivered me yours, gives me to understand, that he was sent to give me notice of your arrival to take possession of this garrison, according to the capitulation made in Canada; that you have likewise a letter from Mons. Vaudreuil directed to me. I beg, Sir, you'll halt your troops at the entrance of the river, till you send me the capitulation and the Marquis de Vaudreuil's letter, that I may act in conformity thereto.

I am surprised there is no French Officer sent to me along with you, as is the custom on such occasions. I have the honour to be, &c. &c.

De Beleter."

" To Mr. *Rogers,* Major and
   Commander of the Eng-
   lish detachment."

Shortly after a French party, under Captain Burrager, beat a parley on the west shore; I sent Mr. M'Cormick to know his business, who returned with the Officer and the following letter :

Detroit, le 25me Novembre, 1760.

" Monsieur,

" Je vous ai déja marqué par Monsieur Burrager les raisons pourquoi je ne puis répondre en détail à la lettre qui m'a été remise le 22me du courant, par l'Officier que vous m'avez detaché.

J'ignore les raisons pourquoi il n'a pas voulu retourner auprès de vous. J'ai envoyé mon interprete. Huron chez cette nation, que l'on me dit être attroupé sur le chemin de les contenir, ne façhant positivement si c'est à vous ou à nous qu'ils en veuillent, & pour leur dire de ma part, qu'ils ayent a se tenir tranquilement ; que je savois ce que je devois à mon General, & que de lorsque l'acte de la capitulation seroit reglé, j'étois obligé d'obéir. Le dit interprete a ordre de vous attendre, & de vous remettre la present. Ne soyez point surpris, Monsieur, si sur le long de la côte vous trouverez nos habitans sur leur garde ; on leur a annoncé qu'il y avoit beaucoup de nations à votre suite, à qui on avois promis le pillage, & que lesdites nations étoient même determinées à vous le demander ; je leur ai permis de regarder, c'est pour vôtre conservation & sureté ainsi que pour la nôtre, en cas que les dites nations devenoient à saire les insolents, vous seul ne seriez peut-être pas dans les circonstances presentes en état de les reduire. Je me flatte, Monsieur, que si tôt que la present vour sera parvenue, vous voudriez bien m'envoyer par quelqu'un de vos Messieurs, & la capitulation & la lettre de Monsieur Vaudreuil. J'ai l'honneur d'ètre,

Monsieur,

Votre tres-humble & obéissant serviteur,

Pign. de Beletere."

A Monsieur Monsieur *Rogers*,
Major, commandant le de-
tachment Anglois au bas de
la riviere,

In English thus :

" Sir, Detroit, 25th Nov. 1760.

" I have already by Mr. Barrager acquainted you with the reasons why I could not answer particularly the letter which was delivered me the 22d instant by the Officer you sent to me.

" I am entirely unacquainted with the reasons of his not returning to you. I sent my Huron interpreter to that nation, and told him to stop them, should they be on the road, not knowing positively whether they were inclined to favour you or us, and to tell them from me they should behave peaceably; that I knew what I owed to my General, and that when the capitulation should be settled I was obliged to obey. The said interpreter has orders to wait on you, and deliver you this.

" Be not surprised, Sir, if along the coast you find the inhabitants upon their guard ; it was told them you had several Indian nations with you, to whom you had promised permission to plunder, nay, that they were even resolved to force you to it. I have therefore allowed the said inhabitants to take to their arms, as it is for your safety and preservation as well as ours ; for should these Indians become insolent, you may not perhaps, in your present situation, .be able to subdue them alone.

" I flatter myself, Sir, that, as soon as that shall come to hand, you will send me by some of the Gentlemen you have with you, both the capitulation and Monsieur Vaudreuil's letter. I have the honour to be,

Sir,

Your very humble and obedient servant,

To Major Rogers.

Pign. Beletere."

We encamped the next day five miles up the river, having rowed against the wind; and on the 29th I dispatched Captain Campbell, with Messieurs Barrager and Babee and their parties, with this letter.

"SIR,

" I acknowledge the receipt of your two letters, both of which were delivered to me yesterday. Mr. Brheme has not yet returned. The inclosed letter from the Marquis de Vaudreuil will inform you of the surrender of all Canada to the King of Great Britain, and of the great indulgence granted to the inhabitants; as also of the terms granted to the troops of his Most Christian Majesty. Captain Campbell, whom I have sent forward with this letter will shew you the capitulation. I desire you will not detain him, as I am determined, agreeable to my instructions from General Amherst, speedily to relieve your post. I shall stop the troops I have with me at the hither end of the town till four o'clock, by which time I expect your answer; your inhabitants under arms will not surprise me, as yet I have seen no other in that position, but savages waiting for my orders. I can assure you, Sir, the inhabitants of Detroit shall not be molested, they and you complying with the capitulation, but be protected in the quiet and peaceable possession of their estates; neither shall they be pillaged by my Indians, nor by your's that have joined me.
I am, &c.

To Capt. Beletere,   *R. Rogers.*"
commanding at Detroit.

I landed at half a mile short of the fort, and fronting it, where I drew my detachment on a field of grass. Here Capt. Campbell joined me, and with him came a French officer, to inform me that he bore Monsieur Beleter's compliments, signifying he was under my command. From hence I sent Lieutenants Leslie and M'Cormack, with thirty-six Royal Americans, to take possession of the fort. The French garrison laid down their arms, English colours were hoisted, and the French taken down, at which about 700 Indians gave a shout, merrily exulting in their prediction being verified, that the crow represented the English.

They seemed amazed at the submissive salutations of the inhabitants, expressed their satisfaction at our generosity in not putting them to death, and said they would always for the future fight for a nation thus favoured by Him that made the world.

I went into the fort, received a plan of it, with a list of the stores, from the commanding officer, and by noon of the 1st of December we had collected the militia, disarmed them, and to them also administered the oaths of allegiance.*

The interval from this time to the 9th was spent in preparing to execute some measures that appeared to be necessary to the service we were upon. I put Monsieur Beletere and the other prisoners under the care of Lieut. Holmes and thirty Rangers, to be carried to Philadelphia ; and ordered Capt. Campbell and his company to keep possession of the fort. Lieut. Butler and Ensign Wait were sent with a detached party of twenty men, to bring the French troops from the forts Miamie and Gatanois. I ordered, that, if possible, a party should subsist at the former this winter, and give the earliest notice at Detroit of the enemy's motions in the country of the Illinois. I sent Mr. M'Gee,

---

* Major Rogers was again sent to Detroit in 1763, and participated in the military operations of that year.

In a work entitled " Diary of the siege of Detroit, in the war with Pontiac," etc.; printed in 1860, under the supervision of the editor of this volume, his Journal is given (pages 121 to 135), covering the period from May 6, to July 4, 1763, and an account of occurrences attending the siege of Detroit under Pontiac, within these dates. The original is found in the *Johnson Manuscripts,* VII, 116.—*Munsell's Historical Series,* No. IV, small 4to, pp. 304.

with a French officer, for the French troops at the Shawa-nese town on the Ohio. And as provisions were scarce, directed Capt. Brewer to repair with the greatest part of the Rangers to Niagara, detaining Lieut. M'Cormack with thirty-seven more, to go with me to Michlimakana.

I made a treaty with the several tribes of Indians living in the neighbouring country ; and having directed Capt. Wait, just arrived from Niagara, to return again thither immediately, I set out for Lake Huron, and on the night of the 10th encamped at the north end of the little Lake St. Clair, and the next evening on the west-side of the streight, at the entrance of a considerable river, where many Indians were hunting. We opened Lake Huron the day following, and saw many Indian hunters on both sides of the mouth of the streights. We coasted along the west shore of the Lake, about twenty miles north-and by west, the next day being the 13th forty, and the 15th thirty-eight miles, passing the cakes of ice with much diffi-culty. We could not advance all the 16th a heavy north-wind setting the cakes of ice on the south-shore in such quantities, that we could find no passage between them. I consulted the Indians about a journey to Michlimakana across by land ; but they declared it impracticable at this season without snow-shoes, and to our great mortification we were obliged to return to Detroit ; the ice obstructing us so much, that with the greatest diligence and fatigue, we did not arrive there till the 21st.

I delivered the ammunition to Capt. Campbell, and on the 23d set out for Pittsburg, marching along the west-end of Lake Erie, till the 2d of January, 1761, when we arrived at Lake Sandusky.

I have a very good opinion of the soil from Detroit to this place ; it is timbered principally with white and black oaks, hickerie, locusts, and maple. We found wild apples along the west-end of Lake Erie, some rich savannahs of several miles extent, without a tree, but cloathed with jointed grass near six feet high, which rotting there every year, adds to the fertility of the soil. The length of Sandusky is about fifteen miles from east to west, and about six miles across it. We came to a town of the Windot Indians, where we halted to refresh.

On January 3d, south-east-by-east three miles, east-by south one mile and a half, south-east a mile through a meadow, crossed a small creek about six yards wide, running east, travelled south-east by-east one mile, passed through Indian houses, south-east three quarters of a mile, and came to a small Indian town of about ten houses. There is a remarkable fine spring at this place, rising out of the side of a small hill with such force, that it boils above the ground in a column three feet high. I imagine it discharges ten hogsheads of water in a minute. From this town our course was south-south-east three miles, south two miles, crossed a brook about five yards wide, running east-south-east, travelled south one mile, crossed a brook about four yards wide, running east-south-east, travelled south-south-east two miles, crossed a brook about eight yards wide. This day we killed plenty of deer and turkies on our march, and encamped.

On the 4th we travelled south-south-east one mile, and come to a river about twenty-five yards wide, crossed the river, where are two Indian houses, from thence south-by east one mile, south-south-east one mile and a half, south-south-east two miles, south-east one mile, and came to an Indian house, where there was a family of Windots hunting, from thence south-by-east a quarter of a mile, south five miles, came to the river we crossed this morning; the course of the river here is west-north-west. This day killed several deer and other game, and encamped.

19

On the 5th traveled south-south-west half a mile, south one mile, south-south-west three quarters of a mile, south half a mile, crossed two small brooks running east, went a south-south-west course half a mile, south half a mile, south-east half a mile, south two miles, south-east one mile, south half a mile, crossed a brook running east-by-north, traveled south by-east half a mile, south-south-east two miles, south-east three quarters of a mile, south-south-east one mile, and came to Maskongom Creek,* about eight yards wide, crossed the creek, and encamped about thirty yards from it. This day killed deer and turkies in our march.

On the 6th we traveled about fourteen or fifteen miles, our general course being about east-south-east, killed plenty of game, and encamped by a very fine spring.

The 7th our general course about south-east, traveled about six miles, and crossed Maskongom Creek, running south, about twenty yards wide. There is an Indian town about twenty yards from the creek, on the east side, which is called the Mingo Cabbins. There were but two or three Indians in the place, the rest were hunting. These Indians have plenty of cows, horses, hogs, &c.

The 8th, halted at this town to mend our mogasons, and kill deer, the provisions I brought from Detroit being entirely expended. I went a-hunting with ten of the Rangers, and by ten o'clock got more venison than we had occasion for.

On the 9th travelled about twelve miles, our general course being about south-east, and encamped by the side of a long meadow, where there were a number of Indians hunting.

---

* Muskingum.

The 10th, about the same course, we travelled eleven miles, and encamped, having killed in our march this day three bears and two elks.

The 12th, continuing near the same course, we travelled thirteen miles and encamped, where were a number of Wyandots and Six Nation Indians hunting.

The 12th, travelled six miles, bearing rather more to the east, and encamped. This evening we killed several beaver.

The 13th, travelled about north-east six miles, and came to the Delaware's town, called Beaver Town. This Indian town stands on good land, on the west side of the Maskongom River; and opposite to the town, on the east-side, is a fine river, which discharges itself into it. The latter is about thirty yards wide, and the Maskongom about forty; so that when they both join, they make a very fine stream, with a swift current, running to the south-west. There are about 3,000 acres of cleared ground round this place. The number of warriors in this town is about 180. All the way from the Lake Sandusky I found level land, and a good country. No pine-trees of any sort; the timber is white, black and yellow oak, black and white walnut, cyprus, chestnut, and locust trees; At this town I staid till the 16th in the morning to refresh my party, and procured some corn of the Indians to boil with our venison.

On the 16th we marched nearly an east course about nine miles, and encamped by the side of a small river.

On the 17th kept much the same course, crossing several rivulets and creeks. We travelled about twenty miles, and encamped by the side of a small river.

On the 18th we travelled about sixteen miles an easterly course, and encamped by a brook.

The 19th, about the same general course, we crossed two considerable streams of water, and some large hills timbered with chestnut and oak, and having travelled about twenty miles, we encamped by the side of a small river, at which place were a number of Delawares hunting.

On the 20th, keeping still an easterly course, and having much the same travelling as the day before, we advanced on our journey about nineteen miles, which brought us to Beaver Creek, where are two or three Indian houses, on the west side of the creek, and in sight of the Ohio.

Bad weather prevented our journeying on the 21st, but the next day we prosecuted our march. Having crossed the creek, we travelled twenty miles, nearly south-east, and encamped with a party of Indian hunters.

On the 23d we came again to the Ohio, opposite to Fort Pitt, from whence I ordered Lieut. M'Cormick to march the party across the country to Albany, and, after tarrying there till the 26th, I came the common road to Philadelphia, from thence to New York, where, after this long, fatiguing tour, I arrived February 14, 1761.

APPENDIX A.

COMMISSION AND INSTRUCTIONS OF SIR WILLIAM JOHNSON, IN THE COMMAND OF PROVINCIAL TROOPS RAISED IN 1755, FOR THE REDUCTION OF THE FRENCH FORT AT CROWN POINT.

Commission of Sir William Johnson, as Commander-in-Chief of the Provincial Forces raised for the Reduction of Crown Point. *

By His Excellency William Shirley, Esq., Captain General and Commander-in-Chief, in and over His Majesty's Province of the Massachusetts Bay in new England, and the Lands and Territories thereon depending; Vice Admiral of the Same, and Colonel in His Majesty's Army.

To WILLIAM JOHNSON, ESQ., GREETING:

Whereas by my messages on the 13th and 15th days of last February to his Majesty's Council and House of Representatives for the aforesaid Province, in Great and General Court Assembled, recommending to them to make provision for carrying on an attempt in conjunction with some of His Majesty's other neighbouring Governments, to erect a Strong fortress upon an Eminence near the French Fort at Crown Point, and other services in the said

---

* Johnson MSS., I, 153.

Messages expressed: In answer to which the said the Houses of the aforesaid Assembly by their message to me, on the eighteenth of the same February, among other things therein contained, desired me forthwith to make the necessary preparations for such an expedition, to appoint and commissionate a general officer, to command the same, to advise His Majesty's other governments thereinafter mentioned, of the said designs, and in such manner as I should think most effectual, to urge them to join therein, and to raise their respective proportions of Men, as follows, vizt: New Hampshire, 600; Connecticut, 1000; Rhode Island, 400; New York, 800, or such larger proportions as each of the said governments should think proper, and to cause twelf hundred men to be enlist d for the service of the Sd Expedition, as the proportion of the Province of Massachusetts Bay, as soon as it should appear that the three thousand men proposed to be raised by the aforesaid Colonies of New Hampshire, Connecticut, Rhode Island and New York, should be agreed to be raised.

And whereas, in consequence of my aforesaid messages, recommending the said Expedition, and of the Resolves of the Assembly of Massachusetts Bay thereupon, (copies of both which I transmitted to the beforementioned four neighbouring Governments together with a letter to each of them, to join in the same, as proposed by the Assembly of the Massachusetts Bay;) and nominally you to be the Commander-in-Chief of the Provincial Forces to be employed in the said Expedition, the Governments of New York, New Hampshire, Connecticut and Rhode Island, have agreed to raise in the whole, 2,900 men, for His Majesty's Service in the said Expedition, which with 1,500 men since agreed to be raised for the aforesaid service, by the Massachusetts Bay, will make up 4,100 men, and acquiesced in my nomination of you to be Commander-in-Chief of the said forces.

And whereas, his Excellency Major General Braddock, Commander-in Chief of All His Majesty's Forces in North America, hath since approved of my appointment of you to the said command : Now reposing especial trust and con fidence in your fidelity, courage and good conduct, I do by Virtue of the authority to me granted in and by His Majesty's Royal Commission, under the Great seal of Great Britain, and in consequence of the several proceedings of the governments of the aforesaid colonies of New England and New York, and of the approbation of Major General Braddock, appoint you to be Major General and Commander-in-Chief of the Forces raised and to be raised, by the aforesaid five Governments, or any of them for the service of the aforesaid expedition, as also of such Indians as shall assist His Majesty in the same : You are therefore to take upon you the command of the said Forces, and diligently to execute the duty and office of commander-in-chief of the said expedition, according to such instructions as you shall receive from me, bearing even date with these presents, and to follow such further orders as you shall from time to time receive from me, or any your superior officer herein : Hereby requiring all officers and soldiers employed, or to be employed by the aforesaid five governments, in the said expedition, to obey you as their commander-in-chief.

> Given under my Hand and Seal at arms, the 16th day of April, in the 28th year of the reign of our Sovereign Lord, George the Second, by the Grace of God, of Great Britain, France and Ireland, King, Defender of the Faith, etc., and in the year of our Lord Christ, 1755.
>
> W. SHIRLEY.

By His Excellency's command,
WM. ALEXANDER,
Secretary pro hac vice.

A commission was also issued by Lieutenant Governor James De Lancey, of New York, of substantially the same import.*

Instructions from Governor Shirley to General Sir William Johnson in his Expedition against the French at Crown Point.†

By his Excellency, William Shirley, Esq., Captain General and Commander-in-Chief in and over the Province of the Massachusetts Bay in New England and of the Lands and Territories thereon depending, Vice Admiral of the Same, and Colonel in His Majesty's army.

To WILLIAM JOHNSON, ESQ., GREETING:

Whereas by my commission dated this day, under my seal at arms, I have appointed you to be Major General and Commander-in-chief, of the forces now raising by the said Goverment of the Massachusetts Bay, New York, New Hampshire, Connecticut and Rhode Island, for an expedition against the French incroachments· at Crown Point and upon the Lake Champlain, as also of such Indians as shall assist in the service of the above expedition ; I do hereby give you the following Instructions and Orders for the regulation of your conduct.

1stly. You are to engage as soon as possible as many of the Indians of the Six Nations, as you can in the aforesaid service, upon the encouragement proposed to be given them by the aforesaid colonies ; as also those ordered by his Excellency's Major General Braddock to be given them

---

* *Johnson MSS.*, 1, 154.
† Johnson MSS., 1, 152.

in his Majesty's name, and you are to appoint such officer to lead and conduct the said Indians as you shall judge for his Majesty's service.

2*dly*. When you shall have finished your aforesaid business with the Indians, you are to repair to the city of Albany, and there wait the arrival of the forces to be employed in the aforesaid expedition and as soon as such number of them shall arrive as you shall judge sufficient for the service, you are to proceed with the train of artillery and ordnance stores provided for the expedition under convoy to Crown Point, clearing as you pass along a practicable road for the transportation of them, and the other stores and to cause such strong houses and places of security to be erected as shall be required to serve for Magazines of stores, places of Shelter for the men in their march, and return to and from the said city of Albany; and you are to leave the necessary orders for such of the said forces as shall not be arrived at the time of your departure from Albany, to follow you to Crown Point as soon as may be.

3*dly*. Upon your arrival at Crown Point, you are to cause one or more Batteries to be erected upon the rocky eminence nigh Fort St. Frederick, or as near as may be to the said fort upon the most advantageous ground for commanding the same, and to point the said Battery or Batteries against the said Fort, and in case you shall Meet with any resistance in the erecting of said Battery or Batteries, from the Garrison of Fort Frederick, you are to attack the same; and use your utmost efforts to dislodge the French Garrison, and take possession thereof.

4*thly*. In case you shall not be interrupted or annoyed by the French in erecting the said Batteries, then, as soon as you shall have finished the same you are to send a summons to the Commandant of Fort St. Frederick, requiring him forthwith to retire with the garrison under his command from the same as being an encroachment upon his Majesty's territories, within the Country belonging to the Indians of the Six Nations, and erected contrary to the Treaty of Utrecht, made between the Crowns of Great Britain and France, whereby the Indians of the then Six Nations are expressly declared to be subject to the Crown of Great Britain ; and in case the the said commandant shall upon such summons, refuse or neglect to evacuate the same, you are to compel him to do it by force of arms, and to break up all the French settlements which you shall find near the said fort, or upon the lake Champlain.

5thly. If you should succeed in your attempt against Fort St. Frederick, you are immediately upon becoming master of it, to strengthen yourself therein, and erect such works, as, with the advice of a Council of War which you shall summon for that purpose, you shall think necessary to preserve that important post ; and you are to put into it such a garrison, as you shall judge sufficient to maintain the same.   But as the said Fort may not be situated in the most convenient or advantageous place for securing the possession of that Country to the English, you are by yourself and your officers to survey and examine the several places upon the Lake Champlain, and to find out such other places as you and a Council of War shall judge best to answer that purpose, of which you are to give me immediate notice, with your and the Council's reasons for making the choice of the place you shall agree upon. that I may be enabled to give the necessary orders for fortifying the same.

6thly. You are to give me a regular and constant account, from time to time, of what you do, in the discharge of the trust reposed in you, which you are to transmit by express to me wherever I shall happen to be.

7thly. You are by means of the Indians, or any other means, to procure the best intelligence you can of the designs and motions of the French, the number of any Body of Troops they may employ to oppose you, or any other of the King's forces, all which you are to communicate to me from time to time.

8thly. You are to acquaint the Indians of the Six Nations, if you shall judge it, from the temper you find them in, proper to do so, with his Majesty's design to recover the lands upon the Niagara and upon the Ohio River out of the hands of the French, and to protect them against future incroachments for the benefit of their tribes and to encourage some of them to meet me at Oswego, in order to assist me thereto, upon such services as I shall order them to go upon; assuring them of my good disposition towards their several castles, and that they shall be generously entertained by me.

Lastly. You are to use your discretion in acting for the good of his Majesty's Service, consistant with the instructions before given you in the business committed to your charge, in any matters concerning which you have no particular instructions given you; acquainting me constantly with your doing there, as soon as possible.

Given under my hand ye sixteenth day of June, 1755.

W. SHIRLEY.

"Lake St. Sacrament, 29th Aug., 1755.

"Sir: We arrived here yesterday evening and made a temporary encampment in which we continue. We found no ground cleared but we are about it. However until Capt. Eyre comes up, a place for a fort fixed on, a more regular encampment made, and ground laid out for the use of the army (all which I hope will be done in a day or two), I must beg you will not move. I would wish the heavy artillery to come along while the weather is dry, but not the stores till you come. A working party must set out a little before to repair the road in those places where it may require. I think 50 men for the guard, 25 working for the road, and 25 to cover them will be sufficient, as I have sent out this morning reconnoitering parties several ways.

"You will take care the waggons now sent return as soon as possible. Upon their return, I shall dispatch them back to you and send orders for your Marching.

" I am sir, your most humble servant,
WM. JOHNSON.

To Maj. Gen. Lyman.

"You must keep a good look out upon the Waggoners or they will desert. If attempted, make an example."

APPENDIX B.

SETTLEMENT OF THE CLAIMS OF MAJOR ROGERS UPON THE PROVINCIAL GOVERNMENT OF NEW HAMPSHIRE.

Entry in the Journal of Council and House. *June* 5, 1761.

" The Memorial of Maj. Robert Rogers setting forth that in the year 1755, he was ordered to remain with a company at Fort William Henry during the Winter of

1755, and till the spring of 1756, &c., for which he nor his Company had received any allowance, and prays the Consideration of the General Assembly that they would set a time for him to produce his vouchers, &c., read and sent down."

House Journal, June 26, 1761.

" The Memorial of Major Robert Rogers and the Muster roll of his Company therein referred to with the certificates thereto relating, read, and Major Rogers being admitted into the House by his desire said what he had to say in order to inforce his Memorial and retired.

" The House took the matter under Consideration immediately, and it being after twelve o'clock, A. M., and the House being informed they were to be prorogued this forenoon, and there being no time for a mature deliberation and debates thereon, and Major Rogers not having his vouchers with him to support his Memorial, he was ordered into the House, and by the Speaker was told the minds of the House, viz :—That the House was ready to do every thing in regard to his Memorial that consisted with Honour and Strict Justice, and that if he had paid any Moneys to any of his Company as therein represented, he must produce the vouchers therefor, and then the House would immediately proceed on the consideration of his Memorial ; but untill that was done and as the House was to be immediately prorogued, they could not with any propriety act thereon now, and then was ordered to withdraw."*

On the 25th of January, 1763, Major Rogers again memorialized the House, and on the 28th, he was admitted, and presented his Roll for a company of men in the service of the colony in 1756, at Fort William Henry, and swore to the same. Finally, on the 1st of February, 1763, an

---

* *New Hampshire Provincial Papers* ; vi, 790, 794.

allowance of £235 11s. 9½d. sterling, was granted for 43 men, in the winter in which this service was rendered.*

The Muster Roll of the New Hampshire Company commanded by Capt. Robert Rogers, left by order of a council of war held at Lake George in November, 1755, in connection with commissions appointed for several provinces of New England, to garrison the forts in the winter of 1755, and under the command of Col. Jonathan Bagley, Esq., from the 25th of November, 1755, to June 6 inclusive, is given in Report of the Adjutant General of New Hampshire for 1866, vol. II, p. 156. Four names on the roll were those of Indians, their pay was £15 per month, old tenor.

At the council of war above mentioned, it was promised that four hundred and fifty men, officers included, should be immediately enlisted or drafted out of the troops then in camp to be employed during the winter to garrison Fort Edward and Fort William Henry, for which they promised both officers and men that their pay should be continued until they were relieved and the commissioners further promised that they would lay the affairs before the General Assembly of the several governments represented, immediately after their return home, for their consideration, for the allowance of a bounty for each man who should then remain.

A memorial of Capt. Rogers addressed to Lord Amherst, and endorsed under date of May 23, 1760, presents his claim for £486 19s. 2d., lawful money of the Province, for services rendered in the winter of 1755–6, with his company.†

---

* *New Hampshire Provincial Papers*, vi, 861, 865, 866; *Adjutant General's Report*, New Hamp., 1866, ii, 157.
† *Johnson MSS.*, xxiv, 84, 86.

In answer to inquiries from Lord Amherst, Sir William Johnson replied : " With regard to Major Roger's affair, my memory does not serve me to recollect particulars of the agreement between him and the Commissioners, but this I know that I recommended him, that he served, and I think he ought to be paid."*

Again in writing Jan. 26, 1760, he says : " I think Rogers has done very well, as he merits y' Excellency's approbation, and I hope Lieut. Holmes will also succeed."†

APPENDIX C.

EXTRACTS FROM CORRESPONDENCE AND DOCUMENTS, RELATING TO MAJOR ROGERS' CONDUCT AT MICHILI-MACKINAC, IN 1766-8.

It will be seen from the following extracts, that Major Rogers, on his return from England, soon after the publication of his " Journals," and the " Concise Account," etc., was appointed commandant of the Military Post at Mishilimackinac, under orders from England, and sadly against the better judgment of Sir William Johnson, whose keen perception of character in this instance was most fully vindicated in the result. Finding this however a matter which he could not prevent this sagacious superintendent of Indian Affairs, lost no time in endeavoring to control Rogers in the

---

* *Johnson MSS.*, xxiv, 87.
† *Johnson MSS.*, xxiv, 93.

best manner he was able, by tying him up in the instructions, and limiting to narrow limits, his authority to incur expense. He repeatedly and forcibly expresses in the very beginning, his utter distrust of the man's principles, and fitness for the post, and declares that however well qualified he might have shown himself to be as a Ranger, he was lacking in judgment, as well as honesty, and wholly untrustworthy in the management of accounts. In his previous employment in the western country, while still a provincial officer, he had engaged in Indian trade, and he foresaw that as commandant on a remote and important trading post, he would inevitably get engaged in speculation, either directly or indirectly, to the detriment of the public service, and the general interests of the Indian trade. It appears that the conduct of Major Rogers, while in transient authority at Oswego, on his way up the lakes, had led an official to remark, that he considered himself " not bound by instructions, unless they conformed to his own interests ;" and he lost no time in following up this loose maxim of policy, as opportunities presented.

Major Rogers' instructions were dated January 10, 1766. He was a short time in the summer following, at Oswego, and on the 23d of July of that year, was present at an Indian Conference held at that place. He probably reached Michilimackinac, in the month of August.

The following letters and documents, are now, in part, for the first time published, and will show his management of affairs, in a station to which, under better counsels, he would never have been appointed. They are arranged somewhat out of their order of time, to present the subject in its proper relations, and are chiefly extracts from letters and documents embracing information upon other subjects here omitted.

*Sir William Johnson to General Thomas Gage.**

[Private.]

* * * " Touching your last favor: I must own it Surprised Me a good deal, to find the papers for some time past, filled with GOVERNOR ROGERS and his Great Appointments.

" He was a Soldier in my army in 1755, and as we were in great want of active men at that time, his readiness recommended him so far to me, that I made him an officer, and got him continued in the Ranging service, where he soon became puffed up with pride and folly, from the extravagant enconiums and notices of some of the provinces. This spoiled a good Ranger, for he was fit for nothing else—neither has nature calculated him for a large Command in that service. He has neither Understanding or principles, as I could sufficiently shew. The character you have given him is exceedingly just, and I am astonished that the government should have thought of such an employment for him: but since it is so, I am of opinion he should be tied up in such a manner as shall best prevent him from doing mischief; and I wish I could well point out how it is to be effected. I apprehend it will chiefly depend on the words of his commission, or appointment. If he is appointed Commandant of Michilimackinac, and a Deputy Agent of Indian Affairs in that quarter, under the Superintendent, and bound by his orders, (except where those of Commander-in-chief for the time being, interfere), in every thing relating thereto, and obliged to transmit regular reports from time to time, of all transactions, I think he will not have it in his power, to do so much harm as otherwise—but to prevent him from doing any, is impossible, for he has been concerned in trade, during the

---

* *Johnson MSS,* XII, 22. Dated January 23, 1766.

time he was in thé service, and will again, with those of
his connections in that Quarter, wheie, by his being Commandant, he will have it in his power to confine the trade
in a great degree to himself and friends ;—neither can I
think he would stick at saying anything to the Indians, to
effect any of his purposes.

" The like objection will be against him if appointed for
any other place. I wish the Government would revise the
case, and put him on full pay, or give him some little appointment as a Barrack Master, Fort Major, &c., of
which there will doubtless be some establishment. In such
offices, it would be out of his power to do harm, either in
accounts or otherwise ; but as Commandant and Indian
Agent, it will be extremely difficult to check him, or
detect him. If, after all, nothing else can be thought on,
I shall, on your being pleased to signify to me the power
contained in his commission, lay before you such articles,
as may in some measure tye up his hands—for I presume
he may not be sent out for his post this winter. In the
meantime, as I observed before ; the only thing to be done
at present is, to point out from whom he is to take his
orders respecting Indian affairs, the channel through which
his reports are to be transmitted, ard to limit his expenses
to pipes, tobacco, and a little liquor, unless when he may
be ordered to meet any body of Indians ; but not of himself, to incur any other expenses, or to assemble or treat
with the Indians ; and whenever they shall address him to
send a faithful copy of his speeches, and to take care of all
their Belts, Calumets, etc.''

'· *Instructions to Major Robert Rogers, Commandant of the
Post of Michilimackinac.**

" His Majesty's pleasure having been signified to me, that
you should be appointed to the command of Michilimackinac,

---

* *Johnson MSS.*, xii, 10.

or some other post in the upper country, I do by these presents, appoint you to be Captain Commandant of the Garrison of Michilimackinac, and you are hereby authorized to take the command of the said garrison, and the officers and soldiers that compose the same are required to obey you as their commanding officer. You are therefore to take the said charge upon you, and carefully and diligently to discharge the duty thereof, by doing and performing all and all manner of things thereunto belonging. And you are to observe and follow such orders and directions as you shall from time to time receive from his Majesty, myself, or any other your superior officer, according to the rules and discipline of war. And for your better guidance and direction, in the great trust reposed in you, you are herewith furnished with such orders as have been given out, during my command, to the officers commanding posts, to which you will pay due attention and obedience ; I can't recommend too strongly to you, the strictest economy in the small expenses that may unavoidably be incurred at this post now put under your command. But nothing new or chargeable, must upon any account, be undertaken by you, of your own head.

As in the course of your command, you must necessarily have some intercourse with the Savages. I have thought proper in *this particular*, to put you under the direction of Sir William Johnson, Bart. His Majesty's sole agent and Superintendent of the Northern Indians, and he will furnish you with proper instructions for your guidance in your transactions with the Indians, who reside near, and may visit the said post of Michilimacknac, to which, and all such future orders as he may judge necessary to send you, *upon this subject*, you are to pay the strictest attention ar.d obedience.

You will as frequently as possible report to the officer commanding at Detroit, under whose immediate command you are,—(Michilimackinac being a post dependant thereon,) the state of the troops under your command, sending the proper returns and acquainting him of every occurrence relative to the better conducting His Majesty's affairs in that country, that you shall think it necessary he should be informed of.　You will likewise correspond with Sir William Johnson, giving him notice of every thing you shall think worthy his knowledge, relative to the conduct and temper of the Indians.

"Given, etc., New York, 10th January, 1766."

" *Sir William Johnson to Major Moncrieffe Gage.** ·

" Johnson Hall, Jan. 30, 1766.

"DEAR SIR, Major Rogers delivered me your favor of the 20th inst., by which I am surprised to find that my letter of July was three months on the road.　Indeed, the irregularity of the Posts, and miscarriages of letters are become very frequent of late, and a subject of general complaint from most of my correspondents.

· "I have known Major Rogers ever since 1755, and should be glad the Government had made a better or more adapted appointment for him.　As Michilimackinack is pointed out, he must go there, where I hope he will act a proper part, prove of service to the public and extricate himself out of his difficulties, and deserve a better character than the public has for some time bestowed upon him, the particulars and causes of which you are so well acquainted

---

* *Johnson MSS.*, xii, 27.

with, that I need say no more than to assure you that your recommendation will always have due weight with me.*

"I heartily thank you for your honest remarks and candid sentiments on our American disputes. They have been always mine, and I trust we shall never differ in opinion thereon. The unconstitutional steps pursued to obtain a constitutional redress, can hardly be parallelled, and I fear they have kindled a fire which all their engines may not extinguish, not withstanding all the paper puffs, and the distresses which they threaten Great Britain.† If I could find one instance of patriotic disinterestedness and moderation—of respect for the Crown and its officers and unprejudiced sentiments of liberty I should esteem them ; but when long experience induces me to think that opposition and bravado are their darling passions, I cannot but condemn their doctrine, and I shudder at the licentiousness it might introduce.‡ A country without fleet, army, or even

---

* In the original draft, in place of the preceding sentence the following had been written and then erased : "I am sorry to say, he does not appear much esteemed, for it gives me a sensible pain to find a useful active man, struggling under the disadvantages of distress, and a bad name, and he would have done much better, if not exalted too much by the people here, who appear now foremost in debasing him."

† In the original draft, the following had been here written and erased :
"I am not friend to any act which may bring difficulty or distress on a free people ; but I love the British Constitution, and would not add £100 a year to my estate, to produce the smallest diminution of the British Rights, I love a monarchy, such as England is, but not such as they would make it.

‡ This passage as first written, in the original draft, and then partly erased, was as follows :
"But when I know by long experience, by good information, and even from their own history, that it is not liberty but faction they court, and that their sentiments and conduct so strongly resembles that of those who once overcast the British Constitution, I shudder at the licentiousness they would introduce ; and if they were absolved from all British tyes, cannot but consider them as a prey for the first maritime power, or rather as fallen to the share of all the maritime powers in Europe."

numbers equal to the smallest Kingdom, and they too, scattered over an extensive tract of country, with few sea ports, and those few, with all their commerce, liable to be totally obstructed by the smallest squadron, must certainly fall a sacrifice if left to themselves, to one, or other, or all the maritime powers, which makes me astonished at the extravagant speeches I daily hear (no doubt brought from good authority) of their strength and resolutions. In a country where we are denied the liberty of altering our thoughts, it is scarcely safe to say much, and I can say little further than to express my wishes, that moderation may become more in esteem, and that the public may at length be convinced by serious reflection, that their violent conduct is in no wise calculated for procuring them redress. or esteem from the mother country. I sincerly thank you for all your good wishes, and if you approve of my sentiments, shall expect a continuance of your friendly correspondence.

"Be assured of my unalterable esteem, of my best wishes for your prosperity, and that I am Dear Moncrieffe, your Sincere Friend,

"WILLIAM JOHNSON."

*Letter from Major Robert Rogers to Sir William Johnson.**

New York, February 14, 1776.

"SIR: I have received orders from General Gage for taking command of the troops and garrison at Michilimakina, a copy of which orders Mr. Croghan will forward to you with this letter. I hope for your approbation, and that I shall have your assistance for any thing that may offer, that is in your Department, as I shall ever be happy to receive, so I shall take pleasure in obeying your commands. I

---

* *Johnson MSS.*, XII, 40.

shall send up my Journals* for your perusal, by the Post. The Packet is hourly expected, should she bring any intelligence worthy your notice, I shall do myself the honour to communicate it to you. The London Papers inform that your son had the honour of a knighthood conferred upon him at his arrival in London.

"I am with great Respect, Sir, your most Obedient and most Humble Servant,

ROBERT ROGERS."

Benjamin Roberts to Sir William Johnson.†

Ontario. [Oswego] July 3, 1766.

"The traders applied to me here to procure liberty to remain on the other side of the river, where they were stationed by Capt. Fuller. I spoke to Captain Rogers to let them remain, but he said he had orders from General Gage to have them at this side the river. I offered to shew him my order from general where all orders concerning Indian affairs were to be obeyed, and that your direction to the Smith was to settle at that side, and I imagined you intended the trade should be there, but t'was all to no purpose.

"I have taken the liberty to mention this to you, as I find he thinks that he is not to obey any orders that don't come directly from the general, least I may meet with any difficulty by others being of the same opinion. I have known as such difficulties, to arise in other departments, till a general order cleared all doubts."

---

* Probably referring to the volume printed in London in 1765, which we here republish.

† *Johnson MSS.*, XII, 232.

*Sir William Johnson to General Gage.**

Johnson Hall, September 11, 1767.

" Tho' I wrote to you a few days ago by Mr. Croghan, yet I could not avoid saying something again on the score of the vast expenses incurred, and as I understand still incurring at Michilimackinac, chiefly on the pretense of making a peace between the Sioux and Chipeweighs, with which I think we have very little to do, in good policy or otherwise. By letters I have this day received from Capt. Claas, I find that further drafts on me have been shown to him at Montreal, to the amount of £1100, and I hear the whole exceeds £5000. In short, from the several accounts I have received, I am induced to think there must be some particular motive for this Expense, and indeed the method practiced in conducting affairs there, tends to strengthen that opinion. The Traders have been vastly indulged to procure their esteem, but are nevertheless very importunate for their money, and I am at a loss what to say to them upon it, for expenses seem to have been made, and Indians called, purely to show authority and gain repu- tation. The business was given into the hands of the Com- missary with a bad grace, and much has been done to draw the latter into large expenses, which however he is suffi- ciently armed against by his instructions as was also the Major. Upon the whole, I have reason to apprehend something more than common is in view, (which may not be a matter of Surprise to you), and I should have given the Secretary of State a hint of it, so that at least he might be sent some where else, but that I would not do it with- out your knowledge and approbation."

* *Johnson MSS.*, xv, 63; *Doc. Hist.*, N. Y., ii, 863. See letter of Sir William Johnson to the Earl of Shelburn, dated Oct. 26, 1767, on a subse- quent page. Also the letter of General Gage to Johnson, dated Oct. 22, 1767.

*General Gage to Sir William Johnson.**

New York, September 21, 1767.·

"With respect to the Commander at Missilimakinak, I could devise no better means to stop his proceedings, and put an immediate end to all the mischiefs he may create, than to remove him immediately from his command. I have therefore done this, and ordered him to meet Mr. Crogan at Detroit ; at which place my letter to Supercede him in the command of Missilimakinak will be delivered to him.† The bills which he has thought proper to draw to so great an amount, pretended to have been incurred on a trifling affair, undertaken solely by his own authority, the expence of it by the same powers only, contrary to the orders and instructions given him by you as well as by me, must be protested ; and I acquaint him that they are protested, and will not be paid. I have send orders that he shall return no more to Missilimakinak, or be permitted to hold any conferences publick or private, with any of the Indian Nations, and to watch his motions very narrowly. Of all this you will take no notice for some time to come,

---

* *Johnson MSS.*, xv. 63. *Doc. Hist.*, N. Y., ii, 863. See letter from Sir William Johnson to the Earl of Shelburne, dated Oct. 26, 1767, on a subsequent page, also letter of Gen. Gage to Johnson, dated Oct. 22, 1767.

† Mr. George Croghan in writing to Sir William Johnson from New York, Sept. 14, 1767, says : The General [Gage] is much displeased with Major Rogers, but I have not had time yet to talk with him on that subject. But from what he has said, I find he wishes he had never been sent there.— [*Johnson MSS.*, xv, 66.]

In writing from Philadelphia, Sept. 25, 1767, he again says : "The General spoke to me about Rogers, and asked my opinion about him which I gave, and the General has sent by me orders to get him down to Detroit, and from thence down here, which the General has no doubt wrote your honor fully about the plan fixed for getting him down the country and which I will endeavor to execute with as much prudence as in my power."—[*Johnson MSS.* xv, 89]. See also MSS., xv, 158, 160, 196; xvi, 55, 65, 144, 177 ; xix, 163.

I have wrote very fully to Lieut. Roberts to send the fullest information upon every part of his conduct, and given orders to the officers to assist him in his inquiries."

*Sir William Johnson to General Gage.**

(Private),

Johnson Hall, October 22, 1767.

"Dear Sir : On my return I found a pacquet just arrived from Montreal, inclosing me the depositions of Mr. Potter, taken before the Chief Justice of Quebec, relative to Major Roger's Schemes and conduct, a copy of which, I am informed, has been sent to you, and also that Potter is gone to England on that occasion.

The Deposition is long, and with the other papers transmitted (one of which is a Letter to my Deputy, Lieut. Johnson) fully shew his views and confirm the strong suspicions we had before entertained concerning him. It appears to me necessary that the Government should be fully informed of these particulars, and you will doubtless agree with me, concerning the necessity there appears for preventing him from putting his resolutions into practice, or eluding the plan you proposed for bringing him from thence. He is a weak vain man ; and however romantick his scheme may appear, I believe him capable of undertaking it, or in short any thing else, and in the present state of affairs, should he escape, he might, I am certain, give us some trouble.

The Traders there tho' ignorant of his particular project, begin to be greatly alarmed on account of their persons and propertys, from some discoveries they have made, and my

---

* *Johnson MSS.,* xv, 105 ; *Doc. Hist.,* N. Y., ii, 883.

opinion is, that as he now knows he is discovered, he will be driven thro' dispair, and that he will leave the Garrison immediately, having concerted a plan with those seduced to follow his fortunes, and I am given to understand, with the assistance of some Indians, to plunder the Traders and go down the Mississippi, or put some of the rest of his plan in execution.

Potter with great difficulty escaped from his clutches and got to Montreal, but on the presumption that you will have received all informations hereon, I will add no more, but beg to be favored with your answer as soon as con venient ; and as my present hurry will not allow me to send copies, should they not be come to your hands, I shall send them in my next."

Sir William Johnson to the Earl of Shelburne.*

Johnson Hall, Oct. 26, 1767.

" My Lord : I think it an essential part of my duty to lay before your Lordship the particulars of a very extraordinary discovery made of the intentions of Major Robert Rogers, Commander of Mishilimacinac, to corroborate which, I transmit to your Lordship the enclosed letter and deposition.

This gentleman has been known to me since 1755, when finding him an active man, I raised him to the rank of a Provincial officer, and employed him on scouting service, there being very few people to be had fit for the purpose. He has since been advanced by several of the Commanders-in-chief, for his alertness in that way, but having mis spent his money, and being reduced in 1763, he was, since recommended by his Majesty's ministers to

---

* *Johnson MSS.*, xv, *N. Y. Colonial Hist.*, vii, 988.

General Gage, to be appointed to his present command, and to act under my direction in Indian Affairs at that post.

From very strong suspicions which now appear well grounded, I took care by the advice of General Gage, to give him very little powers with regard to Ind'n management or expenses there,* the General and myself well knowing the man, the heavy debts he had incurred, and reasonably concluding he ought not to be entrusted with much authority. Some particulars which I had early discovered, contributed to the discovering a villainous correspondence. One letter (of which the enclosed is a copy) of this, would have been earlier laid before your Lordship, but that notwithstanding the motives we had to suspect him, it was nevertheless judged best to wait for stronger proofs, least he might have denied his assent to ye proposals, which we could not then sufficiently disprove—by which means he must have been acquitted; and left perhaps to do much mischief, as he would be furnished with sufficient caution to prevent the future discovery of his designs.

Soon after his arrival at his post, I was informed of his assembling numbers of Indians,† of secret conferences which he held, at which he suffered none to be present of the garrison,—of extraordinary titles he gave himself; ect. To prevent which, with the advice of the Commander in Chief,‡ I appointed and sent a commissary there§ for the

---

* Johnson in writing to Gen. Gage, May 20, 1767, says : " I have received and forwarded the order, respecting the Cloaths remaining at the posts, and shall write to Major Rogers to incur no more Expenses as you desire."— *Johnson MSS.*, xiv, 189 ; *Doc. Hist., N. Y.*, ii, 855.

† See instructions for Mr. Deriver, sent by Rogers to negotiate with the Indians, dated Sept. 2, 1766.—*Johnson's MSS.*, xiii, 74.

‡ Letter dated January 25, 1767, in which Gen. Gage says : " Michilimackinak seems to be the most material post we have, and certainly more necessary for a commissary than any other."—*Doc. Hist., N. Y.*, ii, 837.

§ Lieut. Benjamin Roberts.

management of Indian Affairs, previous to whose arrival, Rogers had incurred a considerable expense, to the amount of several thousands,* and since gave drafts for the same on the Department for Indian Affairs, the pretence alledged on account of part of this expense was to purchase a peace with the Chippawaes, of Lake Superior, and part of the Siouxf, as mentioned in my last,—a peace calculated to serve the purpose of a few Traders, who could not range the country at will, if a variance subsisted between these Tribes, although such variance in no wise affected any other of the Traders, or other his Majesty's Subjects, but should have been as good policy connived at, as it diverted some of the most dangerous Indians from concerting any thing to ye general prejudice.

---

* Sir William Johnson in writing to General Gage, Sept. 6, 1767, says: " I left the Springs sooner than I should have done on account of some letters, etc., transmitted to me by Lt. Johnson, which were received from the frontiers, and from some accounts received from the Indians which I don't much like. On my arrival at Albany, I was surrounded by people with drafts drawn on me by Major Rogers to a very considerable amount. Those I have already seen, come to between £2,000 and £3,000. I must defer saying any thing further on this subject for the present, but referring you to Mr. Croghan for other particulars, conclude, with assuring, etc."—*Johnson MSS.*, xv, 58 ; *Doc. Hist.*, N. Y., ii, 863.

Several of these bills are preserved among the Johnson MSS., viz.:

From Aug. 8, to Sept. 20, 1766, £290 5s. 3d. (MSS., xiii, 89.)
From Sept. 21, 1766 to Feb. 1, 1767, 429 13s. 6d. (MSS., xiv, 42.)
From Feb. 1, to May 23, 1767, 212 19s. 6d. (MSS., xiv, 193.)

See also an answer to a Trader's petition concerning goods advanced to Major Rogers, dated Jan. 7, 1767 (MSS., xiv, 7).

Letter from Major Rogers to Sir William Johnson, dated Aug. 14, 1767, relating to the payment of accounts (MSS., xv, 31).

Letter from Joseph Howard, of Montreal, Oct. 25, 1767, to Sir William Johnson, strongly urging his claims for pay for goods delivered to Major Rogers (MSS., xv, 114).

† See letter to General Gage, dated Sept. 11, 1767.

The bulk of the expence however which he incured, was evidently .calculated to acquire a name and influence amongst the Indians,* for his preconcerted purposes, and of this, the Traders themselves latterly were suspicious, for although his toleration to them to do what . they pleased, at first proved highly agreeable and induced them to accept his drafts for the payment of large sums, yet as he has since drawn so much, has employed so many persons under extravagant promises, and given them rank and powers to go with large Cargoes of goods amongst all the nations. The Traders begin to take the alarm, and from a knowledge of his vanity, and extravagant schemes, (tho' ignorant of the material part), are now in the utmost consternation about the safety of their persons and prop-ertys.

As he is a very illiterate man, he found it necessary to engage some person to do business for him, and accordingly the deponent, Potter, has, on the promise of a handsome allowance, followed his fortune for some time past, How he came to make the discovery of Roger's designs will ap-pear from the deposition which corroborates the particulars which came to the General's, and my knowledge. He has since insulted the Commissary, and interfered with him in his duty, † and the General has taken Measures

---

* *Letter from Daniel Claus to Sir Willlam Johnson.*

Montreal, 16th October, 1766.

" By the last account from Miehilimackina, Major Rogers was arrived there, and immediately without hesitation, gave a general permit to all Traders to go , wintering, for which he is vastly liked and applauded here. The Traders that came from there told me also that his behaviour towards the Indains was liked and approved of by them, as well as the people of the place."—*Johnson MSS.* XIII. 134.

† See Letter of Sir William Johnson to General Gage, dated Oct. 30, 1767, on a subsequent page.

for withdrawing him from thence. * It only remains for me to add thereon, that as his case is now become desperate by Potter's having abandoned his interest, I apprehend he will not wait the General's dispatches, but leave the place, and take some Measures agreable to his own character, which from the present alarming situation of Indian Affairs, may be attended with ill consequences to the public.

The dangerous precedent which he has set to the Indians there, on the article of expense will be productive of much trouble to those who succeed him in the Management of Indian Affairs there, and indeed I cannot avoid observing, that the Indian accounts are greatly inflamed, through the present irregular state of their affairs, and that if, as it was once intended, the Superintendant has orders to procure a certain quantity of articles, for presents, etc., at the Cheapest rates in England, the Indians would be better served, and contented, than at present, when goods are obliged to be brought up in haste, bad in quality, and at the most advanced prices, to answer sudden emergencies — and I am myself obliged, not only to advance my own cash, but very frequently to borrow money to answer the demands and drafts of the several distant officers, all which arises from the want of a regular established fund for the expences of the Department.

This and all other heads, are humbly Submitted to your Lordship's consideration, with a confidence that they will Merit such attention, and produce such powers, as may be thought best, as a remedy against such evils, till when, all I can do is, to propose a General Congress of all the Nations, and in Case my endeavors to prevent hostilities

---

* See Letter of Gen. Gage to Sir William Johnson, dated Sept. 21, 1767, and of Johnson to Gage, dated Oct. 22, 1767.

should prove ineffectual, I persuade myself I can keep some tribes quiet, and even spirit up several partys to àct offensively against the rest, if empowered to do so."

"*Deposition Made by Nathaniel Potter, late of Michilimackina, taken before the Hon. William Hay, His Majesty's Chief Justice of the Province of Quebec, the 28th day of September, 1767.* *

"Mr. Nathaniel Potter, late of Michilimackina, maketh oath, upon the Holy Evangelist and Saith, that about the Month of January in the year of our Lord 1765, he became acquainted with Major Robert Rogers, who is now Commander of the Fort of Michilimackina, and that from that time till this last Summer, he has continued to be much connected with him, and employed by him in various ways, That he has several times observed, that the said Major Rogers was much dissatisfied with his Situation, and expressed a distant design of taking some extraordinary Method to better it. That the said Major Rogers, sent the said Potter last spring to Lake Superior, from whence he returned about the latter end of last June, And in July last, the said Major Rogers had a private conversation with the said Mr. Potter at the Fort at Michilimackina, in which he explained his designs to the said Potter in a fuller manner than he had ever done before. He said he was much in debt to several Traders whom he was unable to pay and that this gave him great uneasiness, That he was therefore resolved to apply to the government of England to do something to better his situation, and he wished that they would erect the country about the Michilimackina, into a Separate Province, and make him governor of it, with a command of three Companies of Rangers, in-

---

* *Johnson MSS.* xv. *N. Y. Colonial Hist,* vii. 990.

dependent of Sir William Johnson, or the Commander-in-Chief of the forces in America—that this would Satisfy him. and make him easy, and nothing else would ; and he purposed to Mr. Potter to go to England to make these proposals to the English Government in his behalf, and to let him know in the speediest manner possible, the success of his negotiations : for if he did not meet with success, he would immediately upon his receiving notice of his disappointment, quit his post, and retire to the French towards the Mississippi, and enter into the service of the French unless he was sure to meet with better encouragement. That he had lately a letter from one Hopkins, who is now in the French Service in one of their West India Islands. That in that letter Hopkins had offered him great encouragement if he would embrace the French interest, and stir up the Indians against the English, That he was sure he would get greater riches, and be a great man, if he was to go over to the French, and therefore he was resolved to do so, if the English Government did not comply with his proposals. And that he advised Potter to do the same, as it would be much for his interest. That upon Potter's expressing some surprise and indignation at this proposal, as being contrary to his duty and Conscience, Rogers told him he was a fool : that he had hitherto taken him for a man of sense, and his friend that would serve him in any scheme to serve him, but that now he found he was mistaken. But he said that for himself, he was resolved to do so, if his proposals were not complyed with :—and he added, that if he did take that step and retire among the Indians and French, he would not go empty handed, but would in that case get into his hands all the goods he could, both from Traders and others — by right or wrong he cared not how, And he said he had already made preparations for such a step, by appointing people to meet him

21

at a place called Lowis Constant, [Wisconsin?], near a
river that falls into the Mississippi.

When Potter refused to engage with Rogers in his
design, the latter flew into a violent passion, and swore
that he would never pay him a farthing of what he owed
him, and said that he supposed, since he would not join
him in his designs, he would go and reveal it, but that if
he did he would certainly kill him. Potter answered him,
that he had always served him faithfully, and wished to do
so still, and had no inclination to reveal any·thing that
might turn to his prejudice, but as he seemed to be so
firmly resolved to take such a dangerous step, that might
be the cause of a new Indian War, or other dreadfull misfortune to the interest of Great Britain, he apprehended
himself to be bound in Conscience, and by the duty which
he owed his country,—to give intelligence of it to proper
persons, in order to prevent its taking place.

Rogers upon this, took an Indian Spear, that was in the
room in which this conversation passed, and pointed it at
Potter, threatening him with instant death, if he did not
swear to keep this matter secret. Potter seeing his life in
danger, cried out for help, but was not heard ; upon which
he fell upon his knees, and begged Rogers to spare·his life
till the next day, when they might converse together upon
the subject again, and he hoped with mutual satisfaction.
That made Rogers grow somewhat cooler. He then
pressed Potter to give him up a note of hand for fifty
pounds, twelve shillings sterling, which he had given him
in New York, and likewise to give him discharges from
several sums of money, which he owed Potter, and which
he knew Potter had set down in his books of accounts—
but Potter did not comply with these demands. Soon
after, Rogers opened the door and went down one of the
steps that were before it ; and Potter, thinking this a good

opportunity to get out of his company, endeavored to push by him and get out of the house. But Rogers would not let him go without blows;—he struck him, and kicked him, saying " damn you, you shant come out yet; I'll cook you, I'll warrant you," besides other very foul language. However by this means, Potter at last got out of his own house, and went to his own lodging. The people were all exceedingly surprised at this behaviour of Rogers, as they had imagined that Potter had been a great friend ard favorite of Rogers as in truth he had been till this extraordinary conversation which he did not at that time, communicate to anybody. The next day, Potter went out to take a walk ; and during his short absence, Rogers took from Potter's lodgings a silver hilted Sword, worth Six Guineas, a Fowling Piece, twenty pound weight of Beaver Skins, a hat and other wearing apparel. Potter on his return from his walk, met Rogers on the Parade, who asked him what he thought of things then, Potter answered, that he continued in the same way of thinking as the day before ; which put Rogers in a violent passion, and made him swear that he would not let Potter go out of the Garrison.

Potter went home, and did not yet tell what had passed. The third day, Rogers again asked Potter what his thoughts were upon the matter he had proposed to him, who again refused to join him in his designs : Whereupon knocked him down, and bid the guard take care of him ; but they, seeing that Rogers was in a violent passion when he gave this order, did not obey it, and Potter was not confined, but went home streight to his lodging. Then several persons who had been witnesses of the ill treatment he had received from Rogers. and were both surprised and shocked at it, went to see him ; and amongst the rest, Mr. Roberts, the Commissary, who advised him to apply to Capt. Spicemaker the Commanding Officer of the Troops for protection. And Potter did so, and received the

Captain's Protection, and received no further injury from Rogers after that time.

On the 29th of August last, he left Michilimackina and the same day, or the day before, he acquainted Mr. Roberts the Commissary, with Roger's private conversation above mentioned, which had been the occasion of their quarrel, before he left Michilimackina. Rogers sent him word, that if he would not hurt him, he would pay him his debt, Potter supposes that by this expression, "if he would not hurt him," Rogers must have meant, if he would not discover the aforesaid private conversation.

Rogers never returned him the sword, and hat, and Beaver Skins, and other things that were taken out of his room. Potter says, that Rogers is in debt to almost all the Traders about Michilimackina, to the amount of 100.000 French Livres, all which debts have been contracted since he has been at Michilimackina. He says that Rogers told him, in the Conversation aforesaid, that he had sent eleven canoes loaded with goods to Lake Superior, and Lake Michigan and other places of Indian trade. Potter says that Rogers seems to him to be collecting an interest with the Indians, in order to retreat to them when he shall execute his purpose of leaving the British Service: and he suspects that one Stoote, and one Atherton, design to go off with him.

Sworn before William Hay, Esq: His Majesty's Chief Justice of the Province of Quebec, at Montreal this 29th day of September, 1767."

Letter of Colonel Hopkins to Major Rogers. *
Au Cap Francois, Isle de St. Domingo,
the 9th of April, 1766.

" My Dear Rojers,

This is the 3d time I've wrote you since our last meeting in New York, and altho' our absence has been long,

---

* *Johnson MSS*, xv. *N. Y. Colonial Hist.* vii, 993.

my ·sentiments of friendship are, and always will be the same — as I promised, you were remembered in my conversations with the Minister of the King I now serve. I have reason to think you would have a reasonable gracious exception, but until my affairs are entirely finished and the promises which were made, amply accomplished, I cannot think of pursuading or enticing you on, until there shall be a certainty fixed for you, or such of our acquaintance as will follow my example. You know the injustices we have suffered, particularly yourself, nor is it in the power of England to recompence you for the disgraces you underwent for . having served them too faithfully. Be assured, my dear friend, of my doing and contributing every thing for your honor and advantage, Seize every opportunity of ingratiating yourself into the favour of the Indians where you are placed Governor, by which means and your own merits, despair not, in case of a change. to be raised to the rank that even the height of your wishes could have expected. Mistrust all the world : have no confidence but in those of whom you have the greatest proofs of their friendship, So soon as the little difficulties I labor under are raised, and my sort fixed you shall know, and also the decision in regard to yourself — a present nous parlerons des affaires publique.

I am not unacquainted with the disturbances in North America. I foresaw the Storm when in London, that lay either with the injustices of the British Minister as my reasons for the steps I've taken, but my dear Rojers, altho' detached from the British Interest, entirely and absolutely, believe me always North America, and ready to render the Continent and my Countrymen all the services which may depend, or which can be expected from me, in risquing for the common liberty not only life and little fortune, but also in being an advocate for them, for any assistance or supplys that the present circumstances of their affairs may exige.   There can be no obstacle to their being a free and independent people (preach this doctrine in the New England Provinces, where you and your family have so much interest.)   You have the means in your own hands; your numbers are far superior to any forces that can be sent against you and I believe there are powers who might think themselves happy in being of the number of your allies and friends, and of giving you the proofs the most effectual of their good intentions for saving you.   Acquaint Baube, and all my friends the Hurons, the Pottawatameys, ye Chippawas, and the Ottawas of the Change I've made and if you have an interview with Londiac [Pontiac ?] take him by the hand for me, and make known to him I serve his Father the King of France, The Reverend Pere Jesuite Portier, pray him de me conserver tojours son amite le famille de Mess'rs Reaumes & St. Martin, particularment ma chere Catharine, donner moi aussi souvant qùi possible de vous nouvelles et croyer moi sincerement votre.   And write me fully without signing your name.

MARYLAND.

Mr. Hopkins is well, and you will address your letters to me under cover to him.   There are continual opportunities from New York and Philadelphia for Monte O'Christ, or by the Mississippi, to write to me.

N. B.—The author of this letter is a Mr. Hopkins, of Maryland, formerly of the 18th Regiment, after which he obtained a Capt's Commission to Command a Corps called the Queen's Independent Company, on the reduction of which, he entered into the French service, and is now a Colonel therein in Hispainola.   A great intimacy always subsisted between him and Rojers."

Sir William Johnson to General Gage.*

Johnson Hall, Oct. 30, 1776.

"Since my last, I have received more letters from Michilimackinac concerning affairs there, by which I find that the Commissary has been led off the parade by a file of men, and confined on account of some words between him and the Commandant, concerning a cargo of Rum, which was siezed on the north shore opposite the fort, the particulars of which are, I apprehend contained in letters which go by this post."†

---

* *Johnson MSS* xv, 121 : *Doc. Hist. N. Y.*, ii, 885.

† The affair of Mr. Roberts, was concisely as follows : As mentioned on a preceding page, he had been appointed Commissary, and was charged with the supervision of the civil affairs pertaining to the Indian trade. He had not been long at his post of duty before he began to observe irregularities and on the 12th of August, 1767, wrote to Sir William Johnson as follows : "Every hour my uneasiness is increased, I fear that in spite of my vigilance, rum will get amongst the Indians and we shall have Mischief done. I hear by some rumors the Christian Indians have been stopped at the Grand Portage who were coming in to hear if Rogers would treat them better than the last Commandant. (*Johnson MSS.* xv, 28.)

On the 20th of August, he was arrested by Major Rogers, under circumstances best shown by his own memorial to Captain-Lieutenant Frederick Christopher Spiessmacher, in command of troops at that place :

The Memorial of Benjamin Roberts, Esq. Commissary for Indian Affairs and Trade for the District of Michilimackinac. To Capt. Lieut. Spiessmacher. Commandant of the Troops. Greeting.

Humbly Sheweth,

That your memorialist received information yesterday of a quantity of Rum being hid in the woods on the island opposite this place : that your memorialist applied to Captain Rogers for assistance to bring into the Fort the Rum that should be found; that then Captain Rogers granted a Sergeant and two men, which your memorialist promised to pay for their trouble ; That your memorialist deputized his clerk, John R. Hanson to seize the Rum, and furnished him also with two Canadians to assist him,—that the rum was actually siezed and landed on the wharf at the Fort gate ;*—that your memorialist desired the Rum should be put into the King's store appointed by General Order, of which the

---

* In a lengthy memorial to Gen. Gage, by Mr. John Weatherhead, dated, Jan. 17, 1773, the details of this seizure are recited.—*Johnson MSS.* xxv, 181.

Mr. Roberts in a lengthy letter to Sir William Johnson, dated Oct. 31, 1767, gives some details of the disturbances

Commissary keeps one key and the Traders another,—that Capt. Rogers ordered the Deputy Commissary of Provisions to take charge of the said Rum ; that your memorialist desired that he might be permitted to keep one key of the store, as well as the Deputy Commissary of Provisions, which was refused with some warmth; that your memorialist said he looked upon himself as seizing officer, and therefore accountable for the Rum ;—therefore would hold the Deputy Commissary of Provisions liable for the Rum. Capt. Rogers told your memorialist he was very impertinent, and said that your memorialist had nothing to say to the affair, your memorialist replied he was acting in Office and that no man but the commanding officer dared tell your memorialist he was impertinent. Then Capt. Rogers got very warm and gave your memorialist the lie. Your memorialist answered that he was a gentleman, and that he would not dare to tell him so out of the limits of his command. Then Captain Rogers cried out he was challenged as commmanding officer, that your memorialist denied having challenged him ; that Capt. Rogers ordered your memorialist in arrest, which your memorialist refused ; that Capt. Rogers called the guard, ordered your memorialist's stick (which your Memorialist used to examine the bales and sacks, that no rum is hid in them) to be wrested out of his hands, and that your memorialist was lifted up, and carried like a criminal through the fort, guarded by soldiers with fixed bayonets, and cast into his house.

Your memorialist from such arbitrary proceeding, has the gravest reason to apprehend the most fatal consequences to his person and effects. He also suffers much in mind from the risque these Traders run, who are ventured into the Indian Country, on the assurance of Rum being prohibited for trade in the Indian Country. Your memorialist must further inform you that Rum was let out of the Fort after tatoo. That after your memorialist made his information to Capt. Rogers that your memorialist saw Capt. Rogers talking to one of the parties concerned in carrying out Rum ; that said party is Stuart (to whom by my information the rum seems to belong) was met crossing over to the island in a Battoe.

Your memorialist apprehends (that as it is His Majesty's Instructions that no person having Command in the Indian Country, Should interpose his authority in anything concerning the trade or civil commerce of the Indians ; but to give the Commissary, or other Civil Magistrate all the assistance in his power), that he has been greatly abused. and has no other resource than your protection, as being Commander of the troops, from further insult, and for the security of the Traders who labor under many grievances.

Your memorialist intreats you to consider the importance of his trust, and the appearance such behaviour must have in the eyes of the savages who are to

created by Rogers not mentioned, in the preceding correspondence. The names Gooddard, Tate, Carver, Engineer,

---

listen to his voice as their father. That his military honor as well as his civil
character, is irreparably sullied by such an unheard of violence, and grant your
memorialist, all the assistance and protection in your power.

Your memorialist must add that he is now on half pay, having resigned
before he could accept of his employment,—therefore don't think himself
subject to arrest; that your memorialist when the necessity of the service
requires it thinks he is in duty bound to set on a Court Martial, if he can
shew no urgent cause to the contrary, being first tendered his full pay. Your
Memorialist is very sorry that any ill bred expressions occasioned warmth
between the Commandant and me, but your memorialist is in duty bound to
protest against the Commandant's proceedings, least part of the general
censure may fall on your memorialist; Taking your memorialists case into
consideration will much contribute to his tranquility tho' your memorialist has
no doubt of your assistance in every legal measure for the security of the
subject, from his own experience and universal good character, yet as your
memorialist is obliged to render an account of his actions and occurances to his
Superiors he is obliged to take this formal manner, Your Memorialist Waiting
the event, will ever pray.

(Signed) B. ROBERTS.

Micilimackinac, 21 August, 1767.
Johnson MSS. xv, 38.

Mr. Roberts had upon the day of his arrest, and having already been informed by Mr. Potter, of the treacherous correspondence that had been going on
wrote to commanding officer of the troops, in the first moments of excitement
this letter :
" SIR :
I impeach Robert Rogers Esq , commandant at Michilimackinac for holding secret correspondence with the enemies of Great Britain and forming con-
spiracies, I desire you in your allegiance, to seize his person and papers, amongst
which you will find sufficient proof.

I am, Sir.
Your humble servant,
B. ROBERTS,
Commissary of Indians Affairs.

I have discharged my duty.
To Capt. Lieut. Spiessmacker
Command't of the troops at
Michilimackinac.

A court of Inquiry was held August 22 by virtue of a warrant from Major
Rogers and the circumstances of the seizure of forty-one kegs of different sizes,
holding from two to eight gallons each, were sworn to by witness. (MSS. xv,
44.)

and one Atherton,* formerly in Wendells Rangers; are mentioned as interested in Roger's plans.

He attributes much of the difficulty among Indians to rum,† and it would prove of great advantage to the trade if all the rum was lodged with the Commissary, and none given or sold to the Indians at that post,—"that then he only having, as they call it, milk to give the Indians," their presents would cost less, and be more acceptable. He thinks the garrison should be often relieved, as the tendency was for the soldiers to become traders. Of Major Rogers he says : "he is very industrious to raise the expense of our department that his might appear small, and is doing everything to undermine me with the Indians and

---

Capt. Speissmacker, in writing to Sir. William Johnson, Sept. 3, after describing the affair more fully described in enclosed papers, stated his belief that both parties had acted imprudently, and says:

"Some time after, they conferred together, and both came to my room, and before Lieut. Christie and me, Lieut. Roberts and the Major asked pardon of each other for the scurilous expression to one and another. Lieut. Roberts said, what he meant by Treason, was by sending him like a criminal to his room." (MSS. xv, 35.)

It appears that Mr. Roberts was a second time arrested, and in writing to Daniel Claus at Montreal, Sept. 21, 1767, he complains of his close confinement, and the probability of his being sent in irons to Montreal. (MSS. xv, 74,90.)

Capt. Spiessmacker wrote to Sir William Johnson Sept. 27, relating the difficulties that had occurred, but without expressing his own opinions concerning them. (MSS. xv, 80.)

Roberts again memorialized Capt. Spiessmacker, October 27, praying for protection, complaining of close confinement without cause, and stating his fears that the public interests would suffer on account of his forced detention from the duties of his office. (MSS. 73.)

* It appears in a letter from Mr. Roberts in London to Sir William Johnson, dated June 7, 1771, that Atherton had commenced legal proceedings for alleged losses, and that he was doing him much injury.—*Johnson's MSS.* xx, 230 : xxi, 32 : xxii, 14, 191.

† In a Memorial of the body of English Traders at Detroit, the same opinion expressed, and the advice is given that the quantity should be limited to 50 gallons to a three-handed battoe load of dry goods.—*Johnson MSS.* xv, 157.

to get a general petition from them that he might be Superintendent to the westward. I believe his endeavours would not prevail was he to remain here. They say he promises more than he can perform,—that he has more love for packs, but less sense than me."

The peace which Rogers had got up at so much expense did not promise to be of long continuance, and troubles between the conciliated tribes ·had again begun. The Indians at Prairie du Chien had shown an insolent preference to the French in the south-west. Rogers had taken into his friendship Mr. John R. Hanson, the clerk of Mr. Roberts and Johnson was cautioned against receiving information through him.—*Johnson's MSS.* xv, 125.

Sir William Johnson to Capt. Cochran.
Johnson Hall, Nov. 17, 1767.

" I believe the public opinion concerning Major Rogers is not ill founded. I raised him in 1755, from the lowest station on account of his abilities as a Ranger, for which duty he seemed well calculated, but how people at home, or any where else, could think him fit for anyother purpose must appear surprising to those acquainted with him. I believe he never confined himself within the *disagreable bounds* of *truth*, as you mention, but I wonder much they did not see through him in time."—*Johnson MSS.* xv, 137.

General Gage to Sir William Johnson.
New York, December 6, 1767.

" Mr. Roberts will no doubt lay his complaints before you. I have near twenty affidavits sent by Major Rogers, which most in fault I can't say. Most probably both of them in some degree. But I, I am apt to believe that the Major would be glad of any excuse to rid himself of an Indian Commissary."

*Sir William Johnson to General Gage.**

Johnson Hall, November 24, 1767.

"I do not doubt but that Potter will make the most of his discovery, from his character, at the same time I believe his account is within Compass, and that probably he could say more if he chose to. Major Rogers has goods trading for his benefit in the Indian Country to a very considerable amount, and the returns may soon be in, as I am informed; for which reason, I thought it best to hint, that it would not be amiss to have them secured for his creditors. I have a letter from Captain Spice Maker on the subject of Lt. Robert's confinement, I hear the latter is near this place on his way down."

Sir William Johnson to the Earl of Shelburne†

Johnson Hall, Dec. 3, 1767.

"MY LORD,

The 26th Ultimo I had the honor to address two letters to your Lordship, the one on the Subject of Indian affairs, the other concerning the Commandant of Michilimackinac, which was accompanied with enclosures on the latter of which subjects we have not heard further since.

The General sent to have him apprehended, but I have received, a very extraordinary plan for a government, etc., to be formed at Michilimackinac, with an estimate of trade, all which I understand has been sent to his Majesty's Ministers.‡ As it is long, and that it speaks for itself,

---

*Johnson MSS. xv, 154. Doc. Hist N. Y. ii, 888.

† Johnson MSS. xv, 167.

‡ An elaborate document of 23 pages, is preserved among the Johnson MSS. (xxv, 108) entitled "An Estimate of the Furr and Peltrey Trade in the District of Michilimacknac, according to the Bounds and Limits assigned to it by the French, when under their "Government, which is set forth in the annexed Map, and the situation and names of the Several Posts specified, etc., etc."

This is evidently the document referred to in the text. The map is not now found with it, as formerly stated.

it is needless here to point out the falsehoods and absurdities contained in it, and shall only remark that it is calculated with an eye to his being Gov'r and to have it in his power to carry on an extensive trade where he pleases, assisted by four or five companys of Rangers, whom he proposes to have established there. In time, we may be form several governments, even, with consent of the Indians, but it is certain, that unless they are framed, and their power executed, by the most disinterested persons, they will totally defeat their intention. A scheme for establishing a needy man, of bad circumstances, and worse principles, in the first authority, and for the next branch of the Legislature of such traders as are at out-posts, is too absurd to deserve any comment. To say that such Traders, (or merchants as they call themselves), will avoid being guilty of wrong, as their own interest would be thereby affected, is a specious tho' false argument, and is what they never yet regarded. It being notorious that men in trade,—much superior in judgment and understanding to any who resort to the frontiers—have constantly sacrificed their own interest together with that of the publick to the present moment, and they must always do so in this country, for reasons that can be easily given.

We have seen how the New York Independent Companies first detached from His Majesty's best troops, degenerated in America, through the avarice of their captains, who to my certain knowledge seldom kept up half their number and these were for the most part, creatures unfit for any duty. How much more may we expect that Rangers, under an interested needy man, in a remote corners without check or control, will be in a short space of time, reduced to a handfull of faggots, or at least a few sufficient to be employed in trade for him, at the charge of the Crown:—but I shall waive this point to proceed to the material objects which have occasioned this letter."

After a lengthy statement of views in respect to a General Indian Congress to settle sundry grievances with respect to boundaries and lands, the necessity of regulating and limiting trade, and the tendencies towards a jealousy between traders from different Colonies, where their interests come in conflict in remote regions, he adduces reasons for encouraging a trade nearer home. He alludes to the successful business formerly carried on by Quebec and Montreal, when in the hands of the French, and the material advantages which the former government had realised from bringing remote tribes into personal contact with the officers of Government, and among the improvements of civilized life. He notices the treachery with which the noted French Partizan Chabert Toncaire had endeavored to stir up discontent and insubordination among the Indians, after being allowed to go among the distant tribes with a large cargo of goods " with many assurances on the word of a gentlemen and an officer, as he expressed it ; that he would not only demean himself as a faithful subject, but even make use of his influence for the public service to show the Indians the absurdity of their expectations from France, and so conciliate them to the British Government."

These fine sayings he repeated at Niagara ; in the presence of Indians, and the officers of the garrison ; but when a little distance beyond " he called a number of Indians together, and told them that they should take no notice of what he had said before—being compelled to do so in the presence of the English ; but that he had brought them assurances from the King of France, of his steady regard for them—that he would shortly show it by the

army he would send to their assistance and that in the
meantime they should begin themselves to do something
against the English." * * *

" But to return to my subject ; I cannot help expressing
my concern to see not only difference of sentiments and
jealousies amongst the traders, but also an infatuation in
favor of their dangerous projects, which induces them to
make misrepresentations to government that might prove,
if credited, fatal to themselves, and dangerous to the public
in general. The public interest is always used as a cloak
to private gain : otherwise they would have no occasion to
disguise their real motive. For the fact is, if we set aside a
few northern people, whose case I have already excepted, all
the rest who hunt in a more favorable climate, are very dif-
ferently circumstanced ; so that if *La Baye*, and the *Miamis*
were re-established, their conveniency would be sufficiently
answered. The Indians have no business to follow when
at peace but hunting. Between each hunt they have a
recess of many months. They are naturally covetous, and
become daily better acquainted with the value of our goods,
and their own peltry. They are everywhere at home, and
travel without the expense or inconvenience attending our
journeys to them. On the other hand, every step our
traders take beyond the posts, is attended with at least some
risque, and very heavy expenses, which the Indians must
feel as heavily in the purchase of their commodities,—all
which considered—is it not reasonable to suppose that, they
would rather employ their idle time in quest of a Cheap
Market than sit down with such slender returns as they
must receive in their own villages ? As a proof of which,
I shall give you one instance concerning *Toronto*, on the
north shore of *Lake Ontario*, formerly dependant on *Niagara* : which, notwithstanding the aspersion of Major
Rogers, that even a *single* trader would think it worth atten-

tion to supply a dependent post—yet I have heard traders of long experience and good circumstances affirm that for the use of that place for one season, they would willingly pay £1000, so certain were they of a quick market, from the cheapness at which they could afford their goods there ; and I am certain that a handsome fund would arise from farming out the places of trade to merchants of fortune and character, they giving security to be answerable for the misconduct of their factors, which could not be more than we find at present."

The writer, after expressing at length his views as to how these irregularities may be best remedied, suggests a series of measures, one of which is as follows : " That all interfering of civil or Military officers be particularly guarded against, by express orders from his Majesty, and that the duty of the Commissaries to them residing at posts, be explained in such a manner, as to prevent disputes between them and Commandants, the superintendent being answerable to removing and otherwise deal with any of the Commissarys who act contrary to instructions, on due complaint made to him.

The necessity of this will appear, from the behaviour of of Major Rogers to my Commissary at Michilimackanac who—remonstrating against his interfering and against his extravagance to the Indians (whom he brought constantly to the company, and insisted on their being loaded with favors, in all appearance to acquire an interest for the dangerous purposes already communicated to your lordship), was insulted, dragged to confinement, and sent prisoner from the post, notwithstanding the military and trading people's application in his favor. From what has been repeated in former letters, and from the many reports transmitted on Indian affairs, concerning the management of these people, I hope will evidently appear, what are the powers necessary to be given to the Department for the purposes of the Crown, and the public advantage ; and therefore it will be unnecessary to repeat them, or to dwell longer upon the want of settling these important points and the alarming prospect of our affairs on that account.

I have therefore only to repeat, that the promoting of religion amongst them is by no means to be neglected, and that the establishment of Missionaries, under proper authority, as promised and expected by the Indians, (many of whom educated in the principles of the Church of England are disgusted at our neglect), would have very happy effects. As I understand, an Episcopate is now solicited for by the National Clergy and their congregations, I am of opinion if this application meets with the success and attention which it appears to deserve, that such an establishment besides its advantage to the National Church, and its members, will tend, in the most effectual manner, to promote religion among the Indians, under a proper Church government, and the auspices of the dignified clergymen in America."

*Sir William Johnson to Gen Gage.**

Johnson Hall, December 26, 1767.

" This will be delivered to you by Lieut. Roberts, who arrived here some days ago. It is judged necessary that as he was sent as a prisoner from Michilimack'c he should wait upon you, notwithstanding he was not received as such by the Commanding Officer at the Detroit, to whom he was ordered to be delivered up, but was left at liberty to go where he pleased.

From the conduct of the commandant of Michilimackinac it is evident that the principal cause of the difference arose from his aversion to an officer who might detect or

22

intererfere with him. The principal · dispute which arose on the seizure of the rum, is certainly in favor of Mr. Roberts, who as he discovered and seized it, was liable to answer for the same, and if a commanding officer will interfere in matters of trade, or any other points which fall within the limits of duty prescribed and approved of by the Government, the appointment of a Commissary is only an unnecessary charge to the Crown—besides that such treatment lessens a Commissary in the eyes of the Indians, who have been told, agreeable to orders, that that officer was to have sole management of their Indian affairs and trade.

Mr. Roberts might have been more cool ; but when we consider the man he had to deal with and the discoveries he had just made of his designs, it will in a great measure account for his conduct, and the letters I have received in his behalf, as well from the officers and traders, appear much in his favor. He thinks himself greatly injured, but you will be the best judge on hearing what he has to say, and examining the papers which he will bring before you. As the bonds, etc., entered into by the Traders are in his hands, and that the most necessary time for a Commissary's presence is early in the spring, I think it best that he should return to his post after waiting upon you, without any other delay than what the season may create, and I believe the most expeditious way for his return will be by Montreal and the Ottawa River, which is generally open some time before the Straits of Niagara.

Mr. Roberts has been not only injured in his character, but put to a great expense by his journey, the amount of which, I think he should be allowed for, and therefore take the liberty to recommend it to you. He has likewise

---

* *Johnson MSS.* xv, 190. *Doc. Hist. N. Y.*, ii, 895.

accounts of expenses incurred lately, which if paid now, would do him real service."*

Earl of Hillsborough to Sir William Johnson.
Whitehall, 12 March, 1768.

" Chabert Joncaire's treacherous conduct, and the wicked and infamous behaviour of Rogers, and his correspondence with Hopkins, which appears from a copy of a letter from the latter which you inclosed in your letter No 7. are of such a nature as require the utmost circumspection and attention of his Majesty's Servants in America ; as in the present state of some mens dispositions in that country when ones correspondence of that dangerous tendancy is discovered, there is reason to apprehend there may be more of the same kind."—*N. Y. Colonial History*, VIII, 36.

Concerning the Instructions received by Major Rogers from the Superintendent of Indian Affairs.†

Sir William Johnson in writing July 23, 1768, to Mr. Hector Theo's Crainahe in transmitting a copy of Roger's instructions on his way to his post, to be used on his trial, says :

" These Instructions merely regarded his conduct towards the Indians.—At his departure he was very desirous of some latitude in the article of Expenses, which I did not then, nor since, think myself justifiable in granting him ; but on the contrary, during a long conversation gave him such verbal orders as I apprehended would have

---

* Roberts returned to Michilimackinac in June, 1768, and in this absence of ten months, the rum was " either stolen or had leaked out of the casks." *Johnson MSS.* xxv, 171.

† *Johnson MSS.*

been a sufficient caution to him to avoid such Expenses, and I make no doubt he had the like from the Commander in Chief. As I could not accept his bills, I did not keep them in my hands, consequently I cannot be exact as to their amount; but to the best of my recollection, the whole of his drafts upon me for Indian Expenses since May 1769, is about £5.000, N. Y. Currency, which were chiefly said to be incurred in the months of June and July, of that year. As to the information which the General desires I should give you concerning the delivery of Hopkin's Letter, and the Conversation that passed thereon, I am to tell you, that Major Rogers was at that time gone to his post: that I enclosed the letter to him, the receipt of which he acknowledged and for which he returned me thanks, in his answer to me, but was silent as to the contents, or any other circumstances regarding it.

This is the whole of what the General has required of me. I have only to add, that I am sorry his conduct has been such as to bring him into his present situation.

I am etc.

WM. JOHNSON.

*Daniel Claus to Sir William Johnson.**

Quebec, 3'd Aug., 1768.

"The Governor asked me at the Same time, whether you did not give me any papers relative to Major Rogers, Affairs, I told him you was not returned from the Sea Coast when I left home. He is an entire stranger to this last plot with the Frenchman, and I could give him no particulars, as I knew but a little about it, and that by hearsay. The Chief Justice Hay told me that in common law the affidavit would not hurt him. Rogers wants to prolong

---

* *Johnson MSS.*, XVI. 123.

his tryal upon several pretences,. and desires to be tried by a civil court. When Mr. Hay told me he would endeavour to evade by having his crime changed to *Mutiny*—he standing now indicted for High Treason, a crime under the cognizance of the civil law, and the former under that of the Military."

Sir William Johnson to the Earl of Hillsborough.

Johnson Hall, Aug. 17, 1768.

" The Indians in the parts adjacent to Michilimackinac have been treated at a very great expense for some time past. Major Rogers brings a considerable charge against the crown for mediating a peace between some tribes of the Sioux and some Chippawaes living about Lake Superior, which, had it been attended with success, would have been only interesting to a very few French, and others that had goods in that part of the Country, but the contrary has happened, and they are more violent than ever against one another, which perhaps is not an unfavorable circumstance to us at this juncture, but the Indians on finding that they are to receive large presents for promising to lay down their arms, will never want occasion to quarrel with one another."

Daniel Claus to Sir William Johnson.†

Williamsburgh 26 Sept., 1768.

" The officers from Michil[a] that are to prosecute Major Rogers were not arrived, when I left Montreal, but hourly expected. If they arrived, the prisoners could not come before the court, having been obliged to begin a Salivation,

---

* *Johnson MSS.*, xvi, 141. *N. Y. Colonial History*, viii, 94.
† *Johnson MSS.*, xvi, 169.

a little before I came away.* The principal paper that is wanted from you, is Potter's affidavit, you having the original. I brought Hopkin's letter back, and left Roger's original; acknowledged the receipt of it as none but original papers may be produced before a court Martial sitting on such occasions, Col. Jones promised to take good care of it."

Sir William Johnson to General Gage.†

Johnson Hall Dec. 16, 1763.

" I hope that any affair of party arising from the late proceedings against Major Rogers may totally subside. If not, it will easy to see what keeps it up. The gentlemen concerned in the prosecution not having the same docu-

---

* Mercurial Medicines administered to the extent of producing ptyalism, were at this period regarded as an essential and radical cure of a certain disease communicated by infection, that need not be here named, and we submit this as a probable explanation of the above statement. The following act of the Legislature of New Hampshire, leads to the inference that Rogers was easily tempted, and that he was not alone in suffering the consequences :

An act to dissolve the Marriage between Robert Rogers and Elizabeth his wife.

Passed March 4, 1778.

Whereas Elizabeth Rogers of Portsmouth, in the County of Rockingham, and State aforesaid, hath petitioned the General Assembly for said State, setting forth, that She was married to the said Robert Rogers about seventeen years ago, for the greater part of which time he had absented himself from, and totally neglected to support and maintain her, and had in the most flagrant manner in a variety of ways, Violated the Marriage Contract; but especially by infidelity to her bed; For which reasons praying that a divorce from the said Robert Rogers, *A Vinculo Matrimonii*, might be granted. The principal facts contained in said petition being made to appear upon a full hearing thereof :

Therefore,

Be it enacted by the Council and House of Representatives for Said State, in General Assembly convened, That the Bonds of Matrimony between the said *Robert* and *Elizabeth*, be and hereby are dissolved.

† *Johnson MSS.*, xvii, 13.

ments to do him a prejudice as himself and sundry others have to manifest his innocence, and induce the publick to deem the whole as a Malicious attack upon a man of worth."

Benjamin Roberts to Sir William Johnson. *
Montreal 11 May, 1769.

Sir : Your favor of the 24ult I received the 8th on my arrival here. It made me much more happy to find I had not forfeited your esteem, than if it had been an order to reinstate me in my office. It came in just time enough to bear up my spirits, under the disagreeable situation I am now in, surrounded by enemies, and threatened with assassination.

My letters were detained in Montreal by Mr. Goddard, who was told I was on my way up, and was waiting in expectation of them at Quebec, that I might decide there, what course to take.

I sent some letters by Colonel Provost inclosing the regulations made here, and advising you of my draft for £100 York, payable at the house of John Weatherhead.

The day before yesterday I waited on Colonel Jones, to let him know of my arrival, and there saw Rogers, I left the house first. He overtook me about 20 yards from the house. He asked me how I did, and then told me he wanted to speak to me. He had in his right hand a stick with a dart in it, and a long spike in the feril, with which he opposed my going further, and asked me if I would give him satisfaction for bribing Potter to swear his life away. I told him, when he was at liberty, I would make him give me satisfaction for the ill usage I had received from him at Michilimacknac. He said he had a case of pistols

* *Johnson MSS.*, xvii, 154.

in his pocket, under his coat, and catched hold of them,—
said I must immediately take one and fire it in the street
with him.   I answered I would chose my own arms and
place ; that the people were beginning to gather and if he
was a brave man, he would not speak loud, or we would
be hindered. He asked me to meet him at the mill, out-
side the Recollet Gate.   I told him I would at 5 the next
morning, but he desired it should be at 10 o'clock, and
alone.   I said I could not trust myself to such a man, who
I heard had neither honor nor courage.   He made use of
many invectives. I asked him, smiling, what became of
all the valor, when he and I was on a footing, and he acknowledged himself a Coward, and begged my pardon.
He told me, he'd blow my brains out and not give me
any fair chance for my life, for he'd kill me whenever he
could.   I all along could not forbear laughing, to see how
he trembled, fumbling under his coat with one hand for
his pistols, and with the other shaking his stick.   He was
pale as death, with his teeth gnashing, I desired him not
to oppose my going about my business,— says he " do you
laugh in my face ? He put his hand to my face and threatened to pull my nose.   I told him he had better let this
alone ; that if I had my sword on or even he thought my
limbs as strong as his, he would not dare to insult me :
but that he was now very brave, with his pistols and a
spear, against a naked man.   He went off, and I went to
Mr. Goddard, and provided myself ; but somebody hearing
he had been twice to look for me at my lodging's and
that he stop'd one in the street, let Mr. Forbishers who is
my friend, know of it, and he told Colonel Jones, who
sent for Rogers, and threatened to put him in close confinement, if he did not give his word and honor he would
neither give nor receive a chalenge from me, or insult me in
any wise.   He sent the town Major to me, to exact my

promise, threatening to put me in arrest if I refused it. I promised I would not accept of, or send him a chalenge. The next morning, I went to the ground, at the hour, but he was not there. I was told he was walking the ramparts. However he gave out he had pulled my nose, and made me go down on my knees in the street, to promise I would go out with him;—that he had been in the field, and [that] I did not appear;—that now he would give me no fair play for my life. I went to Colonel Jones yesterday and told him the affair. He said he had, before witnesses, made Rogers give his word of honor he would not go in my way:—that t'was I that insulted him as he was walking by my door; I desired he might keep the other side of the street;—that he was a Rascal. He answered, was as free for him as for me, and called me a puppy, and that I challenged him.

Think how disagreeable my situation ; obliged to carry pistols in my pocket, and be on my guard against a man who Colonel Jones wont believe carrys arms, Notwithstanding all that is said by everybody seems prepossessed in his favor. What then can I expect, if any accident should happen ? *

Benjamin Roberts to Sir William Johnson.†
New York, Feb. 12, 1770.

" I find by Mr. Wallace and others, that Rogers is making a noise in England—he might keep me in hot

---

* On Mr. Roberts arrival in Albany on the 6th of Dec., 1769, a writ was issued against him, out of the Mayor's Court, in an action of trover commenced by Robert Hensy, John Janell and James Abbott, for the whole amount of the rum seized in 1767, and he was arrested. Not wishing to have his case tried in Albany he procured a transfer of suit to New York, where Mr. Weatherhead became his special bail, and he soon after sailed for England. The trial came on in his absence, and from the want of papers, to prove his case, the jury found a verdict of £171 damages for the plaintiffs besides the costs of suit, which his bail was forced to pay—*Johnson MSS.*, xxv, 191.

† *Johnson MSS.*, xviii, 179.

water, if I have not such letters from you as may gain me protection."

Benjamin Roberts to Sir William Johnson.*

London, 8 August, 1770.

" Vile as Rogers is, his story is much attended to amongst some of the great, who are glad to censure any characters, as they can't bear to see any without a blemish; 't would be so different to their own. So, till that fellow is sent somewhere, I shall be continually plagued with contradicting his vile story."

Benjamin Roberts to Sir William Johnson.*

New York, February 19, 1770.

" Kingston has a most extraordinary letter from London, which says that Major Rogers was presented to His Majesty, and kissed his hand—that he demanded redress and retaliation for his sufferings. The minister asked what would content him. He desired to be made a Baronet, with a pension of £600 St'g, and to be restored to his Government at Michilimackinac, and to have all his accounts paid, Mr. Fitzherbert is his particular friend.

Rogers has got his Salary from G. Carlton as Govr. His expenses at Montreal, etc., were paid him here—he has got them again in England, and also his accounts for his expedition to the North-west.

---

* *Johnson MSS.*, xix, 172.
  In a letter from London dated Oct. 3, 1770, Mr. Roberts says : " I am informed by good authority, that three of the ministry intend providing for Rogers."—*Johnson MSS.*, xix, 226.
† *Johnson MSS.*, xviii, 185.

Stedman has presented large accounts of losses and damages sustained, and is likely to have them paid.

I suppose I shall find a strong party against me by Rogers. The fear of that alone, made me trouble you for a Recommendation. 'Twould be so dishonourable to see that villian taken notice of, and I, that have served thirteen years unblemished, and in many Capacities, employed, not taken notice of. The triumph would be too great for our enemies."

Appendix to a Letter from James Rivington to Sir William Johnson,* dated November 19, 1770.

" The following is an extract from the Letter I received per paquet from England:

" Rogers talks very high of his usages and demands large terms,—to be created an English Baronet, and have £600 a year, with a Majority in the Army, or he would not be Silent. They have given him all his pay as Governor of Michilimackinac, to this time, but they have paid the accounts of the Expedition, and Boats he sent from the above mentioned Post, to make discoveries in the back countries, to one Carver.† Mr. Fitzherbert, who is his friend, says he will give him something, for with his cursed impudence he hums‡ all the great people, and I firmly believe he will succeed beyond what every one in America, who knows him, could expect."

---

* *Johnson MSS.*, XVIII, 186.

† Jonathan Carver, whose travels were published.

‡ A " hum'" (obsolete), is an imposition or hoax.

*Benjamin Roberts to Sir William Johnson.**

London 1 September, 1771.

" Rogers is likely to get his money paid, which was rejected before in England and America. He has many people pushing for him, to whóm he owes money."

Major Robert Rogers to Sir William Johnson.†

"Sir: Having on my way to Michilimackinak in the 1766, been favored with your appointment to manage the Indian Affairs at that post. I request the favor of you to certify that appointment, as also the advance, which commissary who succeeded me had per year, in order that I may be paid by Government for that Service, I am Sir,
Your most obedient and most
humble Servant,
Robert Rogers.
Spring Gardens at Charing Cross,
Monday, 10th August, 1772."

APPENDIX D.

Official Documents and Correspondence relating to Major Rogers, before his open adherence to the Royal Cause in the Revolution.

Major Rogers before the Pennsylvania Committee of Safety.

The records of this Body in their proceedings under date of September 22, 1775(have the following entry :

---

* *Johnson MSS.*, xxi, 82.
† *Johnson MSS.*, xxi, 238.

" Major Rogers having arrived here from England, and being on half pay in the British Army, this Board think it necessary that he should be taken prisoner. Colonel Roberdeau, at the request of this Board, accordingly give directions to Captain Bradford, to take the Said Major Rogers a prisoner and bring him before them."*

Mr. Rogers was accordingly brought as a prisoner before the Board, but not having an answer from the Congress, it was thought proper that he should give his word of honor to appear before the Board the next day, at 9 o'clock, which word he accordingly gave.

In the mean time an answer was received from Congress, in the following Resolve, viz :

" In Congress, Sept. 22, 1775.

Resolved. That in case the committee find nothing against Major Rogers except that of his being a half pay Officer, that he be discharged on giving his parole not to take up arms against the Inhabitants of America, in the present Controversy between Great Britain and America.".

A True Copy from the Minutes :

CHARLES THOMSON, *Secretary.*"

He appeared accordingly, and gave the following Parole :

" I, Robert Rogers, Major on half pay in his Majesty's Army, a prisoner in the custody of the Committee of Safety for the Province of Pennsylvania, and being kindly treated and protected by them, and engaged on parole, do hereby solemnly promise and engage, on the honor of a Soldier and a gentleman, that I will not bear arms against the American United Colonies, in any manner whatever, during the present contest between them and Great Britain ; and that I will not in that time, attempt to give intelligence

---

* *Force's American Archives*, Fourth Series, III, 865.

to General Gage, the British Ministerys or any other person or persons, of any matter relating to America."

ROBERT ROGERS *Major.*

Agreeable to his request, he was furnished with a copy of his Parole, and the following certificate, viz :

" These are to certify to all persons to whom these presents may appear ; that the above writing is a true copy of the Parol of honor given by the bearer, Major Robert Rogers, to the Committee of Safety for the Province of Pennsylvania ; it is therefore recommended to such persons that the said Major Rogers be permitted to pass where his business may lead him, without any hindrance or molestation."*

Major Rogers before the New York Committee of Safety.

In less than a week after receiving the above certificate, Major Rogers appeared before the New York Committee of Safety, and under date of September 27, 1775, we find the following entry :

'' Mr. Robert Rogers, commonly called Major Rogers, according to directions for that purpose, attended on the Committee. He assured the Committee that he was a prisoner on his parole of honor to the Committee of Safety at Philadelphia ; that he received from the said Committee a certified copy of his parole, with a certificate thereof, signed by Benjamin Franklin, which he unfortunately lost ; and Mr. Rogers declared to this Committee, upon his honour as a soldier and a gentlemen, that he will not depart from this city without leave of this Committee, until he shall have recovered the said certified Copy of his parole, or another certified copy thereof,

---

* *American Archives*, Fourth Series, IV, 874.

and produce the same to this Committee : and that, in the mean time, he will, on request, attend upon this Committee. Mr. Rogers informed the Committee that he lodges at Doctor Harrison's in Broadway."*

A certified copy of the lost parole and pass, was received by post from the Philadelphia Committee of Safety, October 5, 1775.†

Extract of a letter from Major General William Howe to the Earl of Dartmouth, dated Boston, November 26, 1775.

" A letter from Major Rogers, at New York, to General Gage, being directed to the Commander in Chief, came to my hand since the General's departure wherein he has made offers of his services ; to which I have given encouragement, by desiring him to make his proposals, and by giving an assurance that I am well inclined to do every thing in my power to afford him an opportunity of recommending himself to His Majesty's future favour. I find from Governour Tryon, that the Rebels have made considerable overtures to him."‡

Letter from President Wheelock of Dartmouth College to General Washington§ dated December 2, 1775.

" MUCH HONOURED AND RESPECTED SIR :

On the 13th Ult., the famous Major Robert Rogers came to my house from a tavern in the neighborhood, where he called for refreshments. I had never seen him

---

*American Archives, Fourth Series, III, 914; Journals N. Y. Provincial Congress, I. 157.

† Ib. III, 1271.—Journal N. Y. Provincial Congress, I, 167.

‡ American Archives, Fourth Series, III, 1674.

§ Then in camp before Boston.

before, He was in but ordinary habit, for one of his character. He treated me with great respect : said he had come from London in July, and had spent twenty days with the Congress in Philadelphia, and I forget how many at New York ; had been offered and urged to take a Commission in favor of the Colonies ; but, as he was on half pay from the Crown, he thought proper not to accept it ; that he had fought two battles in Algiers under the Dey ; that he was now of design to take care of some large grants of land made to him ; that he was going to visit his sister at Morristown, and then return by Merrimac River to visit his wife, whom he had not yet seen since his return from England ; that he had got a pass or license to travel, from the Continental Congress ; that he came in to offer his service to procure a large interest for this College ; the reputation of it was great in England ; that Lord Dartmouth, and many other noblemen had spoken of it, in his hearing with expressions of highest esteem and respect ; that Capt. Holland, Surveyor-General, now at New York, was a great friend to me and the College and would assist me in the affair ; and that now was the most favourable time to apply for a large grant of lands for it.

I thanked him for expressions of his kindness, but, after I had shown some coldness in accepting it, he proposed to write to me in his journey, and let me know where I might write him and he should be ready to perform any friendly office in the affair. He said he was in haste to pursue his journey that evening. He went to the aforesaid tavern, and tarried all night : the next morning told the landlord he was out of money and could not pay his reckoning—which was three shillings, but would pay him on his return, which would be within about three months, and went on his way to Lyme ; since which I have heard nothing from him. But yesterday, two soldiers, viz : Palmer, of Oxford (whom they say was under Colonel Bedel) and Kennedy, of Haver-hill, on their return from Montreal, informed me that our officers were assured by a Frenchman, a Captain in the Artillery, whom they had taken captive, that Major Rogers was second in command under General Carlton ; and that he had lately been in Indian habit through our encamp-ments at St. John's, and had given a plan of them to the General; and suppose that he made his escape with the Indians, which were at St. John's.

This account is according to the best of my remem-brance. If it shall prove of any service to detect such an enemy, I shall be glad ; if not my intention will, I trust, apologize for what I have wrote."*

Letters from Major Rogers to General Washington.†
Medford (Porter's Tavern),
19-December, 1775.

" SIR : I sailed from Gravesend the 4th of June last, in a merchant ship, bound to Baltimore, in Maryland, which was at the time I came away, the nighest passage I could get to Philadelphia, where I waited on the gentle-men that compose the Continental Congress, in order to obtain their permit to settle my private affairs, being much encumbered with debts, chiefly contracted in the Province of New York ; in which settlement my brother, Colonel J mes Rogers who lives in the Province of New York, about twenty miles west of Connecticut river was deeply con-cerned, being bound for me in several sums of money, which made it necessary for me to visit him in my way home ; and for that purpose came by the way of New

---

* *American Archives, Fourth Series,* iv, 159.

† *American Archives, Fourth Series,* iv, 265. *Spark's Correspondence of the Revolution.*

York and Albany to my brother's and from thence to Portsmouth, to my wife and family (a pleasure long wished for), having been six years in Europe.

I have taken the earliest opportunity that would permit to come to this town (where I arrived this morning), in order to lay before your Excellency the purport I received at Philadelphia, from the Committee of Safety there, a copy of which is transmitted at the bottom of this letter, together with the minutes made thereon by the committees of safety of New York and New Hampshire. I do sincerely entreat your Excellency for a continuance of that permission for me to go unmolested where my private business may call me, as it will take some months from this time to settle with all my creditors.

I have leave to retire on my half-pay, and never expect to be called into the service again. I love North America; it is my native country and that of my family, and I intend to spend the evening of my days in it.

I should be glad to pay you my respects personally, but have thought it prudent to first write you this letter, and shall wait at this place for your Excellency's Commands.

I am, Sir, your Excellency's most
Obedient and
most humble servant,
ROBERT ROGERS.

*Letter from Brigadier General Sullivan to General Washington.**

Camp on Winter Hill,
17 December, 1775.

MUCH RESPECTED GENERAL,

Agreeably to your orders, I have again waited on Major Rogers, and strictly examined him, I have seen his several

* *American Archives, Fourth Series,* IV, 300. *Spark's Correspondence of the Revolution,* I, 196.

permits, and think them genuine, and in every respect agreeable to the copy sent you. He says he left New York about the 10th of October, being ill with the fever-and-ague, was ten days in getting to Albany ; and there, and at the place called Stone Arabia [Lansingburgh] he tarried ten days more ; he then passed through Hoosick, Stand-ford, Draper and Hinsdale, is his way to his brother, who lives in Kent ; he was three days in performing this route, and tarried with his brother five or six days more ; he was then three days in going to Westminister, and in his way passed through by Dartmouth College, and saw Mr. Wheelock ; from thence he went to his farm in Pennicook, where he tarried six or eight days ; from thence he went to Newburg, and from thence to Portsmouth, and, after tarrying there some few days, laid his permit before the Committee of Safety.

He owns everything in Mr. Wheelock's letter except that of having been in Canada, which he warmly denies, and says he can prove the route he took, and prove himself to have been in the several towns at or near the days he has mentioned. I asked him why he came to the camp, as he had no business with any particular persons, and had no inclination to offer his service in the American cause ; to which he said he had voluntarily waited upon the committees of several colonies, as he thought it a piece of respect due to them, and would probably prevent his being suspected and treated as a person unfriendly to us ; that he likewise thought it his duty to wait on your Excellency, and ac-quaint you with the situation of his affairs, and if he could to obtain your license to travel unmolested.

These, Sir, are the facts as handed to me by him. What may be his secret designs I am unable to say, and what steps are most proper to be taken respecting him your Ex-cellency can best judge. I am far from thinking he has been in Canada ; but, as he was once governor of Michilimackinac, it is possible he may have a commission to take that command, and stir up the Indians against us, and only waits for an opportunity to get there ; for which reason I would advise, lest some blame might be laid upon your Excellency in future, not to give him any other permit, but let him avail himself of those he has ; and should he prove a traitor, let the blame centre upon those who enlarged him. I beg pardon for intruding my opinion, and subscribe myself,

Your Excellency most obedient Servant
John Sullivan.

Correspondence between General Washington and General Schuyler. *

General Washington in writing to General Schuyler, Dec. 18, 1775, informed him of the report received through Doctor Wheelock, concerning the visit of Major Rogers to the camp at St. John in the disguise of an Indian, and requested him to have the report examined into, and to inform him as to the authenticity or probability of the truth of it. He was then in Massachusetts, and might be apprehended if any circumstances should be discovered to induce a belief that he was there.

To this, General Schuyler, on the 5th of January, 1776, in writing from Albany, replied :

"Since the receipt of your Excelency's of the 18th, Major Rogers is come to this town. I sent to him, and amongst a variety of passes, he produced a late one from the Committee of New Hampshire, to pass unmolested to New York, for which place he sets out to day. I believe there is no truth in the intelligence sent by Mr. Wheelock.

---

* *Am. Archives*, 4 Ser. iv, 311,

for I find upon inquiry that Rogers arrived at this place after St. John was invested, and that he went hence to New England." *

General Washington in writing to General Schuyler January 16, 1776, alluded to Major Rogers as follows :

"I am apt to believe the intelligence given Dr. Wheel-ock, respecting Major Rogers was not true, but being much suspected of unfriendly views to this Country, his conduct should be attended with some degree of Vigilance and Circumspection." †

Extract of a Letter from Lord Germain to General Howe.

Lord George Germain, in writing to Major General Howe, under date of January 5, 1776, says :

"The King approves the arrangement you propose, in respect to an Adjutant General and a Quarter-master General, and also your attention to Major Rogers, of whose firmness and fidelity we have received further testi-mony from Governor Tryon, and there is no doubt you will find the means of making him useful." ‡

Letter from Major Rogers to the President of the New York Provincial Congress.

New York, February 19, 1776.§

SIR : Business of a private nature, and such only as respects myself and creditors, renders my attendance on board the Dutchess of Gordon indispensibly necessary.

---

* *Ib.* 581. *Spark's Washington,* III, 243.

† *Ib.* 695. *Spark's Washington,* III, 208.

‡ *American Archives, Fourth Ser.,* IV, 575.

§ *Journals of New York Provincial Congress,* II, 125. *American Archives, Fourth Series,* IV, 1201 ; *Ib.,* v, 291.

As I am soliciting grants for several tracts of land within this Province, I shall be obliged frequently to attend the Governor and Council to facilitate those grants. I shall be greatly obliged to you if you will be so obliging as to mention these matters to the gentlemen of the Congress, in order that I may obtain a permit to go on board the Governor's ship at any time when my business may require my attendance.†

I am Sir,

Your very Humble Servant

ROBERT ROGERS.

To Colonel Woodhull, President of the
    Honourable Provincial Congress for
    the Province of New York."

---

† The series of *Land Papers* in the office of the Secretary of State at Albany, contains several petitions from Major Rogers and his associates for grants of land, some of which were rejected, and some approved ; but too late to be recognized by the State, which has in its Constitution from the beginning declared that " all grants of land, made by the king of Great Britain, or persons acting under his authority, after the 14th day of October, 1775, shall be null and void." The following is an abstract of all the papers on file referring to Roger's claims for land :

On the 10th of March, 1761, Major Robert Rogers, Dequipe, Esa Putnam, John Miller, Hugh Miller, Roger Prince, Francis Doyne, James Osgood, Samuel Osgood, Ephraim Dickison, Daniel Chase, James Miller, David Thompson, John Taggart, David Hughes, John Herring, Daniel Miller, Robert Miller, James Moores, Daniel Moores, John Evans, David Evans, John Shute, Benjamin Osgood and Jonathan Chace, petitioned for a grant of land on the West side of Lake George, in the County of Albany,—beginning at the garrison lands of Fort William Henry, from thence running west two miles ; thence Northerly to the head of a brook called Putnam's Brook that falls into the northwest Bay of Lake George ; thence easterly to a place called the First Narrows on the said Lake, and from thence along the lake to the place of beginning—containing 25,000 acres of land, including the islands fronting the tract, under quit-rents restrictions and limitations as directed in his Majesty's Instructions.— *Land Papers,* xvi, 36.

(Endorsed May 27, 1761 : " Read in
    Council and granted, and warrant of
    survey issued dated the same day.")

Journal of the New Hampshire House, *June* 25, 1776.
" Voted to choose a Committee of this House to join
a Committee of the Hon'ble Board to confer upon the ex-

A duplicate of this petition (*Land Papers,* xvi, 39), bears the following
agreement, dated New York, March 17, 1761, and signed by Robert Rogers:
" It is agreed, if a patent is obtained for this tract of land, being copy of petition
given in, that Mr. Alexander Colden, Mr. Goldsborough Banyar, Mr. Jacob
Walton, Mr. Waddell Cunningham, Mr. Henry White, and Mr. John Dies,
all of New York, are to be equally concerned in the land granted with me,
they paying third part of all expenses and charges, and assisting all in their
power, in obtaining patents for said Land."
[A letter from Mr. Cunningham to Sir William Johnson, dated New York,
March 1, 1762, strongly urges this claim of Major Rogers, and alludes to an
order from the Home Government, that would stop all further grants of land
from the Government. Mr. Banyar also appears from this correspondence to
be deeply interested in Roger's behalf.—*Johnson MSS.,* v, 198.]
A petition dated January 22, 1776. was presented by Robert Rogers, in
behalf of himself, and twenty-four associates named, asking for a grant of land
in Charlotte Co., between Lake George and Hudsons River—beginning on
the west side of Lake George 58 chains N. 16° W. from Fort George, and
25 chains from the old Fort called Fort William Henry ; thence W. 160
chains ; thence N. 51° W. 463 chains, to the Hudson river ; thence up said
river, as it winds, to a marked tree 623 chains from the S. bounds of this
tract, measured on a course running north from said South bounds ; thence E.
352 chains to Lake George, and along said lake to the place of beginning—
together with the islands fronting said lands, containing in all, 25,000 acres,
with the usual allowances for roads, etc., and under the customary quit-rents,
provisoes, limitations and restrictions,—and that the same be erected into a
township, by the name of MOUNT ROGERS, with the usual privileges.
This petition states that a Warrant of Survey dated May 27, 1761, had
been issued by Cadwallader Colden, then President of the Council and that a
return of this survey had been made April 5, 1763, by Alexander Colden, then
Surveyor General of the Province.—*Land Papers,* xxxv, 132, Secretary's
Office.
(Endorsed Feb. 26, 1776, " Read in
Council and postponed for further consideration.")
On the same date, Rogers and eight associates named, addressed a petition
to the Governor in which he stated that he had discovered a tract of vacant
land in Albany Co., between lots 7 and 9, of the Wosen Hook Claim, and
the line of the Manor of Rensselaer Manner proper, containing about 4,200
acres, being lot 8, surrendered by John Van Rensselaer to the Crown :—And
also another tract of land within the county of Charlotte, on the east side of

pediency of securing Major Robert Rogers in Consequence
of Sundry informations against him as inimical to the rights

Hudson's River, beginning at the S. E. cor. of a tract of land belonging to
Edward and Ebenezer Jessup (opposite the mouth of the Sacondaga River),
from thence Northerly about two miles ; thence easterly, towards Queensbury,
about one mile and a half; thence Southerly about four miles ; thence
Westerly, about two miles, to the South bounds of the said tract, and from
thence to the place of beginning—the two tracts containing about 9,200
acres of land, with usual allowances and customary quit-rents.—*Land Papers*,
xxxv, 133.

(Endorsed, Jan. 29, 1776 : " Read in
Council and rejected, the prayer being
contrary to His Majesty's Instructions.")

On the same date, Rogers individually petitioned, for a tract of vacant
land, known by the name of " Nipper Mosbee," in Albany Co. ; beginning
on the N. bounds of the Manor of Rensselaerwyck, at the S. E. cor. of
Pittstown ; thence northerly, on the E. and N. bounds of said Pittstown, to
the N. W. cor., and thence from the E. and N. lines of Pittstown, easterly
and northerly to the W. and S. bounds of Hoosic Patent,—including all the
unpatented lands between the E. and N. bounds of Pittstown, and the W. and
S. bounds of Hoosick, being about 4,000 acres of land.—Also another tract
of vacant land, bounded westerly by the E. bounds of the Township of
Cambridge, easterly by lands granted to Aaron Van Corlear and others,
Southerly by lands granted to reduced officers, and northerly by lands granted
to Ryer Schermerhorn, containing about 800 acres of land, in Albany Co.—
Also another tract of vacant land in Albany Co., bounded Westerly by Saratoga,
Northerly by Cambridge, and Southerly by Hooseck Patents, containing about
200 acres,—being in all 5000 acres, more or less.   To this grant he expressed
the belief that he was entitled by Royal proclamation dated Oct. 7, 1763, as
compensation for services during the late war,—with usual allowances, and
customary quitrents.

To this petition an affidavit was appended, declaring that he had not received any grants of land as a reduced Major, under the above proclamation,
by any of His Majesty's Governors in America.—*Land Papers*, xxxv, 136.

(Endorsed, Jan. 29, 1767 : " Read in Council and rejected,
as to the first tract, it having been prior located and
petitioned for, and the petitioner to exhibit a map certified
by the Surveyor General, and showing the second and
third tracts herein prayed for.")

On the 7th of December, 1775, Major Rogers certified that Ensign
William Philips had served under his command in the late war, and had been
reduced at the conclusion thereof.—*Land Papers*, xxxv, 191.

and Liberties of this Country, and to make report thereon to this House as soon as may be ; and that Capt. Harriman,

On the 22d of January, 1776, Major Rogers as agent of Mark Noble, Thomas Read, Henry Phillips and William Phillips petitioned for a grant of land for services, adjoining Rensselaerwick on the North, Pownell on the east, the Massachusetts line on the south and by east, and Stephentown on the west, containing about 8,000 acres of land.—*Land Papers*, xxxv, 131.

(Endorsed Jan. 29, 1776, " Read
    in Council and granted.")

On the 6th of February, 1776, Rogers and 22 associates named, petitioned in relation to a grant of land in the town of *Hubbardton* on the Connecticut river, previously granted (June 15, 1764), by the Governor of New Hampshire, and containing 23,000 acres of land. The petitioners stated that they were owners of the greater part of the said townships.—*Land Papers*, xxxv, 137.

(Endorsed, Feb. 19, 1776, " Read in Council and
    granted—not interfering with any prior grant.
    The petitioner to produce a map of the lands
    prayed for, certified by the Surveyor General
    prior to any further proceedings.") ·
        [See also in relation to Hubbardton Grant, the *English Colonial MSS.*, CL, 138 ; Secretary's Office.]

A similar petition on the same date, from Rogers and 22 other associates, prayed for the grant of the township of land, previously granted by the Governor of New Hampshire, June 17, 1764, under the name of ", Dunbar," which they asked to have granted under the name of ROGERSBOROUGH.— *Land Papers*, xxxv, 138.

(Endorsed, Feb. 14, 1776, ". Read in Council, and
    granted on the equity herein set forth. The
    Petitioners to give bond to convey to the persons
    claiming Rights in the said pretended grant of
    " Dunbar," their respective and proportionable
    shares in the within mentioned lands.")

A warrant of Survey of the above township was issued to Edmund Fanning Surveyor General of the Province, March 20, 1776.—*Land Papers*, xxxv, 145.

On the 7th of February, 1776, Rogers and 23 associates named, petioned for a grant of land on the east side of Lake Champlain, previously granted in 1763 to Samuel Willis, Edward Burling and others, and bounded northerly by Onion River westerly by the Lake by common land and easterly by Deerfield, containing 23,040 acres, and named " ROGERSTON."—*Land Papers*, xxxv, 139.

(Endorsed, Feb. 14, 1776 : " Read in Council and
    rejected, it interfering with the Canada claims.")

Major Philbrick and Mr. Bell be the Committee of this House for that purpose."*

On the 2d of July, the following entry was made on the Journal of the House:

" Whereas it is strongly suspected that Major·Robert Rogers and one Samuel Dwyer are inimical to the Rights and Liberty of Americans.

Therefore voted, that it be and hereby is strongly recommended to the several Committees of Safety and of Correspondence in this Colony, or either of them. That they [take] effectual care to seize the bodies of the said Samuel Dwyer and Robert Rogers or either of them under proper guard and convey them, or either of them to this House or Committee of Safety of this Colony, as soon as may be for examination."†

Extract of a Letter from General Washington to the President of Congress, dated June 27, 1776.

" Upon information that Major Rogers was travelling through the country under suspicious circumstances, I thought it necessary to have him secured. I therefore sent after him. He was taken at South Amboy, and brought up to New York. Upon examination he informed me that he came from New Hampshire, the country of his usual abode, where he had left his family ; and pretended he was destined to Philadelphia, on business with Congress.

As by his own Confession he had crossed Hudson's River at New Windsor, and was taken so far out of his proper and direct route to Philadelphia, this consideration

* *Provincial Papers, N. H.,* viii, 163.
† *State Papers New Hampshire,* viii, 185.

added to the length of time he had taken to perform this journey, his being found in so suspicious a place as Amboy, his unnecessary stay there on a pretence of getting some baggage from New York, and an expectation of receiving money from a person here, of bad character, and in no cir-cumstances to furnish him out of his own stock, the Major's reputation, and his being a half pay officer, have increased my jealousies about him. The business which he informs me he has with Congress, is a secret offer of his services, to the end that, in case it should be rejected, he might have his way left open to an employment in the East Indies, to which he is assigned; and in that case he flatters himself, he will obtain leave of Congress to go to Great Britain.

As he had been put upon his parole by Congress, I thought it would be improper to stay his progress to Philadelphia, should he be in fact destined thither, I there-fore sent him forward, but, to prevent imposition, under the care of an officer, with letters found upon him which from their tenor, seem calculated to recommend him to Congress. I submit it to their consideration, whether it would be dangerous to accept the offer of his services."—*Spark's Life and Writings of Washington*, III, 440.

Letter from the President of the Continental Congress to General Washington.

On the 1st of July, 1776, John Hancock, President of Congress wrote to General Washington as follows :

" Sir : I wrote you by the express on Saturday last, since which nothing has occured worthy of your notice. The sole reason of troubling you with this is to acquaint you, that in consequence of your orders to Captain Peters, he proceeded with Major Rogers to this city, and called on me on Saturday last. and in the evening of that day I relieved him of his charge, and put Major Rogers under guard at the barracks, where he now remains, the Congress having, by a particular appointment, had under consideration a momentous matter this day, which prevented their attention to Major Rogers. My next will inform you, I hope, of some very decisive measures."*

Congress in a communication to the New Hampshire Assembly, July 6, 1776, informed them that Major Rogers would be sent to that state to be disposed of as that Government should judge best.† Upon which that body appointed Captain Harriman, Major Philbrick and Mr. Bell as a Committee for that purpose.‡ An order for his arrest was voted, as also of one Samuel Dyer, and that effectual measures be taken to seize them, or either of them wherever found in the Colony, and to bring them to the House, or Committee of Safety of the Colony for examination.§

Before he was sent off from Philadelphia, Rogers found means to escape,|| and found his way to General Howe, by whom he was empowered to raise a battalion of Rangers.**

---

* *American Archives.* Fifth Series, 1, 1.

† Ib, 1, 33, 136, 1568.

‡ Ib. 1, 72.

§ Ib, 1, 80.

|| A reward of £50 was offered by the Committee of Safety for his arrest.— *Ib.* 1, 348, 1291.

** Gen. Howe, in a letter dated August 6. 1776, wrote :—" Major Rogers having escaped to us from Philadelphia, is empowered to raise a battalion of Rangers, which I hope may be useful in the course of the campaign."—*Spark's Washington*, iv, 520.

Governor Tryon in writing to Lord George Germain, Sept. 27, 1776, says that Major Rogers was then raising a Corps of Provincials for the war generally.—*N. Y. Colonial History*, viii, 687.

It appears that Rogers lost no time in accepting this appointment, for in a letter from William Duer, to Gen. Washington dated at Harlem, Aug. 30, 1776. He says:

" I have likewise to inform your Excellency, that on yesterday Morning, one Lounsberry, in Westchester County, who had headed a body of about fourteen tories, was killed by an officer named Flood, on his refusal to surrender himself prisoner ; that in his pocket book was found a Commission signed by General Howe to Major Rogers, empowering him to raise a battalion of Rangers, with the rank of Lieutenant-Colonel Commandant ; that annexed to this was a warrant to this Lounsberry signed by Major Rogers, appointing him a Captain of one of these companies, as likewise a muster-roll of the men already inlisted.—Ib. 1, 789, 1236.

APPENDIX E.

CORRESPONDENCE AND STATEMENTS CONCERNING THE ATTACK UPON LIEUT. COL. ROGER'S PARTIZAN CORPS AT MAMARONEC, *N. Y.*, *October* 21, 1776.

Extract of a Letter from Colonel Robert H. Harrison, Secretary to General Washington, To the President of Congress.

Headquaters White Plains 25 October, 1776.

* * * On Monday night a detachment of our men under the command of Colonel Haslet was sent out to surprise and cut off Major Rogers if possible, with his regiment which was posted there. By some accident or other the expedition did not succeed so well as I could have wished. However our advanced party led on by Major Green, of the first Virginia Regiment, fell in with their out-guard, and brought off thirty-six prisoners, sixty muskets, and some blankets. The number killed is not certainly known ; but it is reported by an officer who was there, that he counted about twenty-five. Our loss was two killed and ten or twelve wounded ; among the latter Major (John) Green, whose recovery is very doubtful.*" *Sparks Life of Washington*, IV, 524.

Extract of a Letter from Colonel John Haslet, to General Cæfar Rodney, dated White Plains, N. Y., Oct. 28, 1776.

"On Monday Night, Lord Sterling ordered me out with seven hundred and fifty men to attack the enemy's outposts ten miles from this place , at the village of Mamaronec ; which was done, and their guards forced. We brought in thirty-six prisoners a pair of colors, sixty stand of arms, and a variety of plunder besides. The party we fell in with was Colonel Rogers's, the late worthless Major. On the first fire he skulked off in the dark. His Lieutenant, and a number of others were left dead on the spot. Had not our guards [guides?] deserted us on the first outset, he and his whole party must have been taken. On our side three or four were left dead and about fifteen wounded. Among the latter is Major Green of the second Virginia Regiment wounded in the shoulder ; and Captain Rope who acted as Major, and behaved with

---

*Major Green recovered and subsequently became a Lieutenant Colonel.

The affair is mentioned in a letter from Major General Greene to General Washington dated Oct. 4, 1776, but without material addition. He laments the loss of Major Greene, who is mentioned as a brave officer, and mortally wounded.—*Spark's Official Correspondence of the Revolution*, I, 299.

An extract from a letter of Gen. Heath, referring to the above affair, is given in *Bolton's History of Westchester Co., N. Y.* I, 311.

great bravery wounded in his leg; both likely to recover. As this was the first effort of the kind, and a plan of his Lordship's he was so highly pleased with our success, that he thanked us publicly on the parade."—*Spark's life of Washington*, IV. 526.

The following account of this affair was published in a Hartford newspaper of the day :

" On Monday last (October 21st) a party of Tories (100), Some of whom came from Long Island, under the command of the infamous Major Rogers, made an attack upon an advanced party of our Men, when a smart en gagement ensued, in which the enemy were totally routed. About twenty were killed on the spot, and thirty-six taken prisoners who were safely lodged in the goal at White Plains. Their gallant Commander, with his usual bravery, left his men in time of action, and made his escape."—*Stark's Memoirs*, p. 389.

Enlisting orders issued by Rogers in the British Service.

Valentine's Hill, 30 December, 1776.

" Whereas, his Majesty's service makes it absolutely necessary that recruits should be raised, this is to certify that Mr. Daniel Strang, or any other gentlemen who may bring in recruits, shall have commissions according to the number he or they shall bring in for the Queen's American Rangers. No more than forty shillings bounty is to be given to any man which is to be applied towards purchasing necessaries to serve during the present Rebellion, and no longer. They will have their proportion of all rebel lands, and all privileges equal to any of any of his Majesty's troops. The officers are to be the best judges in what manner they will get their men in; either by parties, detachments, or otherwise, as may seem most advantageous ; which men are to be attested before the first Magistrate within the Brstish lines."

ROBERT ROGERS,

Lieutenant Colonel Commandant of the Queen's Rangers.

Strang, who had the above paper in his possession, was taken up near the American Camp at Peekskill. He was tried by Court Martial, and making no defence was con-, demned to suffer death, on the charge of holding correspondence with the enemy, and lurking around the camp as a spy. General Washington approved the sentence.*

Extract from a Letter of Governor Trumbull, of Connecticut, to Colonel Livingston, dated October 13, 1776.*

" I have received intelligence which I believe may be depended on, that Major Rogers, now employed by General Howe, and who you know was a famous partisan or ranger, in the last war, is collecting a battalion of Tories on Long Island, and that he proposes soon to make a sudden attack in the night on Norfolk, to take the continental stores, and lay waste the town. I hope we shall be able to frustrate his designs. I have no need to apprize you of the art of this Rogers, He has been a famous scouter, or woods-hunter, skilled in waylaying, ambuscade, and sudden attack. I dare say you will guard against being surprised by his or any other party."

---

* *Spark's Washington*, IV. 520.
* *Spark's Washington*, IV. 125.

INDEX.